M. J. C. Vile

M. J. C. Vile is Professor of Political Science and Pro-Vice-Chancellor of the University of Kent. Born in 1927 in London he studied at the London School of Economics for the B.Sc.(Econ.) degree and later obtained his Ph.D. there. After teaching at the University of Exeter he was for a time a Fellow of Nuffield College, Oxford. He has also been a Visiting Teacher at the University of Massachusetts, Smith College, Massachusetts, and other American Universities. His other publications include *The Structure of American Federalism* (1961), *Constitutionalism and the Separation of Powers* (1967), *Federalism in the United States, Canada and Australia, Commission on the Constitution* (1973), and *The Presidency: American Historical Documents* (1974).

Politics in the U.S.A.

M. J. C. Vile
*Professor of Political
Science at the
University of Kent*

Hutchinson
London Melbourne Sydney
Auckland Johannesburg

Hutchinson & Co. (Publishers) Ltd

An imprint of the Hutchinson Publishing Group

17–21 Conway Street, London W1P 6JD

Hutchinson Group (Australia) Pty Ltd
30–32 Cremorne Street, Richmond South, Victoria 3121
PO Box 151, Broadway, New South Wales 2007

Hutchinson Group (NZ) Ltd
32–34 View Road, PO Box 40–086, Glenfield, Auckland 10

Hutchinson Group (SA) (Pty) Ltd
PO Box 337, Bergvlei 2012, South Africa

First published by Allen Lane 1970
This edition published by Hutchinson 1976
Reprinted 1977, 1982

Printed in Great Britain by The Anchor Press Ltd
and bound by Wm Brendon & Son Ltd, both of Tiptree, Essex

ISBN 0 09 127541 5

Contents

Contents

Preface to the Revised Edition

The first edition of this work appeared in 1970. Since then the American political system has endured its most traumatic experience since the Civil War. In revising the book I have incorporated the main changes in the structure of government, and brought the details up to date wherever possible. I have tried also to take account of the Watergate Affair in the revision of the chapter on the presidency, and in the final chapter, by giving an assessment of the central problem of the American system as it appears now that the excitement has died down. However, the main body of the work remains unchanged; partly because it is too soon to evaluate fully the impact of these events upon American political behaviour, and partly because, in spite of the almost incredible history of the Nixon Administration, the basic nature of the American political system, of which the presidency is the most visible, but not necessarily the most critical element, seems to have been left fundamentally unchanged by this experience.

M. J. C. VILE
January 1976

Introduction 1

The United States is the most powerful nation on earth today, but for many who, like the present writer, find it also the most fascinating, it is not this position of world power that is the only, or indeed the main, focus of their interest. The great attraction that the American scene exerts upon the sympathetic observer is twofold: of all political systems this is perhaps the most complex that the modern world has evolved, and it is also one which is the conscious creation of the mind of man. The United States is in a real sense an artificial creation, fashioned out of the wilderness within the past 350 years. The most striking aspect of the story of this achievement is not the technological, the economic, or the material aspect of America, which has so often claimed attention in the past; it is rather the human story of the establishment of a society, a nation, and a political system, out of such diverse materials in such a relatively short time. If the political system of a country is determined by its social composition, its history, and its constitutional structure, then an understanding of American politics will have to begin with these three factors. The relative influence of these factors differs from country to country, and from one age to another, and the importance of each of them for a particular political system may be hotly disputed by students of politics; but there can be little doubt that in the case of the United States each of these three factors plays a significant role in the way in which politics is conducted in that country.

THE CHALLENGE OF AMERICAN HISTORY

Although the history of the United States is short by the standards of European or Asian societies, it is a history packed with

incident, for the United States has had only 300 years in which
to pass through those stages which elsewhere have taken 1,000 or
2,000 years. We cannot here survey even the main outlines of that
history, for our main concern must be with the politics of the
United States today, but certain essential facts of history must
be borne in mind if the complexities of the American political scene are to be fully understood. Only by observing the main
characteristics of the American development, from the establishment of the first permanent settlements in the early seventeenth
century to the position of the United States in the world today,
can we understand both the magnitude of the achievements of
American politics, and the nature of the strains, sometimes very
serious strains, to which it is subjected. For if the working of the
American political system seems so incomprehensible to many
Europeans, it is to the unique character of American history that
we must turn for the roots of the differences between American
politics and those of every other country in the world.

When the original colonists sailed for America they went for
two main reasons – either to escape from religious oppression, or
to make their fortune in the New World. When they arrived they
had to govern themselves as well as to combat the wilderness and
the Indians. The ideas they held about government were inevitably largely drawn from the society which they had left behind.
The men of Massachusetts, Rhode Island and Connecticut established their own forms of government, but throughout most of
the period up until the Revolution, colonial political ideas followed closely upon those of the mother country. Nevertheless
there was, from the beginning, a basic incompatibility between
these European ideas about politics and the actual circumstances
of American life, an incompatibility which became more and
more evident as the eighteenth century progressed, and which
burst into the open with the outbreak of the Revolution. For the
society which established itself in America was not composed of a
cross-section of the then existing European society, neither were
the circumstances in which it found itself those of Europe. As
the American writer, Louis Hartz, has so brilliantly explained,
the most important factor of American history is that it lacked
altogether an ancien régime; feudalism never existed in

America in spite of the existence of the great land-owner 'aristo-crat' of colonial times, or of the bond-slaves who arrived from Europe to serve out their time under their American masters. America is not, and never has been, a 'classless society', but there is a very real sense in which it has always been a middle-class society, without the extremes, except in relation to Negro slavery, of European class attitudes. In an age when Europe was domi-nated by kings and nobles, America represented an ideal of a more egalitarian society in which, with ability and industry, a man might easily rise to the highest positions. The absence of a socialist tradition in America is in large part the result of the fact that there was not the same class structure for the socialist to react against. Thus the American 'liberal' is a very different being from the European who bears the same label. Similarly the American 'conservative' is a very different animal from the Euro-pean conservative, and it is necessary to arrive at a proper understanding of these differences before American politics becomes comprehensible.

There was always an underlying conviction among Americans that they had broken away from the corruption of old Europe to create a new and clean society. They were influenced, it is true, by European institutions and European ideas, for they had no other source upon which to draw, but they felt able, by the exer-cise of human reason, to select those things which were good and to reject those which were bad. Thus when they came to write the Federal Constitution they were deeply influenced by the balanced constitution of eighteenth-century England. But they did not copy it slavishly. They created something new, something unique, and they were aware that they were doing so. The *Federalist Papers*, written in 1787-8 by Alexander Hamilton, James Madison and John Jay, urging the acceptance of the proposed Constitution, provide perhaps the greatest example of human reason attempting to combine the wisdom of tradition with the rational solution of new and unprecedented problems. There is, therefore, a sense of uniqueness in the Ameri-can experience which ensures the autonomy of the American political tradition. Suggestions that America should follow Europe's example, or more specifically the pattern of British government, are rarely well received, and probably with good reason. As we shall see in later chapters, the conditions of American political life are so different from those of Britain that it is extremely unlikely that the same institutions would produce the same results.

The fact that the American polity is a conscious creation is an explanation of its American-ness, but it is also the explanation, in part at least, of other aspects of American life which it is harder for the outsider to understand. Isolationism became associated in the thirties and forties of this century with particular groups who seemed to have a particular reason, usually their ethnic origins, for not becoming involved in Europe's quarrels. But isolationism went deeper than this, and its reappearance in different guises in America in the 1960s must be seen in the context of an antipathy towards becoming tainted by that corrupting influence of Europe that Thomas Jefferson feared in the eighteenth century. Yet perhaps the most pervasive effect of the fact that America is a conscious, artificial creation from diverse materials is that at no time in its history has it been able to enjoy the luxury of allowing feelings of nationality and community to grow naturally and in an unrestricted way, allowing, as in other countries, the process to take many centuries. There has always been a conscious social policy of Americanization, one might almost say of indoctrination in the values and ideals of American society. A society which has had to cope with a continuous influx of immigrants of varying nationalities and creeds could not allow itself to be indifferent about their mode of assimilation into the American way of life, or to allow them to give full rein to the ideas and customs which they brought from their homelands. America is a free society, in which the freedom of speech and the press are jealously guarded, yet the limits of what is socially or politically acceptable are more clearly drawn, more consciously maintained, than in older, more self-confident societies. Thus the proscription of the Communist party in a country where communism seems unlikely to have the slightest hope of success is understandable only in the light of this feeling of a need to control extreme, or un-American attitudes. In such a society it is felt that political freedom can be safeguarded only if the minimum degree of conformity deemed necessary for its survival is actively maintained. The American political system has to encompass great diversity within certain boundaries of accepted actions and beliefs. The fear is ever present that to open the gates too far is to invite the waters of diversity to overflow the banks of an orderly society. The tensions which this situation creates can be seen at every level of American political life today, for one of the major functions of the American political system must be seen as its task of ensuring a minimum uniformity in a situation of potentially explosive diversity. This is the challenge which the history of the United States has set its political system.

A further aspect of this characteristic of America as a consciously created entity is the revolutionary tradition. The mere act of travelling to the New World to settle was, for many of the early Americans, itself an act of rebellion against the rulers and religions of Europe. The breaking of the ties with Great Britain in a violent and glorious act of defiance set the seal upon the American image as the propagator of revolutionary ideals of freedom and democracy. America became to the downtrodden peoples of Europe the symbol of the ability of man to break the shackles of tradition and to triumph through reason and determination. No American could declare allegiance to the principles of true conservatism, that is of utter resistance to all change, and remain an American. Yet the American revolutionary tradition is of a very special variety. Those 'aristocratic' leaders of the American Revolution who took their places at the head of the movement for independence were not fire-brand revolutionaries with extreme ideas of democracy and equality. They achieved the remarkable feat of leading a revolutionary war to a successful conclusion whilst maintaining the existing structure of American society. They enshrined in their Constitution a respect for the slow processes of the law, for the sanctity of property and contract, and for the leadership of the solid men who had a stake in the community. The counter-revolutionaries of 1787 who wrote the American Constitution were the same men who had led the revolution itself in 1775–6. Thus we find even today in America an equivocal reaction to the idea of democratic revolutionary movements in the rest of the world. Americans are democrats, but conservative democrats; they are revolutionaries who oppose revolution.

UNITY AND DIVERSITY

The settlement of the area which now forms the United States involved a long, continuous process of expansion from the original settlements on the Eastern seaboard: a process which has not ended even at the present time, for the vast influx of population into California in recent years, and the development of Alaska, represent, in differing ways, the last stages of the passing of that phenomenon which dominated the history of America throughout the eighteenth and nineteenth centuries – the frontier. The moving frontier of settlers, with its saga of pioneering feats, of cowboys, of Indian fighters, and of the life of its frontier towns (see map), has been proposed by some historians as the prime explanation of the nature of American politics, American society, and even of American national character. Whatever the exact importance of the frontier the broad outlines of its significance for America can hardly be in dispute. The frontier was a continuous re-creation of the story of American society. It was a reminder of the 'open', democratic, character of America, in which a man might carve out his own fortune from the wilderness; it was a constant portrayal of the opportunities which America offered, for although the hopes of the pioneers were sometimes sadly disappointed, they were often glowingly realized. The continued westward expansion gave to American society and politics some of its most persistent traits. It helped to perpetuate those characteristics which had marked America from the beginning. If socialism failed to find a root in America because feudal class structures had never existed, it was certainly excluded from later development by the open conditions created by the frontier. It was not until the era of expansion was over, and America began to resemble rather more closely the economic systems of 'closed' European nations, in the 1920s and 30s, that American politics took on something of the attitudes of Western Europe.

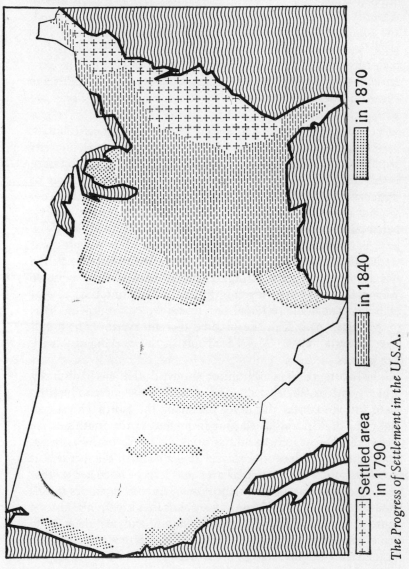

Settled area in 1790 +++++

in 1840

in 1870

The Progress of Settlement in the U.S.A.

Even in the early stages of American history the regional differences in climate, soil and natural resources gave rise to distinctive interests and differing ways of life in the colonies. New England, the Middle-Atlantic States, and the South, differed in the crops they produced, in the role of commerce in their economic life, and, particularly because of the existence of slavery, in the very structure of their society. As settlement progressed inland, there began that series of tensions between the more highly developed areas and the farmers and settlers on the frontier that have provided some of the most persistent themes of American politics. Farmers resented the Eastern commercial and financial interests which provided the material resources and the capital necessary to subdue the wilderness – at a price. The concentration of industry and commerce near the Eastern seaports, and the consequent growth of urban centres in the north-east region, exacerbated all the traditional differences between city and rural dwellers. Furthermore, as each new area of the United States was settled it acquired a character of its own, partly because of the nature of its economic structure, partly because of the people who settled it. The moving frontier became the unrolling of that map of regional and sectional differences which formed the basis of American politics in the nineteenth century, and which still today plays a muted but essential role in the working of American politics.

The existence of the frontier provided the mechanism by which some of the most divisive elements in American politics were introduced. As the development of the South progressed, the value of African slave-labour in producing the South's staple commodities, first tobacco and at a later stage cotton, was recognized; the establishment of slavery, together with the fact that it was best suited to a particular area and largely restricted to that area, have been cardinal influences upon American politics to this day. The place of the Negro in American society, his historic sense of resentment at his former status, and his struggle to achieve social and economic equality with white Americans, is a major factor in American politics, not merely in the South, but across the nation. Furthermore, as westward expansion continued in the first half of the nineteenth century, with the con-

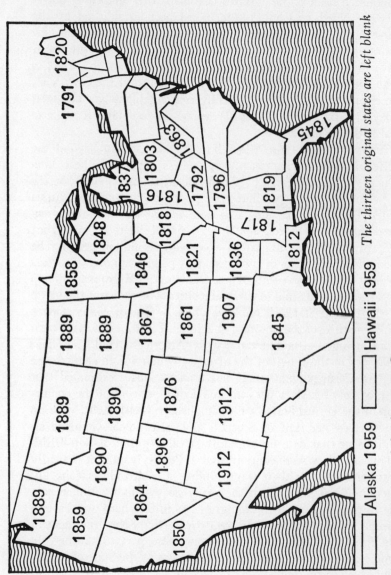

Alaska 1959   Hawaii 1959   *The thirteen original states are left blank*

The Establishment of the American States

tinuous creation of new States (see map) the balance of power
between North and South which had been established by the
Constitution was endangered. The problem of whether the new
States would be slave or free dominated the politics of the era. If
slave they could be expected to side with the South; if free, to
align themselves with the North. The holocaust of the Civil War,
the effects of which have not fully worked themselves out even
today, was the result of inability to find an acceptable formula to
deal with this problem.

Westward expansion, the filling of the vacuum beyond the
frontier, provided that seemingly endless supply of cheap land
which was, particularly in the period after the Civil War, the
engine which made possible mass immigration into the United
States. Between 1865 and 1920 over 28,000,000 immigrants entered the United States, and in six separate years between 1905
and 1914 the yearly migration exceeded one million people. The
changing composition of the immigrant population over the years
meant that concentrations of particular national groups built up
in particular areas, and in particular cities. The choice of the motto
of the United States, E pluribus unum – Out of Many, One –
which applied to the union of the States, could hardly have been
more fitting – although those early Americans could not have
conceived of the extent of the diversity which was to characterize
the American population. It has been variously estimated that
in 1790 between sixty per cent and eighty per cent of the population of the United States was of English or Welsh stock, with up
to fourteen per cent of Scottish and Irish stock. Germans ac-
counted at that date for the only sizeable group of non-British
origin, and they were concentrated in Pennsylvania. In the early
nineteenth century there was an influx of Irish and Germans, but
after the Civil War, when the really heavy immigration began,
the emphasis changed to immigrants from Southern and Eastern
Europe. In the peak year of 1914 over seventy-three per cent of
the 1,218,000 immigrants were from these parts of Europe. In
1790 eighty-two per cent of the population of the State of Massachusetts was of English stock, but in 1920 two thirds of the
population of the State were immigrants or the children of immigrants, and the Irish, Italians, Poles and Jews, together with

a number of minor groups such as Lithuanians, Greeks, Armenians and Syrians far outweighed the 'old-stock' inhabitants.

At the end of the nineteenth century the expansive movement within the United States overflowed into a relatively mild episode of imperialism, as a result of which Puerto Rico, Hawaii and the Philippines were acquired. The Philippines have since gained full independence, but Hawaii followed a different course, and in 1959 it became the fiftieth State of the Union, and the first State to have Asians as the largest racial group in its population. Puerto Rico has provided the human material for yet another racial complication by the extent of Puerto Rican immigration into New York City. The problems which face a political system and a society in attempting to assimilate different nationalities and races on this scale are indeed daunting to say the least. The influx of immigrants brought with it the elements of diversity, in language, in religion, in colour, in social customs, and in attitudes towards social and political problems, which provide the warp and woof of American life today. That the United States has largely achieved the creation of a single nation from such varied peoples is little short of a modern miracle. In an age when racial problems are in the news from all parts of the world, it is as well to bear in mind the American achievement, even though its success is not total. Nevertheless, this background of national and racial heterogeneity must be remembered when we look at the workings of American politics, for beneath the superficial conformity of dress, and of mass-produced consumer goods, there lies, not too far from the surface, a pervasive diversity.

POLITICS AND THE CONSTITUTION

The relationship of the political life of a country to the formal and informal structures of its constitution is a matter of great complexity. For centuries men, particularly Americans, have considered the nature of the constitution to be a vital factor in maintaining freedom and the rights of the individual, as well as ensuring order and stability in society. In recent decades, however, the view has been increasingly expressed that constitutional provisions, and particularly the more formal, legalistic aspects of the constitution, have little or no importance in determining the outcome of political struggles; rather, it is argued, it is to 'social forces' that we must direct our attention if we are to understand the working of politics. It is perhaps surprising that this point of view has been expressed more forcibly in modern America than in most other countries of the world, in spite of the fact that constitutions and constitutionalism would seem to have played such a significant part in American history. In this work we shall attempt to give full weight to 'social forces' in our description of the working of American politics, but it would be pointless to attempt to describe American political processes other than within the detailed framework of the American constitutional system. Social groups and movements are the raw material and the driving force of the political process, but the exact form in which they operate, and the precise results which they achieve, must depend to a considerable extent upon the nature of the channels through which they have to work; more precisely, the channels through which the social forces must operate are part of the whole complex of influences which have made these social forces of America just what they are.

It will become apparent during the course of the discussion that the American Constitution has indeed an important impact upon the way in which politics are carried on, but it must be made somewhat clearer what we mean by 'the Constitution'. The formal Constitution, the document which emerged from the Philadelphia Convention in 1787, remains very little changed to this day. Fundamentally it remains the same, in spite of the mere twenty-six amendments which have been made in the course of 170 years or so. Thus to the problems of meeting the challenges set by American society and history there is added the difficulty of working a Constitution which was devised by the men of the eighteenth century to meet eighteenth-century needs, and in accordance with eighteenth-century ideas about a desirable system of government. The Founding Fathers had not heard of atomic power, Keynesian economics, radio and television, or the aeroplane; yet the American system of government has to deal with these aspects of modern life, and many others unknown to the founders of the American polity. Much of this burden is carried by the Supreme Court of the United States, which has the task of interpreting an eighteenth-century Constitution in a way which makes sense in the twentieth-century world. But it is the working political system which has to translate this Constitution into action, and to produce results which will be satisfactory in the modern American context. To gain some idea of the extent of this problem let us look for a moment at the Constitution and the philosophy behind it.

Like most of the men of wealth and property in the eighteenth century, the framers of the Federal Constitution did not believe that government should exercise considerable power. They were frightened by two spectres – autocracy and democracy. They wished to avoid the tyranny of one man, or of many. They therefore constructed a constitution which would avoid both evils, by separating the parts of government, and by balancing them against each other. The twin doctrines of the separation of powers, and checks and balances, therefore characterize the American Constitution. The President was to be elected indirectly by means of an Electoral College, which would remove the choice of this officer from the hurly-burly of mob politics. The Congress was to be divided into a House of Representatives which represented the people in proportion to population, and a Senate which gave equal representation to the States. The judicial power was to be vested in a Supreme Court. No member of one branch was allowed to be a member of any other branch of the government, thus ruling out cabinet government on the English model, which at that time was seen as a monarchical or aristocratic device to control the representatives of the people. The personnel of the three branches of government, legislature, executive and judiciary, were, therefore, strictly separated. But the Founders were not satisfied that this alone was a sufficient check to the abuse of power, in particular the abuse of power by the legislature. They had witnessed the experience of the American States during and after the Revolution, when the State legislatures had interfered in executive and judicial affairs, and there had been nothing to prevent them from doing so, except as Jefferson put it, 'parchment barriers'. They therefore instituted a number of checks to the exercise of power. The President was given the

power to veto legislation, and the Supreme Court would interpret the laws and the Constitution, although the latter power was
implicit rather than explicit in the Constitution. The Americans moved back somewhat, therefore, towards the ideas behind
the eighteenth-century constitution of England, but they did not
go all the way. They were not prepared to give to their President
the prerogatives which the British Crown exercised. They gave
to Congress the power to declare war, they subjected the making
of treaties and of appointments to the approval of the Senate,
and they provided that the President's legislative veto could be
overridden by a two-thirds majority of both Houses of Congress.
Thus they erected the structure of government in such a way that
no single part could of itself exercise supreme power. To obtain
effective action there had to be agreement between the differing
parts of the system of government. To ensure the stability of this
system they provided that the Constitution could be amended
only by a long and difficult process, which required the agreement of three quarters of the legislatures of the States. Thus a
major *political* problem in the United States has been the working of this Constitution, particularly in moments of crisis, in
order to get the necessary decisions taken.

Of course, the above description relates only to the formal,
written Constitution, but many aspects of it have been profoundly altered in practice, and certain modes of behaviour,
although not written in the Constitution, have become just as
fixed as if they were rigid constitutional rules. We shall see this in
particular in the working of the system of electing the President,
which operates in strict law as laid down in the Constitution, but
in fact produces exactly the opposite result from that which the
Founders intended. Then there is a whole range of political institutions, such as the congressional committee system, and the
White House Office, which have grown up as a means of ensuring
a much greater degree of contact between the legislative and
executive branches than the Constitution intended. Furthermore, the working of the party system, and the existence of
pressure-groups, provide extra-legal links between the parts of
government, and thus articulate them in practice.

The complexity of the American Federal Government structure is, however, only a part of the story. The United States is a federal system of government in which fifty individual States each has its own position of legal autonomy and political significance. These States are not of course sovereign bodies, but they do exercise powers and carry out functions which in other countries are normally attributed to the central authority. The Constitution set up a division of power between the Federal and State governments which initially limited the former principally to the fields of defence, foreign affairs, the control of the currency, and the control over commerce among the States. This division of power has been eroded with time so that today the functions of the Federal Government have been extended beyond all recognition, touching most of the important concerns of the citizens of the United States. Nevertheless, although the relative power of the States has been considerably diminished they continue to be extremely important and politically powerful centres of government activity.

Furthermore, the local sub-divisions of the States, the cities, counties, towns, and myriad different elective bodies at local level, also exercise varying degrees of political power. The decentralization of American political power can best be seen by examining the autonomy and the political role of a city such as New York, or the relationship between towns or counties with the State governments which legally are their masters. It becomes clear immediately that local *government* has a significance in America that it has long lost in Europe. Thus to understand the politics of the Presidency, or the workings of the Congress of the United States, it is necessary to start by looking at the roots of American politics, at the characteristics of the electorate, at regional variations in political style and behaviour, at the way in which politics is conducted at the State and local level. Only then can we understand the nature of the Presidency, its strengths and its weaknesses; only then can we understand the contradictions of a Congress which can be at one and the same time a parochial assembly and a body of national legislators. The study of American politics must build up from its local components in a way which is no longer so true of the study of most European countries, for the diversity which remains at the base of American life prohibits either the easy generalization or the simple explanation of political behaviour. It is this pattern that we shall follow, building up a picture of the American scene that will help to make explicable what happens at the more glamorous level of President and Congress, and without which the events which make the headlines in the newspapers of the world are often quite incomprehensible. It is a complicated story, which requires much detail if the overall picture is to be appreciated, but it is the story of the political life of a fascinating and complex people, whose behaviour may sometimes be difficult to comprehend, but which is never dull.

The Nature
of American
Politics

2

In attempting to describe and explain the operation of a political
system it is necessary to arrange a vast amount of detailed information into a recognizable pattern which will give meaning
and shape to the activities of those who live in it and make it
work. In the case of the United States, the problem of identify-
ing the major determinants of political behaviour is complicated
by the enormous diversity of American life, and by the way in
which constitutional structures and the patterns of political
action are continually acting and reacting upon each other. Before we plunge into the detail of American politics, therefore,
it is necessary to reflect for a moment upon possible explanations
of the motive forces behind political systems, which have been
isolated in discussions of politics, and of the implications of these
differing explanations for our understanding of the American
system. These 'models' of political life will help us through the
complexities of American politics at all levels of activity, in the
electorate at large, in the structures of party and pressure-group,
and in the workings of congressional and presidential politics.

MODELS OF POLITICS

One of the most powerful sources of man's political loyalty and
action has always been his sense of attachment to a region or
community. When he identifies himself very closely with the interests of a particular area or a particular group of people to the
point where his life ceases to have any real importance other
than within that context, then he has been prepared if necessary
to die to defend those interests. In countries with a very highly
developed national consciousness, it is the nation itself which
becomes the sole focus for this sort of loyalty, but on the way to

the realization of complete national solidarity there are many stages, in which local and regional loyalties can be as important, sometimes more so, as the attachment to the country as a whole. The United States grew out of distinct colonial communities and gradually extended across a continent in a way that tended to emphasize local loyalties, and the constitutional structure of federalism that was evolved in 1787 gave great opportunities for the continued expression of these loyalties. Thus American political history has been strongly characterized by *sectional* patterns of behaviour, in which the inhabitants of a particular region, at all levels of society, have felt themselves united against the conflicting interests of other areas. The most dramatic confrontation of this sort was, of course, the Civil War in which North and South became for a time distinct warring nations. But at a less dramatic level, sectionalism has been a moving force in American politics throughout its history. The unity of the section was dependent upon some common interest which set it off from the rest of the country and which was of sufficient importance to unite its inhabitants in spite of class or other internal divisions. Frequently this common interest was economic, a crop or product upon which their whole livelihood depended. Thus throughout the nineteenth century agricultural sectionalism deeply affected American political behaviour. The historian Frederick Jackson Turner described the sections of the country as faint reflections of European nations. The extreme example of sectional loyalty was provided by the presidential election of 1860 in which in the whole of ten Southern States not a single vote was cast for the candidate of the Republican party, Abraham Lincoln.

Such extremes of sectionalism are not found in the United States today, yet sectional politics continue to have an effect out of all proportion to the actual solidarity of opinion within the different regions of America. The reasons for this will become clearer later, for the impact of local and regional loyalties are to be observed in the stubborn decentralization of the party system, in the machinery of elections, in patterns of voting behaviour, in the working of Congressional politics, and, indeed, in the very nature of the Presidency itself.

The second model of political motivation is that which looks to the class structure of society as the major determinant of political behaviour. Taken to extremes this is, of course, quite incompatible with sectionalism as a force in politics. If political loyalty is really a matter of social class, then regional loyalties will have no part to play in the political system, and to the extent that these regional loyalties continue to exist, then class solidarity across the nation will be diminished. In fact, recent American political history is, in part, the story of the complex interaction of these two political motivations, with sectionalism declining as class consciousness waxed. Each of these styles of political behaviour has, of course, very different implications for the type of party system one would expect to find. Indeed, if either sectional or class politics is taken to the extreme then party politics as we understand it would be ruled out: there would simply be civil war, either between geographical regions or between classes. The working of the democratic system depends upon the fact that these extremes are never realized, and that political parties must appeal both to different sections of the country and to different classes of the population.

Our third approach to the political system we may describe as the *pluralistic* approach. This views the political system as a large number of groups each with a different interest, so that politics is a continually changing pattern of group activities and inter-actions. Economic, class, and geographic factors are important parts of the pattern, but many other types of groups are also important; religious groups, ethnic groups, and other social groupings. Furthermore, although economic groups play an important part in the political system they do not coalesce into two or three big classes for purposes of political action; they are divided among themselves, union opposing union, one type of producer battling with his competitors, agriculture ranged against industry, small businessman against big businessman, the re-tailer against the manufacturer, and so on without end. Class and regional loyalties are fragmented, each group seeking for support to win its battles wherever that support is to be found. Thus we have a picture of the political system as a collection of a very large number of groups, of varying size and importance, battling for their interests in a society where no single group dominates. Since the membership of these groups overlaps considerably – there are Catholic businessmen and Protestant businessmen, Irish-American labour leaders and Italian-American labour leaders – there is a continual set of cross-pressures upon the leaders of these groups which helps the processes of compromise between them and moderates their demands. At the extreme the role of government in such a society is simply to hold the ring, to act as referee between the groups to enable the necessary bargaining and compromise to take place. The political machinery becomes simply the mechanism through which an equilibrium is achieved between the contending interests. As the government's main autonomous interest becomes that of maintaining law and order, there is little scope for active leadership to give direction to national policy, and political parties have little coherence or discipline, being merely organizational devices devoid of policy content. Pluralism is very much an American view of the political process, and many accounts of the working of the system of government, and in particular the role of interest groups in it, are couched in these terms. It is essential to approach American politics from a pluralistic viewpoint, but as with the other models so far discussed, the temptation to push it to an extreme as the *sole* explanation must be resisted.

A rather different approach to the nature of the American system, but one closely related to both class and pluralistic theories of politics, is the belief that the United States is governed by a series of *élites*, or indeed by a single power *élite*. This view, associated with the name of C. Wright Mills, tends to place great emphasis upon the power and wealth of those groups in the population that control crucial areas of the economy and government, in particular the chief executives of large corporations and military leaders, the military-industrial complex against which President Eisenhower delivered a warning to the American people when he came to the end of his term of office. Thus certain relatively small groups of men cease to be just part of an internal bargaining process and become in fact, behind the scenes, the real rulers of the country. The formal political machinery becomes less and less important in the taking of the really important decisions, and the electorate, and even the Congress, are by-passed. This interpretation of American politics, even though it can degenerate into a conspiracy-theory which attempts to explain every important decision as the results of the secret manipulations of the power *élite*, must be given serious consideration. There are *élite* groups in the United States, as in any large industrial society, and they may have great influence in certain circumstances.

The final model of political behaviour we must employ in the analysis of American politics is *individualism*. In the other accounts of the political system to which we have referred, the individual is swallowed up by a class, section, or group, his behaviour is 'determined' by class ideology, regional loyalty, or group interest, and as an individual he has little or no significance in political situations. Such interpretations of political life bear little relation to the long tradition of democratic thought in which the individual citizen was the central concern of writers on politics, and in which personality and individual choice were crucial elements in the political situation. It is ironic that it is in America, the land of individualism *par excellence*, that students of political behaviour have demolished the classical description of the democratic political system as composed of rational, informed individuals each making up his own mind on political issues on the basis of a cool appraisal of the facts. They have suggested that, in the mid twentieth century Western democracies at any rate, the influence of family, of class, of the local community or other relevant social groupings, is far more important in determining voting behaviour than knowledge of the issues which face the electorate. Nevertheless, it would be rash indeed to attempt to describe the working of the American political system without paying great attention to the importance of personal factors in the choice of candidates, and in the influence of personality on voting behaviour, or to fail to give due weight to the role of individualism in such things as 'ticket-splitting', and in the evolving patterns of suburban politics. Sometimes, perhaps because of their closeness to their own political system, American students of politics seem

unaware of the importance of the individual in politics in the
United States compared with his role in the politics of other
countries.

Each of these 'models' of political behaviour and motivation
has, of course, very different implications for the type of party
organization which we would expect to find in systems of government in which they played a dominant role, very different roles
for personality and leadership in the political system, very different attitudes towards ideology and 'issues' in the political
process, and very different results in terms of party cohesion
and discipline, particularly in the legislature. Taken to extremes
these models of the political system are mutually exclusive, each
giving rise to a very different style of political life. The fascination of the American political system lies in the fact that it represents a complex amalgam of all these different patterns of politics,
in a constantly changing kaleidoscope of sectional, class, pluralistic and individualistic styles of politics. None of these 'explanations' of political behaviour can be written off as insignificant,
and equally none of them can be considered to be the dominant
pattern of American political life. The significance of each of
these elements differs from time to time, from issue to issue. At
one point of time, because of economic circumstances, the class
factor may become relatively more important in the understanding of the political situation; at another point of time, because
of the cold war or other external forces, the 'military-industrial
complex' may exercise considerable influence; when economic
and external crises recede, personal and pluralistic factors may
dominate the political scene. Furthermore, because American
politics are conducted at several levels, the significance of one
or other political style may be different at the level of presidential
politics from that of congressional politics, or at State level from
that of the Federal level, or in the party system as compared with
the structure of pressure-groups.

It is in this spirit that we must approach the study of American politics, seeking out the elements of class, sectional, pluralistic and individualistic politics, putting them in perspective
at the different levels of political life, and exploring their implications for political organization. Only in this way can we hope

to make sense of the complexity and diversity of American political patterns and to see the political system as a whole.

THE DECLINE OF SECTIONALISM

Sectionalism has been a factor in American politics ever since the differing characteristics of the seventeenth-century settlements in Virginia and Massachusetts began to interact with the differing climatic and economic conditions to be found on the south-eastern and north-eastern seaboards. The Constitution adopted in 1789 represented in part a bargain between North and South which provided the uneasy basis for American political life till the outbreak of the Civil War. The position of the Republican Party as the representative of the victorious North in that war and the association of the Democratic Party with the South, gave a twist to the distribution of political power which persists to the present day. It is the election of 1896, however, which sets the high-water mark of sectionalism as a political force in modern politics. The Populist supporters of William Jennings Bryan gained control of the Democratic Party's Convention in that year, and secured his nomination as the party's presidential candidate. Populism represented an attack upon privilege and upon the power of financiers and industrialists; it was a movement of the 'common man', and as such it would seem to mean an injection of a strong class element into the American political scene. But although the Democratic Party platform of 1896 pledged the party to support the interests of the farmer and the labourer it was only able to capture the votes of the agrarians of the South and West. The industrial workers of the East voted strongly for the Republicans and the extreme sectional pattern of politics in that election can be gauged from the following map.

The reaction to the rise of the Populists was even more significant for the nature of politics at the turn of the century. There was a revulsion against this upsurge of the common man, and conservatives in North and South alike set about the creation of political machines in which they could maintain their ascendency, working through the medium of the Republican Party in the

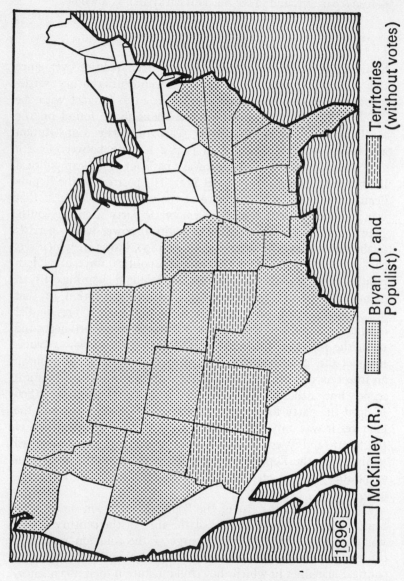

McKinley (R.) Bryan (D. and Populist). Territories (without votes)

1896

The Presidential Election of 1896

North and through the Democratic Party in the South. Before 1896 the two parties had been relatively well balanced throughout the country, but by 1904 there remained only six States in which the parties were evenly matched. The Republican party almost ceased to exist in the South, while the Democrats were almost as powerless in the North.

As the twentieth century progressed, however, the forces which had produced and maintained this sectional alignment were gradually eroded. The nationalizing influences of the growth of communications and of America's involvement in world affairs tended to diminish local patriotisms, but perhaps the most important factor was the economic problem of an economy which was no longer 'open' in the sense in which it had been in the expansive years of the nineteenth century. The years of depression were the background to the Democratic victories of Franklin D. Roosevelt, in 1932 when the old sectional alignment was shattered, and in 1936 when he won every State in the Union with the exception of Maine and Vermont. Genuine competition between the two parties gradually spread into more and more of the States, and this process is now beginning to affect even the States of the Deep South.

Yet important as sectionalism undoubtedly was at the beginning of the century, we must not overstate its importance. Although one party might consistently win elections in a particular State or region over a long period of time, this fact might mask the existence of a strong minority, and as the century progressed this minority gradually began to achieve some sort of parity with the previously dominant group. This is not true of the really Deep South, but V. O. Key has recently shown that even in that most distinctive of regions, it is only in matters concerning racial problems that the South differs profoundly from other regions in the make-up of public opinion. Much of the impression of Southern conservatism in economic and social matters is largely due to the way in which the one-party politics of the Southern variety distorts the operation of the machinery of representative government. However, even if opinions are not radically different in different parts of the country, the fact that the working of politics produces sectional differences in the

attitudes of Senators and Representatives is of the greatest importance, for we are concerned here with the outcomes of political
situations, and the transformation of raw public opinion into
sectional politics in Congress, and in the Presidency, is the vital
stuff of our study.

Thus sectionalism has declined in importance, and no doubt
will continue to do so as the nationalizing forces at work in
America continue to create a more homogeneous community.
Nevertheless regional and local factors continue to play a very
important part in American politics today. We shall look later
at the variety of the patterns of State and local politics, and
at their impact upon the voting behaviour of Congressmen
and Senators; but even in the sphere of the presidential election,
the most national event in the American political calendar, the
importance of sectional influences is very considerable. The impact of sectionalism varies in significance from election to election.
In 1964 the landslide victory of President Johnson swamped most
sectional influences, for he won forty-two of the fifty States, with
an overall sixty-one per cent of the total vote cast, against thirty-
eight and a half per cent for Senator Goldwater. Such an overwhelming victory makes the differences between the regions of
the country in their support of one candidate or the other seem
quite insignificant. Even in 1964, however, there were some remarkable regional differences in the pattern of voting. Of the six
States won by the Republican candidate, Senator Goldwater, five
formed a block of States in the Deep South – Mississippi,
Alabama, Louisiana, South Carolina and Georgia – States which
normally are solidly Democratic. On the other hand, there was
a large swing to the Democrats in the Prairie States and the States
of the Mid-West, which in the previous election the Republicans
had won handsomely.

In a more closely contested election, however, sectional differences may be critical. Thus in 1960 the victory of the Democratic candidate was achieved by the slimmest possible margin of
0.1 per cent of the total votes cast, and the significance of
sectionalism in the result can be judged from the map below.

Kennedy won a majority of the States of the South and East,
whilst Nixon almost swept the board in the West and Mid West.

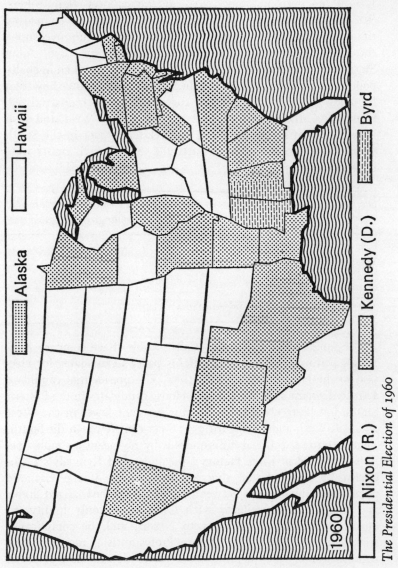

Nixon (R.)   Kennedy (D.)   Byrd

Alaska   Hawaii

1960

The Presidential Election of 1960

For a number of reasons, particularly his religion, Kennedy performed less well in some parts of the country than others.
We can get a picture of these sectional differences by comparing
the percentage in each region by which Kennedy improved upon
the performance of the Democratic candidate in 1956, Adlai
Stevenson, who had had to do battle against the phenomenally
popular President Eisenhower. The figures given below show that
Kennedy was very much more successful in the industrialized,
relatively Catholic Eastern States, than in the West and Mid
West, and that his performance was relatively poor in the South
where his Catholicism and his attitude towards civil rights were
both against him.

Section	Democratic percentage change from 1956
East	+13·9
West	+ 6·1
Mid West	+ 5·1
South and Border (excluding Mississippi and Alabama)	+ 2·5

The same sectional pattern is discernible if we compare Kennedy's performance with that of his party's candidates for election to the House of Representatives. The presidential candidate
attracted almost as many votes as House candidates in the Eastern
States, but he received three to four per cent fewer in the West
and Mid West, and a staggering 15.8 per cent fewer in the South.
This pattern of sectional differences is by no means a simple one.
It is composed of three factors: the impact of Kennedy's Catholicism, because of the uneven distribution of the Catholic
population; the division between the highly industrialized States
and the less industrialized, with Ohio as the only highly industrialized State which went to Nixon; and the complicated
sectionalism of the South, where Protestantism, racialism and
ruralism combined to deprive the Democratic candidate of seven
Southern and Border States.

In the election of 1968 the sectional nature of American

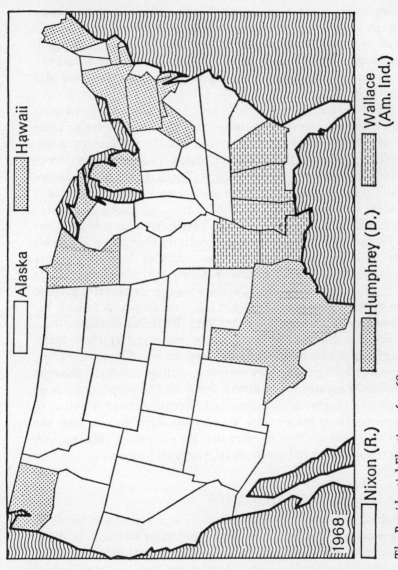

Alaska   Hawaii

Nixon (R.)   Humphrey (D.)   Wallace
(Am. Ind.)

1968

The Presidential Election of 1968

politics was demonstrated again, in one sense indeed in a rather more extreme way than in 1960. A bloc of five States in the Deep South were captured by George Wallace; the rest of the South (except Texas), and almost the whole of the West and the Mid West went to Richard Nixon; Hubert Humphrey won the populous Eastern States, including New York, Pennsylvania, and the southern New England States, together with the industrial Mid West State of Michigan.

However, the above map both underestimates and at the same time overstates the sectional forces at work in this election. Three of the States which Humphrey won outside the Eastern industrial bloc, Texas, Minnesota and Maine, probably went Democratic only for very special reasons. Texas stayed in the Democratic column only by a wafer-thin margin, and in spite of a sizeable vote for Wallace (see Table 5 at end of book), presumably because of the support which the Texan President Johnson gave to Humphrey. Similarly personal loyalty to Humphrey and to his vice-presidential candidate, Senator Muskie of Maine, may have been significant in the results in Minnesota and Maine. If one were to exclude these three States from the Democratic pattern, the sectional character of the election would be stark indeed. Yet Humphrey polled only 0.1 per cent fewer votes than Nixon throughout the country as a whole, and some of those States which are shown in white on the map, such as Illinois and Ohio, were won by Nixon by very narrow majorities. Similarly although Wallace won only five Southern States he had surprisingly large votes in a number of Northern and Western States, as well as in Southern States which were won by the Republicans. Thus the sectional map obscures the fact that the election of 1968 was one of the most 'national' elections in American history.

CLASS IN AMERICAN POLITICS

That class-oriented political behaviour is a significant factor in American politics cannot be denied, but the problem is to determine how significant it is. At the end of the nineteenth century the triumph of sectionalism had as its corollary a relative lack of emphasis upon class in American voting behaviour; but as sectionalism declined in importance, the class alignments of American voters became more significant. The events of the 1920s and 1930s, and the appeal of Roosevelt's New Deal measures to the underprivileged, established a distinct relationship between class and party allegiance, though one which is subject to considerable variation from election to election. Alford gives the following figures of the differences in the preferences of manual and non-manual workers for the Democratic Presidential candidates over the past thirty years.

Percentage preference for Democratic party among manual and non-manual workers

	Manual workers	Non-manual workers
1936	67	52
1940	65	40
1944	67	46
1948	79	38
1952	57	34
1956	52	39
1960	60	46

The preference of a majority of manual workers for the Democrats and of a majority of non-manual workers for the Republicans is found in every election except that of 1936. Using similar figures S. M. Lipset has recently given considerable emphasis to the class element in American voting behaviour. He has pointed out that if the above occupational categories are broken down, the further down the social scale, the greater the percentage preference for the Democratic party. In 1948, he notes, nearly eighty per cent of American manual workers voted for the Democrats, a higher percentage than most left-wing parties in European countries can achieve. Nevertheless, as in the case of sectional influences, the significance of social class as a factor in electoral behaviour must not be overstated. The 1948 election was certainly one in which the class factor was important, because the issues before the electorate were largely of an economic kind, but if we look at the election of 1956 we get a very different picture. In 1956 almost as many manual workers voted for the

Republican candidate as for the Democrat, but we would not be justified in concluding from this isolated fact that class was irrelevant to American politics.

Perhaps the first point to note about the role of class in American politics is the considerable variation in the percentage of manual workers voting for the Democratic party in these years. Over a period of only eight years, 1948–56, there was a difference of twenty-seven per cent in the proportion of the manual working-class vote going to the Democrats. It can be argued, of course, that the elections of 1952 and 1956 were 'abnormal' because of the enormous personal appeal of the Republican candidate, Dwight Eisenhower, but this very fact highlights the potential role of personality and other factors in determining the result of American elections. The high proportion of manual workers voting Democratic in 1948 was as 'exceptional' as the low proportion voting Democratic in 1956. Indeed every American election might be said to be 'exceptional' for there is no single determining factor which can be said to be always dominant in American politics.

In fact, of course, the attribution of sectional or class motivations on the basis of the sort of statistics quoted above is a very difficult exercise. What is apparently class voting may be motivated in quite different ways, because religious, ethnic and regional groupings all overlap with class to a very considerable extent. Exactly why a low-paid Irish Catholic industrial worker in the North East votes Democratic rather than Republican is hardly to be explained by any simple formula. Thus Angus Campbell and his co-authors in their study The American Voter found that one third of the American population is 'unaware' of its class position, and that social class plays a significant role at a conscious level in the political behaviour of only a fairly restricted and sophisticated portion of the population. Furthermore, the relative volatility of the American electorate, the readiness to change parties, is also a measure of the limitations upon appeals to class orientation as a source of voting behaviour. American elections can produce 'landslide' results which would be unlikely in a system where stable class voting was the norm. The figures below give the percentage of the total vote cast, that has gone to the Democratic Party in presidential elections over the past thirty years. There is a difference of nineteen per cent between the low-water mark of 1956 and the record level set by President Johnson in 1964, indicating a potential switching of voters of quite startling proportions. With the intervention of a strong third party in 1968 the Democratic proportion of the vote fell back almost as far as it had been in 1956.

Democratic percentage of the total Presidential vote

1936	60·8	1956	42·0
1940	54·7	1960	49·7
1944	53·4	1964	61·0
1948	49·5	1968	42·7
1952	44·5	1972	60·7

URBAN – RURAL – SUBURBAN POLITICS

The relatively straightforward categories with which we began this chapter soon begin to look somewhat inadequate when we delve into the rich detail of the American political scene, for sectional, class and other aspects of the political pattern overlap and intermingle. The first major overlap is represented by the blending of geographical sectionalism and class politics due to the uneven distribution of industry across the country, and to the consequent divisions between the urban and rural populations. During the nineteenth century sectionalism was largely the consequence of the differing crops and products resulting from different climatic and soil conditions; with the enormous growth of industrial power and the rapid concentration of population in urban centres, however, the clash of interest between city and country became a dominant factor in the political scene. The greatest impact of the flood of poor immigrants at the turn of the century was felt in the cities, and at the same time there was an internal migration from the farms to the cities. The result was the concentration of the underprivileged, the poor, and less well-educated, in the great cities of the North and East. The proportion of the population of the United States

living in cities of over 100,000 people rose from 12·4 per cent in
1880 to nearly thirty per cent in 1930, during which time the
total number of people living in such cities shot up from six
million to thirty-six million. Here was the raw material for
the transformation of the political system of the United States
into something very different from that of the sectional alignment of 1896, but one in which geography continued to play a
part.

The Great Depression of the 1930s was the catalytic agent
which transformed this vast mass of human beings into what has
come to be called the 'normal' Democratic majority. Samuel
Lubell has shown that it was Alfred E. Smith, the unsuccessful
Democratic candidate for the Presidency in 1928 before the
Depression actually began, who first drew the political battle
lines between the cities and the rural areas; but it was the New
Deal policies of Franklin D. Roosevelt that fixed the urban
masses of the North and East in the Democratic column. In 1924
in the twelve largest cities in the United States the Republicans
had an overall majority over the Democrats of 1,252,000 votes.
Twenty years later in the same twelve cities the Democratic
majority over the Republicans was 2,296,000 votes. This enormous change of allegiance represented, in Lubell's phrase, the
revolt-of the underdog. Economic, ethnic and religious factors
combined to create a body of support for the Democratic Party
which broke the hold which the Republicans had had upon the
Presidency, with short breaks, since the Civil War. The urban
masses of the North became one prop of the Democratic party,
in uneasy alliance with the rural southern whites who used the
Democratic Party to maintain their position locally and to
resist interference at the Federal level. This remarkable coalition,
papering over deep ideological cleavages because historical
accident and existing organizational structures provided both
wings of the Party with an unprecedented opportunity to
exercise power, has dominated American politics since the election of Roosevelt in 1932, and only now shows signs of breaking
up. The Northern wing of the Party dominated the Presidency,
whilst the Southern wing gained a strategically vital position in
Congress, in particular by its control of committee chairman-

ships. As we shall see the Presidency and the Congress may be said to have different 'constituencies' because of the methods of their election. To gain election to the Presidency a candidate must woo the great populous urban States of the North and East, whilst Congress has in the past been more representative of, and more responsive to, rural interests. The resulting tension between President and Congress on a wide range of policies became, because of the coalition nature of both great political parties, a great source of internal strife *within* the parties as well as between them.

The years since the end of the Second World War have, however, brought a new complication to this pattern of urban-rural politics. The rapid development of suburbia has begun to transform America both visually and politically. These suburbs spreading out many miles into the country around urban areas represent a whole new way of life, and potentially their impact upon politics may be as great as that of the Roosevelt revolution. They represent a new type of community in which the old guidelines to political behaviour are no longer so reliable. The population of the suburbs is ethnically diverse whilst its economic composition is relatively homogeneous. Neither the old pattern of city politics based upon ethnic differences, nor the urban-rural alignment, seem any longer relevant. As Robert C. Wood has pointed out, the suburbs fit neither into the class patterns of the early twentieth century, nor into the sectional patterns of the nineteenth. Yet old political loyalties die hard, and the persistence of party allegiance is one of the facts of political behaviour, even when the original reasons for choosing one side rather than another have long become irrelevent. It is therefore very difficult to predict the way in which the suburbs will affect relative party strengths in the future. During the nineteen-fifties the suburban vote was strongly Republican; in this decade there is a suggestion of increasing Democratic strength. Perhaps the greatest significance of the rise of suburbia is to provide an overlap with another of our patterns of political behaviour, individualism, for suburbanites tend to think of themselves as independents in politics, discriminating between candidates rather than parties, paying attention to different issues at the various levels of govern-

ment, and making use of all the opportunities for ticket-splitting
that the American electoral system provides.

PLURALISM IN AMERICAN POLITICS

The group basis of politics has become the subject of intensive
study only in the twentieth century, and significantly it is in
two American works, *The Process of Government* by Arthur F.
Bentley published in 1908, and David B. Truman's *The Governmental Process* of 1951, that this approach has been developed.
We shall look closely at this view of the political system in a
later chapter when discussing interest group politics, but here we
shall concentrate upon two aspects of group politics of particular
significance at the level of electoral behaviour – the politics of
ethnic and religious groups.

ETHNIC POLITICS

Since the early 1930s minority groups such as Italian-Ameri-
cans, Irish-Americans, the Jewish community, the Negroes,
have tended to vote for the Democratic party. The tendency is
particularly noticeable in the large cities, but in 1948 in the
small city of Elmira, New York, Berelson and his collaborators
found that whilst eighty-one per cent of the white native-born
protestants voted Republican, only thirty-three per cent of the
Jews, nineteen per cent of the Negroes and eighteen per cent of
the Italian-American voters followed suit. Here again there is an
overlapping of our simple categories, for minority groups, and
particularly the Negroes and foreign-born immigrants, belong
also to the lower-income groups; nevertheless Berelson found
that the tendency of these groups to vote Democrat was not
particularly affected by their socio-economic position. The
significance of such group voting can be very great. Thus one of
the many 'decisive' factors in the victory of John F. Kennedy in
1960 was the way in which the Negroes in a few Southern States,
by voting solidly Democratic, delivered those States to Kennedy
instead of Nixon. In the nineteenth and early twentieth centuries the Negro had traditionally been loyal to the Republicans,

the party of Lincoln, but Roosevelt's economic policies, and the commitment of the Democratic party at the national level to civil rights programmes, led the Negro to support the Democrats in ever-growing numbers. As Negro voting registrations increase in the Southern States the politics of that section must be transformed by the political cohesiveness of the Negro community.

Other ethnic groups play less dramatic but no less significant roles in electoral behaviour. Samuel Lubell in his *Revolt of the Moderates* found that the power-base of the late Republican Senator Joseph McCarthy could be traced to those ethnic groups who were deeply affected by the cross-pressures they experienced as a result of America's involvement in two World Wars. Lubell showed that in McCarthy's home State of Wisconsin there had been a considerable shift away from the Democratic Party by German-Americans, because that Party was associated with the policy of war against Germany. In 1932 eight largely German Catholic counties in Wisconsin voted seventy-four per cent Democratic, but by 1952 the Democratic vote had dropped to thirty-two per cent. This change was reflected in German-American communities throughout the country. Lubell emphasized that, as the second most numerous 'foreign-stock', the German-Americans held the balance of power in many States, especially in the Mid West. Such support provided a formidable reservoir of emotion upon which a man like McCarthy could draw, for these people wished to emphasize their American patriotism, and at the same time to give expression to attitudes towards communism which were related to their religious beliefs. In the same way the complex inter-relationship between Catholic doctrine and the need to assert their Americanness led the Irish Catholics of New York to give overwhelming support to McCarthy.

At the lower levels of the political system ethnic divisions play a crucial role. The politics of New York City present the extreme picture of ethnic diversity and its effects. Over half the population of New York is of Jewish, Italian, German or Irish origin, and nearly a quarter is negro or Puerto Rican. Only about one twentieth of the population are 'old-stock' white Anglo-Saxon protestants – or WASPs. In 1960 almost half the population of the city was foreign-born or the children of immigrants. Glazer and Moynihan, the authors of a work on the racial character of New York politics, described the election of Mayor Wagner in 1961 in the following terms: Wagner won, they say, 'with the support of lower-class Negro and Puerto-Rican voters, and middle-class Jewish voters, who together were enough to overcome the opposition of Italian, Irish and white Protestant middle-class and upper-working-class voters'. This complex of criss-crossing ethnic and class divisions has implications not only for local or city elections, but may be a decisive factor in congressional politics, or even in the complex processes by which the President of the United States is chosen. Furthermore, it is possible that differing attitudes towards such concepts as 'the public interest' may be affected by ethnic origins, although it is very difficult to demonstrate direct relationships between particular ethnic groups and specific attitudes towards governmental structure or policy. James Wilson and Edward Banfield have suggested that 'Anglo-Saxon' and Jewish voters in certain Ohio communities were more favourably disposed to increasing public expenditure than were Polish or Czech voters enjoying the same level of income. What does seem to be incontestable is that Jewish voters, at all income levels, tend to adopt 'liberal' attitudes on political issues, and to discriminate in their voting in favour of those candidates, of whichever party, that they consider to be liberal.

Some of the ethnic divisions within American society cut very deep, as is evidenced by the position of the Negro, yet one might expect that as groups of 'hyphenated Americans' become assimilated both culturally and economically, they would become indistinguishable in their political behaviour from the rest of the population. This 'assimilation theory' may well be correct, *in the long run*, but it is important to remember that the great waves of immigrants were still flowing into the United States just over forty-five years ago. Furthermore it is one of the most frequently observed facts of political life that political loyalties tend to outlive the factors which created them. Local conditions and local leadership can give a quite remarkable persistence and coherence to ethnic political behaviour. In a study of the city of

New Haven in Connecticut, R. E. Wolfinger has shown that the Italian-American community, although belonging to the poorest segment of the population, persists as a strong Republican voting bloc, although in the North East in general Italians tend to vote Democratic. In the same city the Irish-Americans, who have now almost all risen to the ranks of the middle class, remain staunch Democrats. The end of ethnic politics in the United States is still a long way off.

RELIGION IN POLITICS

Religion has been a factor in American politics ever since the Pilgrim Fathers made landfall on Cape Cod. Furthermore the regional distribution of religious belief has served to complicate the sectional differences of American politics. In colonial times Puritan New England and Anglican Virginia were separated by Quaker-dominated Pennsylvania, the Roman Catholics of Maryland, and the Dutch Reformed church in New York. The mass immigration of the nineteenth and twentieth centuries transformed the pattern of religious affiliation, for a very high proportion of the immigrants were Catholic. Today it is estimated that there are over forty-five million Catholics in the United States, making the American Catholic community one of the largest in the world. Because the waves of immigrants headed for the cities of the North and East, the pattern of sectional attitudes became further complicated, and because they were poor, Catholic immigrants contributed a further dimension to the pattern of sectional, class and religious influences which today form the fabric of American politics. Thus the electorate of the Southern States remains almost completely Protestant in composition, whereas the concentration of Catholics in Northern States such as Massachusetts gives to those States a quite distinctive political style.

Like the other factors in American politics, religion plays a significant but varying role in national politics. In State and local politics its impact varies greatly from area to area, and from issue to issue; but of its importance there can be little doubt. Religious factors have played an important role in Presidential politics, in helping to influence the voting behaviour of Senators and Congressmen, or in the determination of political battles over the contraception laws in Massachusetts or the closed-shop in Ohio. The candidacy of two Catholics for the Presidency in this century has shown the potential importance of religion in politics. The candidacy of Al Smith in 1928 showed the extent of the bitterness against Catholics, although his defeat cannot be attributed primarily to religious motivations among the electorate. Religious influences on voting behaviour are not confined, however, to elections in which Catholics are candidates. Even in the most class-conscious election of recent years, that of 1948, Berelson found that Catholics in Elmira voted more Democratic than did Protestants, regardless of class status or identification, or of national origin. In 1956, when Eisenhower's personal appeal was so great, Catholics split almost fifty-fifty between the parties, but four years later roughly eighty per cent of Catholics voted for the Catholic candidate, John F. Kennedy, and only twenty per cent for his Protestant opponent.

The significance of religion in the election of 1960 is suggested by the way in which Kennedy's vote-pulling power, as compared with that of his predecessor Adlai Stevenson, varied State by State according to the percentage of Catholics in the population.

States with Catholic percentage of total .population of	Democratic vote, percentage change from 1956*
Over 40	+19·7
30–9	+16·3
20–9	+ 7·3
10–19	+ 5·0
Below 10	+ 2·6

*Excluding Hawaii, Alaska, Mississippi and Alabama

The difference between Kennedy's performance in States with a high percentage of Catholics from his vote-attracting power in States with relatively few Catholics is very marked. The following example, given by John H. Fenton, of the effect of religious divisions within a community, although it may not be typical, shows the effect that religious affiliation can have on politics. In Nelson County, Kentucky, which is half Baptist, half Catholic, Kennedy only received thirty-five per cent of the vote in four predominantly Baptist precincts, but in five largely Catholic precincts he received eighty-eight per cent of the total vote. Nationally, the tendency of Catholics to vote for a member of their own church was, however, more than offset by those Protestant voters who switched to the support of Nixon on religious grounds. For the importance of religion as a political issue is by no means confined to the question of Catholicism. Richard Hofstadter has argued that fundamentalist religious beliefs, still very much alive in the United States today, lie at the heart of much of the extremist right-wing political sentiment which sustains the John Birch Society and similar groups. The problem of the relationship between church and State, particularly in regard to government aid to parochial schools, continues to raise much discussion and argument amongst people who are far from extreme in their views: in recent years the United States has been reminded that there are important non-Christian groups in the population, Muslims and atheists among them, who feel that their way of life is adversely affected by the *de facto* establishment of Protestantism in a country where the Constitution forbids the establishment by the State of any church or religion.

THE ROLE OF INDIVIDUALISM AND PERSONALITY

The patterns of sectional, class, and ethnic and religious politics that we have looked at so far would seem to leave little room for the emergence of truly individualistic behaviour on the part of the electors or their representatives, and yet if we look at the trends of political behaviour in America during this century we find that individualism in politics has become increasingly important. Indeed, we find ourselves here at the very heart of the American political system in the mid twentieth century, faced with an apparent paradox which must be resolved if we are to understand the nature of this system. We have already seen that one of the major developments of this century has been the increasing importance to be attached to the role of class status as a determinant of voting behaviour. As sectionalism declined, class-oriented voting patterns emerged more into prominence. Now if this was an example of class-conscious political behaviour along European lines we should expect certain changes in the political sytem as a consequence. Presumably the role of ideology would have become much greater as a result of the intensification of the theme of class-war, party discipline would have been more rigidly applied because of the sense of class solidarity within the parties, and the role of the individual would have declined because his interest would have been sacrificed to that of the party. Yet in each of these respects just the opposite has in fact taken place. After an initial outburst of ideological fervour in the nineteen-thirties, fashionable works of the fifties and sixties deal with 'the end of ideology'. Party discipline in Congress today is looser than at the end of the nineteenth century. The role of individualism in voting behaviour seems to be on the increase.

Part of the explanation of these phenomena lies in the nature and operation of the machinery of representation which we shall examine later, but certain basic facts about the nature of the electorate lie at the centre of these apparently contradictory trends. At the end of the last century American political attitudes were strongly party-oriented, that is to say that voters identified themselves very strongly with a particular political party. It was in the nature of politics at that time that party identification was founded largely upon historical and regional loyalties rather than class, but as the twentieth century progressed and class voting increased in importance, the ties between the voter and his party progressively declined. That these two things happened at one and the same time was a reflection both of the extreme nature of the sectional alignment after 1896, and of the fact that as the century progressed, much of the electorate became increasingly alienated from political life. Walter D. Burnham has pointed out that an increasingly large proportion of the electorate are 'peripheral voters' who are not closely tied to one party or another, and who participate in elections only when they feel strongly moved to do so by the impact of a personality or an issue sufficiently strong to make them re-enter the political universe. Burnham gives the following figures of voting turnout to illustrate this decline in political activity in the electorate.

Voting turnout by periods, 1848–1960
(Presidential years only)

1848–72	75·1%	1920–28	51·7%
1876–96	78·5%	1932–44	59·1%
1900–16	64·8%	1948–60	60·3%

Voters have also been more ready to change sides in this century, so that the swing from one party to another in successive elections has been greater than in the last century, and landslides have been more common, as illustrated by the elections of 1964 and 1972.

One of the most important manifestations of this decline in close party identification is to be found in the phenomenon of 'split-ticket' voting. At each election the American voter is confronted by a ballot-paper, or a voting-machine, which allows him to vote for a number of candidates for different offices at Federal, State and local level. Each of the major parties, and perhaps some minor ones, will have candidates for all or some of these offices on the ballot. If he so wishes, the voter may simply vote for all the Republican candidates, or all the Democrats. If he does so he is said to vote 'the straight ticket', and usually it is much simpler to do this, requiring only a single mark on the ballot-paper or the operation of a single lever on the machine. Equally, however, he is free to 'split the ticket', that is to vote for one or more Republicans for some offices, and for Democrats for the others, or indeed, where three or more parties appear on the ballot, to spread his votes across them all, voting for individual candidates, regardless of party, as he sees fit. At the Federal level the voter can discriminate between candidates for the Presidency, the Senate, and the House of Representatives, voting Republican for one or two of these offices, and Democrat for the third, or any combination he wishes.

The complexity of the ballot-paper and the trouble involved

in making the necessary discrimination between candidates
might suggest that split-ticket voting was relatively rare. Not so!
Campbell and Miller found that in 1952 as many as one third of
the voters split the ticket and in 1956 two fifths of the electorate
did so. The potential importance of this practice at the Federal
level is illustrated by the vote in 1952 when nearly forty million
Americans voted for the Republican candidate for the Presidency, Eisenhower, but only twenty-eight million voted for Republican candidates for the House of Representatives. In recent
years this pattern of voting Republican for the Presidency and
Democrat for Senate and House candidates – *Presidential Republicanism* – has become increasingly important, particularly in the
Southern States. The following remarkable results in the 1960
elections in Virginia and Tennessee illustrate the extent to which
the electorate discriminated between Presidential and Senatorial
candidates:

Percentage of vote cast for Democratic Presidential candidate		Percentage of vote cast for Democratic Senatorial candidate
Virginia	47·0	82·7
Tennessee	45·8	71·2

It is true, of course, that much of this ticket-splitting should
be attributed to sectional or pluralistic influences rather than to
individualism, for it results from regional antipathies to a particular candidate or set of policies, as in the case of the South, or
from the reactions of a particular group to a candidate's religious
background, as in the case of Kennedy's Catholicism. Nevertheless the election of 1960 provides endless examples of the
importance of this form of political behaviour, which although
influenced by sectional and group loyalties, reflect also the impact of the personality of the candidates upon the voters, and
the extent to which the American voter can break away from
strict party-line voting. Thus in six of the States which produced
a majority for the Republican, Richard Nixon, Democrats were
successful in winning seats in the Senate, whilst in three of

the States which voted for Kennedy, Republican Senators were returned by the same State-wide electorate. Other examples can be drawn from the results of elections to the House of Representatives. In the nineteenth Congressional District of California a Democrat was returned with a majority of 100,000 votes whereas Kennedy won the District by a very narrow margin. In Hawaii the presidential race was decided only after recounts in which the lead changed from one candidate to another, and Kennedy's final majority was little more than a hundred votes, but a single Hawaiian Congressman, a Democrat, was elected with a majority of 88,500 votes.

Perhaps, however, it is the politics of the State of Massachusetts, from which the successful presidential candidate came in 1960, that best illustrates the extent to which split-ticket voting can go. Massachusetts has traditionally split its vote, and in 1960 it outdid itself. The population of the State is approximately fifty per cent Catholic, has a large Irish-American element and is highly industrialized, so that it is hardly surprising that the Irish Catholic Democratic Senator Kennedy from Massachusetts achieved a majority over his rival for the Presidency of over half a million votes out of a total of less than two and a half million. At the same time as this landslide for Kennedy was taking place, and on the same ballot papers, the Democratic candidate for Senator was being beaten by a majority of 300,000 votes, by the incumbent Republican, Leverett Saltonstall.

It is always difficult to assess the importance of the personality of a candidate upon voting decisions, and, as Samuel Lubell has suggested, it may well be that personality alone is not enough, and will not sway the voters unless there is some other latent factor which the personal appeal of the candidate serves to bring into operation. The importance of personality will also vary according to circumstances. Thus in areas where party organization is minimal, personality may be decisive in some State and local elections. Even at the Presidential level the fact that Eisenhower could attract the votes of a quarter of those who normally vote Democratic was startling evidence of what personal appeal can achieve if the circumstances are favourable. Eisenhower would have won the election whichever party he stood for, and at one time or another was considered as a candidate by both parties. Similarly when he was active in Californian politics, the future Chief Justice of the U.S. Supreme Court, Earl Warren, was able to win the nomination of both parties at the same election for the post of State Governor. Senator Wayne Morse of Oregon was able to change his party allegiance during his term of office and still gain re-election to the Senate. These are extreme examples, but they indicate that we ignore the importance of personality in American politics only at the risk of altogether failing to understand it.

*

We have tried to isolate four main strands of political behaviour in the electorate and we shall see in later chapters how these strands lead right through the political system. Of course the patterns of political behaviour are more complicated than this, for in reality sectional, class, pluralistic, and individualistic influences overlap and interact. Each election, each political situation, becomes a unique combination of these elements, and we are faced with an ever-changing panorama of political life, responding to changing social, economic and strategic forces, internal and external. However, though in constant change, and although the patterns never repeat themselves, there are certain restraints and certain persistent structures which give continuity and shape to the political system. Constitutional forces, the electoral system, the party system, these provide the framework within which more transient political forces work themselves out, and it is to these that we must now turn our attention.

The Two-Party System

3

The patterns of sectional, class, pluralistic and individualistic political behaviour in the American electorate suggest, at first sight, that the most likely shape for the party system would be a number of different parties each giving expression to the interest of an important section of the political universe. Surely only a multi-party system could give expression to such diversity. Yet a second look at the evidence of the previous chapter throws some doubt on this conclusion. Are the numerous cross-pressures of American politics, the overlapping patterns of group behaviour, consistent with the existence of a number of relatively stable political parties of the kind to be found in continental European countries? Such questions seem purely academic, for in fact two political parties, the Democrats and the Republicans, dominate the scene without any serious rivals on the horizon. There have been important third-party movements in American history, and even today there are many minor parties. In 1968, George Wallace, the candidate of the American Independent Party, polled 13.5 per cent of the total vote, and in 1924 Robert La Follette, the Progressive candidate for the Presidency, attracted the vote of one sixth of those who went to the polls. Another type of third-party movement, the break-away States Rights Party of 1948, won five of the Southern States which normally went to the Democratic Party. The Socialist Party, the Socialist Labor Party, and the Prohibition Party appear regularly on the ballots in a number of States. In 1964 there were six minor candidates for the Presidency, including the first Negro ever to run for the office. Nevertheless, when there is no stimulus for a party of protest to gather an exceptional number of votes, the combined total of the two giants may reach 99.3 per cent of the total vote cast, as it did both in 1952 and 1960.

Thus the diversities of political life suggest that we might expect to find a multi-party system of the most thoroughgoing and unstable variety, and yet there is in fact an established two-party system in operation of the most inclusive sort. How is it that from the morass of groups and interests two parties emerge with a seemingly unchallengeable grip on political power? The answer lies in the complex relationships between the constitutional framework of government, the organizational structure of the political parties, and the ideological bases of political behaviour. For the American party system is a two-party system only in a very special sense. We must not look at the American party system simply in a two-dimensional way, for it has many dimensions, and only becomes a 'two-party system' if viewed from a particular standpoint. From another point of view it is an agglomeration of many parties centred around the governments of the fifty States and their subdivisions, and from yet another point of view it is a loosely articulated four-party system based upon Congress and the Presidency. The names 'Democrat' and 'Republican' are not meaningless labels as Lord Bryce suggested they were at the end of the last century; nevertheless they do tend to obscure the fact that for most purposes America operates under a multi-party system which coalesces into two great coalitions for strictly limited purposes.

FIFTY PARTY SYSTEMS

The major function of American political parties is to provide candidates for office and to secure their election. The effective offices for which candidates have to be nominated are very numerous, particularly at State and local levels. The rewards of office, the spoils, as they are sometimes referred to, are to be found at all levels of government, and there are important policy decisions to be taken, often involving the expenditure of millions of dollars, by Federal, State and local officials. The fact that the Constitution diffuses authority among these levels of government has had a strong disintegrating effect upon party structure. The constitutional division of authority between the Federal government and the States is reflected in the realities of the distribution of effective political power. Conceivably the effects of the constitutional fragmentation of authority might have been offset by a strongly centralized party system binding the parts of the government together, but the conditions which might have led to such a centralization of power have not so far been present in the system. As a result, national party organizations have had a very restricted function to perform in the political system, concerning themselves mainly with the nomination and election of presidential candidates. The national parties have tended to be coalitions of State and local parties, forming and re-forming every four years for this purpose. Thus rather than a single party system we have fifty State party systems with the national political parties related to them in a complex pattern of alliances.

It is by no means fanciful to think of politics in the United States operating within a framework of fifty party systems rather than one. A great centralization of government power has undeniably taken place during this century, giving to the Federal government in Washington an interest, and an influence, in a large number of fields of government action which in earlier decades were almost exclusively the concern of the States, and yet these States are by no means political dodos. They continue to exercise important governmental functions themselves. Perhaps the most important single fact about American politics today is that the centralization of decision-taking power in the hands of the Federal government has *not* been accompanied by a corresponding increase in the power of the national political parties over the State and local organizations. Governmental power has been centralized but political power has remained diffuse. This is one of the crucial facts about American politics which helps to explain why the most powerful government in the world may, at certain times, be directed by political forces originating from remote parts of the country with seemingly little relevance to the problems under consideration. Organizationally, the national parties are weak and sporadic in operation. The continuously operative and powerful political organizations are at the State and local level, although their degree of coherence and effectiveness varies considerably from place to place. The constitutional basis of this diffusion of power is reinforced by historical events, such as the Civil War, which have tended to entrench a particular political pattern in a region, by the regional differences of interest that characterize the sub-continent, by a general resistance to the idea of 'big government', and by the vested interests of those groups, particularly local politicians, who benefit from the *status quo*. Thus there exists a whole network of disintegrating factors which reinforce each other and prevent the emergence of powerful national parties which could coerce State and local parties.

There are good reasons for describing politics in say, Mississippi, as constituting a different and distinct political system from that of New York or Michigan. The very quality and nature of political life differs greatly from State to State. Only in about one third of the States does a truly competitive two-party system exist. In many States, although rival Republican and Democratic organizations exist, only one of the parties is strong enough to win elections for the major offices, so that the minor party tends to perform the role of a highly organized pressure-group rather than a genuine competitor for office. In some States of the Deep South the Democratic Party has for a long period been the only effective political organization. In such one-party States the whole nature of politics differs from the competitive two-party model. The political battle is conducted *within* the party, between differing factions and competing leaders. On the other hand, in some cities and counties outside the South a multi-party pattern operates in spite of the overall commitment to the two-party system. Thus New York City politics consists in a battle between Democrats, Republicans, the Liberal Party and the American Labor Party.

THE PRESIDENTIAL AND THE CONGRESSIONAL PARTIES

The structure of American federalism provides one of the most important disintegrating influences on American politics, but the Constitution struck a further blow at the basis of any attempt to centralize political power. The Founding Fathers in their determination to limit the power of government also established a strict separation of personnel between Congress and the President's Administration, and gave to President and Congress a different electoral basis and in fact different constituencies. The President cannot dissolve Congress if it displeases him, nor does he resign if his proposals are rejected by it. Thus although both President and Congress are concerned with the passage of legislation and with the way in which it is put into effect there are very few formal links between them. A major function of the political parties throughout their history has been to provide such links between the separated branches of government, but their success in coordinating these activities has only been partial. Indeed as a result of this institutional division of governmental power each of the political parties themselves has been divided into a *Presidential wing* and a *Congressional wing*.

The distinctive quality of these two wings of each of the major political parties has led James McGregor Burns to describe the American party system as a four-party system. The Presidential Democrats, the Presidential Republicans, the Congressional Democrats, and the Congressional Republicans are, he argues 'separate though overlapping parties'. Each has its own institutional patterns and ideology, representing a different style of politics. The Presidential Democrats differ from the Congressional Democrats in their electoral base, appealing, in part at least, to different sections of the population. The Presidential party seeks its major support in the urban areas of the large industrialized States, whilst the majority of Democratic Senators and Congressmen are much more responsive to rural and suburban influences. The Presidential wings of both parties tend to be closer together doctrinally than they are to the respective Congressional wings of their own parties. Indeed the conflict between the two wings of a party may be more bitter and intense than the conflict between the parties.

It is, of course, difficult to draw precise lines between the Presidential and Congressional wings of the party. Some members of Congress must be numbered among the supporters of the Presidential wing, although usually they are relatively few in number, and each of the two wings will make attempts to influence or even control the other. The nomination of Barry Goldwater by the Republicans in 1964 represented the success of the Congressional Republicans over the Presidential Republicans, and his ensuing defeat at the hands of the electorate illustrated the differing bases of support upon which the two wings of the party must depend. Goldwater was out of his element in Presidential politics and never seemed able to come to terms with the new context in which he found himself. In the past, relatively few Senators have been able to make the transition to the Presidency, most candidates for this office having served their political apprenticeship as State Governors, although John F. Kennedy was able to move out of the Congressional party as a prerequisite to his assault on the Presidency.

WHY TWO PARTIES?

So far we have described American politics as four national parties or 'wings' floating upon a potentially disruptive multi-party system at the State and local level. The disintegrating factors are very evident, but how then do we account for the fact that there are still essentially only two parties, Republicans and Democrats? Why is it still meaningful to talk in some sense of an American two-party system? Part of the answer to this question lies in the role of ideology in the American political system, which we will examine in a following section, but undoubtedly institutional considerations are very important here. From a historical and constitutional point of view the greatest force towards the creation and maintenance of the two-party system would seem to be the office of the Presidency and the mode of election to it. This is the one national office to be fought for; it is the focal point of all national political life. The simple, obvious fact about the office of President is that it can be filled only by one person. The Senate or the House of Representatives could dissolve into a multitude of factional groups, but only one man can occupy the President's chair in the White House.

This simple fact immediately tends to polarize the political spectrum. The most successful strategy for the capture of the Presidency is to create a great coalition behind one man, and the only potentially successful *riposte* is the creation of a second similar coalition. To create or encourage splinter-groups is to lose all hope of controlling this vital position. The method of election prescribed by the Constitution, and the conventions which have grown up around it, powerfully reinforce this polarizing influence of the Presidency. As we shall see later, the campaign manager of a presidential aspirant has to think in terms of gaining an *absolute* majority of votes in the Electoral College which chooses the President, and this fact encourages him very strongly to avoid divisions within the party on polling day. The ability of a party to master the technique of coalition-building is the measure of its ability to command the Presidency. Once in that position the advantage which it has gained is to a considerable extent self-perpetuating. Thus American political history is the history of long periods of domination of the Presidency by one party, with lasting changes of control occurring only in circumstances which bring about a revolutionary change in the assumptions upon which the coalition was built. The 'swing of the pendulum' in American presidential politics is, therefore, generally a long, slow, ponderous swing.

This is an explanation of two-party politics at the presidential level, but not at the congressional level. In a sense, as we shall see when we come to look at congressional politics, the two-party system in Congress is more apparent than real. Congress tends to dissolve into voting blocs in which party allegiance is a factor, but only one among many. Nevertheless, Congressmen do divide into Democrats and Republicans. One contributory factor, no doubt, is the well-known tendency of single-member simple majority electoral systems, of the Anglo-American variety, to discourage the election of third-party candidates. However, although this system discourages minor parties in each separate constituency, it does not necessarily discourage the emergence of three or more parties at the national level, particularly where there are strong regional forces at work, as there are in the United States. The electoral system would not of itself prevent the emergence of a Southern States Rights party, a party representing Western farmers, an urban workers' party of the North and East, and so on. Because America does not have a system of responsible parliamentary government on the English model, the impulse to vote only for a candidate of a party which seems likely to be able to form a majority in Congress does not have the same force as it does in parliamentary systems.

Within Congress, however, there are organizational reasons for the maintenance of two parties: in particular the organization of the committees of Congress, and the desire to control the chairmanships of committees and the office of Speaker; but again, perhaps the most important factor tending to maintain two and only two parties in Congress is the existence of the Presidency, and the consequent relationships that have developed between Presidential and Congressional politics. We shall look later at the ways in which both President and Congress attempt to influence the behaviour of the other; these links between the two institutional structures are promoted by the two-party system and help in turn to prevent the submerged multi-party system from becoming an open one.

The explanation of the persistence of the two-party system at State and local level is rather more difficult. It is true, of course, that over large sections of the country the two-party system does not really exist at all at this level. In the one-party States of the South, and in other States where there is no genuine inter-party competition, the battle between the parties is replaced by intra-party factionalism. At the local level true two-party competition is probably the exception rather than the rule. The labels 'Democrat' and 'Republican' may be adopted for historical or purely expedient reasons rather than as a true commitment to a particular political party. In so far as two-party politics does operate in the States, however, the prevalence of the Republican–Democratic division would seem to be the result of a projection downwards of the Presidential and congressional battles. Furthermore, the distribution of patronage, the spoils of office, from the Presidency downwards was, in the past at least, a powerful force for maintaining the links between party organization at the various levels. Thus the most powerful institutional mechanism for the purposes of maintaining the coherence of the American 'two-party' system is the way in which politics revolve around the Presidency, permeating the whole structure to provide the integrating forces which alone prevent the disruption of the parties into many fragments.

This is not to suggest that political power simply flows downwards in the United States – far from it! Rather it is to point to the *interdependence* of the various levels of political activity. And this is a true interdependence, for the politics of the Presidency are affected by developments in local politics just as much as they are by what happens in Washington. Indeed, the interrelationships between Federal, State and local politics in the United States are much more genuine and alive than the connexion between national and local politics in a more highly centralized country like Great Britain. In Britain national politics have an autonomy of their own, operating seemingly in a sphere almost unconnected with what happens at the lower levels. It would be a foolish Senator or Congressman, or indeed a foolish President, who acted upon such an assumption in America.

GRASS ROOTS DEMOCRACY

It is difficult to generalize about the politics of the States, cities, and counties of America because they vary so much, both in formal structure, and in political practice; but given their importance for the way in which decisions are taken at higher levels, it is necessary to explore this diversity. Do these innumerable units of government provide a lower level of political behaviour which is majoritarian, pluralistic or *élite*-ist?

It is usually assumed that 'democracy' is more characteristic of small, well integrated societies than of large complex societies. As society develops, the argument goes, the division of labour and the increasing technicality of the decisions to be made lead inevitably to *élite*-ist rule, or at the very least to a modern group pluralism which may be far removed from the ideals of majority rule and direct participation associated with the Greek origins of democracy. Although it may be true from the point of view of the machinery of government that direct participation is conceivable in small societies but not in large ones, it does not necessarily follow, either that a small society will be democratic, or that even if majority rule prevails *social* equality and *social* democracy will follow on political equality. Sometimes small communities are much more intolerant of deviant or eccentric behaviour than large ones. Thus we have to tread warily when relating generalizations about the nature and extent of 'democracy' to the size of a community, or even simply to the degree of majority rule in a community.

However, the closeness of local government to the people provides the *opportunity*, at least, of greater participation, and from this point of view the most democratic political institutions in America are the New England towns. When the first settlers landed in New England they divided up their new territory into 'towns' as it was settlèd. A map of 1755 shows a projected line of these towns to be established in the Province of New Hampshire as a frontier against the Indians. However, the towns were not urban areas. They were large tracts of virgin territory, at the centre of which a village or hamlet would be built. The whole area of New England was eventually divided up in this way, and the towns still exist as the basic unit of government in the New England States, and in the State of New York. The system of government adopted for these towns was extremely democratic in form, all the major business being dealt with by a town meeting at which all the citizens attended and voted. They might have voted in the seventeenth century for measures which we today would consider harsh and unjust, but this was the spirit of the age.

A few New England towns in rural areas still operate this system of direct democracy. In Western Massachusetts for example one may find towns with a population of less than a thousand people still running their local affairs by an annual Town Meeting at which the tax rates are fixed, the budget for the coming year is approved, and the town officers, the selectmen, the constable, the fire chief and others, are elected. The Town Meeting may be an all-day affair, with the citizens coming and going, listening to the discussion, casting their votes, and enjoying the New England dishes prepared by the townsfolk. The views of the selectmen who carry out the town's decisions and prepare the budget are listened to with respect, but they are not always accepted. The arguments about whether or not to construct a new bridge, or about the amount of salt and grit to be used on the roads in winter, end in a vote which the citizens may well soon regret, but at least they will have decided it themselves. However, direct democracy has its disadvantages and limitations. Decisions on technical matters may be swayed by the eloquence of the ill-informed, and the town's votes may leave the programme presented by the selectmen in disarray. Such direct democracy is only possible, however, in the small rural towns. With growth, and the increasing complexity of government business, towns have been forced to adopt a representative town meeting, and to supplement the activities of part-time selectmen with the services of a professional town manager.

There are over three thousand counties in the United States, and outside New England the county is the most significant unit of local government. The vitality of the New England towns makes the counties in those States relatively unimportant, but outside New England the relationship is reversed. Townships exist in many areas, originally based upon the example of the New England towns, but they have few functions and little power. It is usually the county which provides the major local services, such as law enforcement, highways, education and welfare services. A county board of supervisors or commissioners is elected to oversee the county's affairs, but there may be quite a large number of other elected officials or boards concerned with one or other of the county's services, in particular the sheriff, and the district, or county, attorney. This pattern of counties covers the whole of the United States with the exception of Alaska, Connecticut and Rhode Island, but they vary enormously in size and importance. Some have a population of only a few hundred, whilst others may include large urban areas, or even great cities, or parts of cities. Thus Cook County, Illinois, contains the city of Chicago, and Los Angeles County, California, had in 1960 a population of over six million.

Superimposed upon this pattern of counties, towns and townships is the vast fabric of cities spreading across the continent. Municipal corporations with their charters were established in the colonies along English lines from the beginning. The enormous growth of urbanization created a situation in which in the nineteen-sixties there were over 5,000 places classified as 'urban' in the United States, and no fewer than two thirds of the

total population live in the great metropolitan areas. The status
and power of the governments which serve these urban areas are
so varied that it is very difficult to formulate generalizations
about them. At one extreme is the small city of a few thousands,
and at the other the City of New York with a population of
eight million. Most cities have a city council of up to thirty or
so members, and a directly elected Mayor. Senior officials of the
city may also be directly elected, and the relative power of council
and mayor vary greatly. In the strong-mayor plan, executive
authority is concentrated in his hands to the point where his
power over the city administration is almost absolute. At the
other extreme the mayor is little more than a figurehead with
authority vested in the hands of boards and commissions with
whose operations the mayor has little to do. Between these extremes there is a variety of gradations of mayoral authority.
Other major systems of city government are the commission plan
and the city-manager system. The former replaces mayor and
council by a small elected commission, usually of five members,
to exercise both the legislative and executive authority of the city
government. The city-manager system has been increasing in
popularity since it was first tried in the early decades of this
century. An elected council with a ceremonial mayor at its head
appoints a professional manager who is responsible to them for
the conduct of the city government. The council passes ordin-
ances and the manager carries them out, having also the responsibility for appointing and dismissing the city's employees. The
city-manager plan reflects the attempt, which we shall come
across in other areas of American government, to take administration out of politics. It is not likely to succeed in doing this,
but at least where this system has been adopted it has resulted in
the introduction of highly qualified professional administrators
into the realm of local government.

LOCAL POLITICS

The decisions which these numerous and varied authorities take
are of considerable importance for the local communities which
they govern. Local government in America is very much alive

and enjoys considerable autonomy. Furthermore the cities and counties form the real foci of political power, the basic organizational units of the party system upon which the State and Federal parties must attempt to build their coalitions. Local governments have patronage to dispense, and lucrative contracts to award, which may be worth, in the case of the larger cities, millions of dollars. The machinery of city and county government provides a relatively secure base for the local politician who maintains himself in office by his ability to influence or persuade the local electorate, and who can survive his party's political disasters at State and Federal level.

The nature and quality of city and county politics is the product of a complex interaction of a number of factors: the size of the community, the economic basis of its life, the structure of the ethnic, religious and other social groups that compose it, its institutional structure, the nature of the leadership in the community, and the range of problems and needs which the government faces. The way in which local politics work depends in large part on the extent to which decision-making is concentrated in a few hands, or in a number of competing groups. Even in the smallest of towns, with their survivals of direct democracy, the impact of personality and leadership will raise some members of the community into positions of power and influence. Vidich and Bensman, in their study of a small town in New York State with a population of only three thousand, describe how the three men who formed the core of the local Republican committee ran the affairs of the town, forming an 'invisible government' which operated largely behind the scenes. Through control of the process of nominating candidates for election, and as a result of the apathy of the citizens of the town, the Republican organization was able to keep a tight control over town affairs. If a dissident Republican challenged the dominance of this leading group they were quite prepared to throw their support behind a Democrat rather than allow the challenge from within their own party to succeed.

As the size of the governmental unit increases so does the need for complex structures to articulate and aggregate the interests of the community. The recognition of this fact has led to an emphasis in studies of local communities on the power of *élite* groups. Lane W. Lancaster has asserted: 'It is safe to say that, in nine tenths of the counties in the United States, public affairs are in the hands of what the irreverent call the "courthouse gang".' This 'gang' is described as a more or less permanent group of elected and appointed office-holders, together with a number of private individuals whose business normally brings them into contact with public officials. The role of businessmen as the dominant influence in local politics, particularly the politics of the cities, has been heavily stressed, to the point where some students of community power structure raised this view to the status of an ideology. Floyd Hunter in his study of *Regional City* (Atlanta, Georgia) argued that the real decision-makers in the city were the leaders of the business community, who manipulated the politicians and local leaders. Other students have arrived at similar conclusions. However some studies emphasize that the relations between the business community and the city government may vary considerably from situation to situation.

Edward C. Banfield and James Q. Wilson in their *City Politics* suggest six principal types of interaction between business groups and the city. In Dallas, Texas, they found that a Citizens' Council composed exclusively of presidents or general managers of business enterprises directly dominated the city council. In other cities the business *élite* control the political machine indirectly through the medium of a political boss. The Republican machine in Philadelphia under the Vare brothers is given as an example. The third type is characterized by powerful business interests facing a powerful, but by no means subservient, political machine. In this situation, characterized by Pittsburgh when Richard Mellon the industrialist faced David Lawrence, the boss of the Democratic machine in the city, there is a bargaining relationship between the two powers in which neither can simply impose his will on the other. The fourth type of city politics which Banfield and Wilson describe is characterized by a powerful political machine, like the Democratic machine of Mayor Daley in Chicago, which is faced by important but diverse business interests in the city, so that the latter have relatively little influence on the mayor. The reverse situation is to be found, however, in Los Angeles, where the power of business is relatively strong and well-organized but the political system highly decentralized. Authority is fragmented on the city council, and the use of the referendum makes it very difficult for the businessmen to exercise any effective control. The final category offered by Banfield and Wilson is the type of city where both business power and political power are fragmented, so that no single group has the ability to dominate the political system. Boston, with its ethnic divisions and its decentralization of political power is an example of this type.

Thus the role of the business *élite*, or of the political *élite*, varies considerably according to the circumstances in each city. The pluralistic approach to the understanding of city politics has been championed by Robert A. Dahl and Nelson Polsby. Their study of New Haven, Connecticut, an ethnically diverse community, found that there was not a single, coherent *élite* group, but a number of specialized groups interested in and influential upon the decisions taken on specific issues, rather than across the whole field of political life. The pluralist argument is based upon the contention that most American communities, small or large, are too heterogeneous to be dominated by a single small group of men who can enforce their commands upon the community. The divisions of class, ethnic origin, economic interest, and religion, and the very real impact of individualism and personality that we found in American electoral behaviour, have their effect throughout the political system. Contending groups bargain and compromise, settling each particular issue in an ever-changing kaleidoscope of political influence. In these situations political leadership acts simply as a broker among these contending interests. Frank Munger writing on the politics of Syracuse in New York State expressed the pluralist view in this way: 'There tend to be as many decision centers as there are important decision areas, which means that the decision-making power is fragmented among the institutions, agencies, and individuals which cluster about these areas.' Although the extreme pluralist explanation of American politics at the local or the national level tends to under-emphasize important structural factors in

the working of the political system, it does seem to offer a more
effective description and explanation of the complexity of the
political scene than that which sees it simply as dominated by a
single coherent *élite*.

The fragmentation of political organizations and of decision-
making is most evident in the government of the great metropolitan areas which are emerging as the dominant pattern of life in
modern America. These great conglomerations of urban development, with populations running into several millions, may extend across State boundaries and encompass a number of cities
as well as numerous other semi-autonomous local government
units. The New York metropolitan area bridges three States,
New York, New Jersey and Connecticut, engulfing the cities of
New York, Jersey City and Newark and many hundreds of
other governmental units. Whilst the economic and social problems of the metropolis are closely inter-related throughout the
whole area, the political organization of the metropolis is decentralized along historical boundaries which seem to have little
relevance to modern problems.

THE STRUCTURE OF THE PARTIES

The different patterns of political behaviour that we found in the
American electorate, if they are truly reflective of deeply significant attitudes, must be reflected in, and work through, the political structures which alone can reconcile these potentially conflicting forces. The political structures of the United States
are likely therefore to be as complex as the diversity of American
political attitudes suggests, and we find in fact that the party
system, the electoral system, and the complex of interest groups,
the three basic structures through which political attitudes are
transmitted to the decision-making institutions of government,
reflect these different styles of political thought and behaviour.
Thus the party system is expressive of the sectional characteristics of the American polity to a very high degree. At the same
time the parties can reflect class and pluralistic interests because
of the way in which the electoral system enables strongly marked
regional groupings, such as the urban areas of the East, or the

farmers of the Mid West, to gain representation. The electoral system also, as we shall see, through the complex machinery of American elections, allows the individualistic elements in American politics full expression. Finally, the interest group structure is the vehicle *par excellence* for the articulation of group demands, including those with a marked sectional or class bias.

American government is divided government, and the fragmented structure of the political parties reflects this fact, but the parties must also transcend these divisions for certain purposes, and above all for the purpose of electing the President. The electoral machinery, and party organization, differ from State to State, from county to county, and from city to city. In some areas political organizations are highly developed and efficient. Thus in Michigan the political activity of the automobile workers' union (the United Auto Workers) resulted in what John H. Fenton has described as 'issue-oriented' politics. As a result politics became more ideological, and voting behaviour in the legislature was more disciplined than in other States. At the other extreme party organization may be almost non-existent as a continuing factor in the political process. At each election the candidates in such areas create their own organizations, gathering around them friends and supporters to organize their campaigns. Indeed this creation of campaign organizations on an *ad hoc* basis to fight elections is by no means confined to the local level. Presidential candidates do not depend solely upon the formal party machinery to conduct their campaigns. They gather round themselves groups of men dedicated to their support who will organize the fight from the primary stage to the general election. Thus the party machine which fought for John F. Kennedy in 1960 was very different from that which secured President Johnson's re-election in 1964, and the Republican organization of Senator Goldwater was very different from that of his predecessor, Richard Nixon. The personnel are different because a candidate wants his own men to run his campaign, and the style of the campaign is different because it reflects the personality of the candidate and of the men who advise him.

American political battles cannot simply be viewed as contests between two rival organizations representing the views of fairly cohesive sections of the electorate. The 'official' party machinery is often involved in bitter disputes with rival factions in the party, and it is by no means a foregone conclusion that the official party organization will be successful in promoting its own candidates for office. More and more the practice of 'unofficial' organizations taking part in elections is growing. 'Spontaneous' citizens' groups, or groups of doctors or lawyers, or ethnic interest groups may set up campaign headquarters and work, with a greater or lesser degree of coordination with the official party, in support of the candidate they favour.

Thus much of the real stuff of American politics is not the battle *between* party organizations, but the battle over who shall take control of the party. This is true from the Presidency downwards. The early stages of a Presidential election are occupied with the conflict between rival candidates for their party's nomination. Every contender for the office of President has first to build himself a power base in State politics, either as Senator or Governor, and then make a bid to take over the national party organization in one way or another. Each candidate will start off with a group of dedicated workers around him, usually drawn largely from his home State. If he is successful in becoming the representative of his party at the presidential level, these men will probably be the leading organizers of his campaign at the national level.

Thus national politics and State politics are inextricably interwoven, but the fragmentation of party organization and power goes much further down the line. It is difficult to build a cohesive party organization even at State level. The diffusion of authority which the Founding Fathers sought in the United States Constitution is taken to almost ridiculous lengths in the States. Not only do State Constitutions enshrine the separation of powers and checks and balances, with an elected Governor faced with two legislative assemblies; the officials of State and local governments have also been subjected to a system of direct election, and the electorate may intervene in the policy-making process through the medium of the initiative (legislation proposed by the people), the referendum (the submission of legislative proposals to the people), or the recall (the ability of electors to have the official removed from his office). Thus the major State officials such as Secretary of State, Attorney-General, Treasurer, Auditor and others, may be elected. These officials all exercise statutory powers weakening the position of the Governor. Furthermore they may not be members of the same political party. Thus in Massachusetts in 1945–6 the Democratic Governor was faced with a Republican Lieutenant-Governor and Secretary of State, a Democratic Treasurer and Auditor, and a Republican Attorney-General. In many States officials such as the Secretary of Agriculture or the Superintendent of Public Instruction may also be elected. A wide variety of offices at county and other levels of government are elective – sheriff, superintendent of schools, county surveyor, coroner, constable or fire chief, although in the larger cities these posts may be appointive offices. All these elected offices are, of course, in addition to the more 'normal' elected positions of State Senator or Representative, mayor, councilman, or county commissioner. Even the judiciary is elective in a majority of the States.

Thus there is a plethora of elective offices, legislative, administrative and judicial, many of them with their own special powers, and able to resist direction or domination from above. This combination of direct election and checks and balances provides a political system of such complexity that few of those involved in it, either as electors or officials, can hope fully to grasp its implications, or to know how to work it. It is this complexity which gave rise to the 'politocrat' or political 'boss' whose ability to work the machinery of government, usually by erecting a system of corruption and influence, made him enormously powerful. The boss could create a political 'machine' based upon the provision of rewards to supporters and party workers in return for their unquestioning allegiance. The enormous numbers of poor and illiterate immigrants at the turn of the century provided a clientèle which needed services in the form of help with finding jobs, relief when sick or unemployed, or help with legal problems, and who were prepared to give their support in the form of votes to whoever provided these services. This unquestioning electoral support gave to the political machine the ability to dominate the government of a county or city, and to use its financial resources to its own ends. Inevitably such an operation involved corruption and intimidation, and often also connexions between the machine and organized crime. The boss might not even himself hold an elective office but direct affairs from behind the scenes through his control over the party machine. Thus the system which aimed at the extreme of responsibility of government to the people resulted in the exercise of power in a quite irresponsible way.

However, although county and city bosses at the turn of the century could be all-powerful in their own bailiwick, it was a political system which it was very difficult to extend to encompass the politics of a whole State. A few men, notably Huey Long of Louisiana, became State bosses, but generally the system added to, rather than detracted from, the decentralized character of American politics. Really cohesive power and organization was to be found at the county level, but rarely above that level.

The circumstances which gave rise to the machines and their bosses have altered, and the mainstay of their power has vanished. The immigrant is now a citizen who understands the language and his rights. More important the social security programmes of the Federal government have removed much of the demand for relief services upon which machine politics was based. The machines have lost their power and the great bosses of the past no longer dominate. But the decline of the boss and of the machine has not been paralleled by the rise of any other political organization which could give cohesion to politics. The remnants of the machines, often locked in battle with citizen reform groups, still provide the political structure of many cities and counties. The philosophy of the machine, which was to treat politics as a business – the business of getting votes and winning elections, as Banfield and Wilson put it – still persists. The old machine was really non-partisan, although it might have been nominally Republican or Democratic, and this non-partisan, non-ideological approach is still typical of urban government. The spoils of office are still considerable and attractive. Patronage is important, with many jobs to be distributed and contracts worth millions to be awarded for highway construction, parking facilities, and public buildings. The line between 'honest graft' and 'dishonest graft' is often difficult to draw. Thus although the problems facing American governments are quite staggering in their complexity and difficulty, and day-by-day decisions are taken which deeply affect the lives and conditions of their citizens, there is often a strange hiatus between the working of politics and the people most closely affected by it.

PARTY ORGANIZATION

Thus the 'informal' elements of the American party structure may well be, in practice, the most important, but there is a formal structure of organizations rising up from the local level to the national. This formal party organization consists of a pyramid of committees starting at the base with ward, precinct, town and township committees, up through city and county committees, and the State committees, to the national party committee. Within each State there is great variation in the way in which these committees are constituted. Broadly speaking the practice is for the lowest level of committees to be elected by the voters, and for the higher levels to be selected from the membership of these lower levels, although direct election may also be used for selection further up the scale. The national committee is responsible for conducting the party's presidential election campaign, but there are also Congressional and Senatorial campaign committees, emphasizing the fact that Presidential and Congressional politics are distinct.

The national committees are Federal in composition. The 1974 Constitution of the Democratic Party provides that, in addition to 'the chairperson and the highest ranking officer of the opposite sex of each recognized State Democratic Party', a further two hundred members shall be elected by State parties, apportioned according to a formula taking into account each State's population and the size of its Democratic presidential vote during the previous election. Representative Democratic congressional leaders, State Governors, Mayors and Young Democrats are also included. The Republican National Committee consists of a man and a woman from each State, with extra representation for

States with a Republican Governor, those where a majority of the
congressional delegation is Republican, or which cast a majority
vote for the Republican candidate at the previous election. The
great size of the national committees make them ineffective for
conducting electoral campaigns, the real responsibility falling
upon the party's national chairman who is formally selected by
the national committee, but is in practice the nominee of the
party's presidential candidate.

Thus the really important part of the national party machinery,
except for the nominating conventions which we shall look at
later, is the national chairman and his staff, which is strongly
augmented in an election year. The national chairman is there
simply to promote the candidature of his party's Presidential
candidate, but after the election is over the chairman of the
defeated party may remain in office till the next convention four
years later, although the man to whom he was committed may
no longer be even the titular head of the party. A defeated Presidential candidate has no automatic claim to the leadership of his
party, and usually the defeated party goes virtually leaderless
through the lean years between elections. Once the election is
over the staff of the national committees are cut back to a
minimum and the national party lies dormant till the next
Presidential election. Even in the non-Presidential election years
when Congressional elections are taking place, the national committee is largely dormant. Senators and Congressmen resent
attempts by national chairmen to dictate policy or to interfere in
Congressional affairs. Thus Congressional leaders were largely
antagonistic to the Democratic Advisory Council, consisting of
eminent Democrats, which was set up after Eisenhower's re-
election in 1956. The Democrats controlled the Congress in spite
of the re-election of the Republican President, and there was
therefore a felt need to 'co-ordinate and advance efforts on behalf of Democratic programmes and principles'. Members of
Congress felt, however, that the Advisory Council represented
an attempt to dictate policy to them and was an unwarrantable
interference in their affairs.

Party organization consists, therefore, of a 'pyramid' of committees, but this does not in any way imply that the lower levels

of the pyramid are subject to control or direction by the levels above them. In a highly organized city party the city leaders may be in a position to appoint and replace ward leaders at will, and some county chairmen still exercise a power reminiscent of the old-time bosses. But the State chairman is not in a position to issue orders to city and county leaders. Still less can the national committee give directions to State chairmen or committees; it can only work towards gaining their cooperation. The sanctions which are available to central party committees in more highly centralized countries have no place in American national politics. The ideological links between party members are weak, so that mere appeals to party allegiance will have little impact. The selection of party candidates at State and local level is completely outside the control of national party leaders. Even President Franklin D. Roosevelt at the height of his popularity with the electorate could not influence his party to the point of obtaining the removal or defeat of candidates of whom he disapproved. The national committee does not have control over the enormous sums of money expended in American election campaigns, for it must concentrate its efforts upon finding the twelve million or so dollars that it needs for the presidential campaign, leaving State and county committees and individual candidates to find the rest of the money, which, it has been estimated, may amount to a grand total of $150,000,000 for both parties throughout the country. The patronage power is perhaps the only real weapon left to national leaders to try to obtain the cooperation of local political leaders, but the growth of civil service requirements at the Federal level has greatly reduced the number of jobs to be distributed, and most of these are handed out at the beginning of the President's term of office.

Thus the power of national party leaders, including the power of the President over his own party, is very limited indeed. Institutional factors, the separation of powers and the structure of the federal system, destroy the basis of any attempt by party leaders to centralize authority in a few hands; the President cannot discipline Congress by dissolving it if it displeases him, nor can he use his position as leader of the party to undermine the power of Congressmen or Senators in their constituencies. The President of the United States is not without power, as we shall see later, but his power and influence must be used in ways very different from that of a British Prime Minister. Presidential politics is a very special game with rules all of its own. Thus national party organization 'floats' upon the shifting sands of State and local politics. The national parties are great coalitions of State and local organizations, and as such they tend to change with the tides of events rather than attempting to direct them.

THE IDEOLOGICAL CONTENT OF AMERICAN POLITICS

The constitutional and structural aspects of the party system that we have surveyed are understandable so far as they go, but something more is needed to comprehend fully the reasons why America has a 'two-party' system. What is politics about in America, and what role do ideas play in the working of the system? What are the issues that give life to the political system? The relation between ideas and political structures is always a very complex one, and nowhere more so than in the United States. Political ideas take different forms, and exist at different levels of consciousness. The term 'ideology' is usually applied to a system of thought in which a number of ideas about the nature of the political system and the role of government are logically related to each other, and developed as a consciously-held guide to political action. Communism or fascism are the prime examples of such ideologies. In this sense ideology plays a very small, indeed an almost negligible, role in American politics. And yet there is an important role for ideas in American politics, and indeed an understanding of the 'American ideology' is essential for a full understanding of the two-party system.

The American ideology is fundamentally the ideology of Western liberal democracy, but whereas in Britain this set of ideas can almost be taken for granted, in the United States it has to be continuously and consciously asserted. The apparent contradictions in American life stem very largely from this felt need to *impose* an ideology which has as its main tenets *freedom* of speech, and *freedom* of political action. The diverse characteristics of American society are such that most Americans seem to feel that the

toleration of unusual behaviour or unusual ideas might lead to
the break-up of their society. There must be a minimum conformity enforced by the state, and yet it is conformity with a
liberal ideal. No ideas can be tolerated which threaten the basis
of that liberalism, or which seem to introduce the germ of a
divisive force into the community.

Thus all tendencies towards a sharp polarization of ideas must
be consciously resisted. Both major parties shy away from ideological commitments, and those issues which cut deepest into
American society usually also cut across the parties. When important problems of a potentially divisive nature arise, such as
the Vietnam war, policy towards China, or civil rights, the tendency of the national leaders of both parties is to move towards
a middle course, avoiding extremes. Thus there arises what has
been described as a *consensus* of ideas, a broad agreement upon
the basic attitudes towards the political system and political
problems which is shared by the vast majority of the American
people.

The consensual basis of American politics has a number of important results. First, it allows particular issues to be discussed as
isolated problems to be solved empirically without reference to
any set of fundamental principles, so that, within the accepted
limits of what is considered an 'American' solution, compromises
can be found both within and between the parties. Second, as a
corollary to this, it makes possible the cross-party voting which
is so characteristic of the American legislature. Here constitutional and ideological factors reinforce each other. Congressmen
when casting their votes do not have to worry about governmental instability of the sort which would result from cross-
voting in a parliamentary system. The legislator can make up his
mind on the merits of the proposals in front of him, or he can
respond to constituency or other pressures. American Senators
and Congressmen therefore vote against their party leadership with a frequency and a regularity which would be intolerable in a more ideological context. Party loyalty is a factor in the
legislator's behaviour, but it is valued for its results rather than as
an end in itself. Furthermore it leaves much more room for the
play of personalities in politics than when there is a strong ideo-

logical background to the division between the parties. Third, consensus politics creates, in the American context, a positive need for outlets for extremist views, *outside* the party system. Those minorities, either of the left or of the right, who feel that American society needs fundamental change, can see no hope of obtaining it through the established parties. The moderating effect of the two-party system, appealing as it does to the vast majority of Americans (or at least of white Americans) drives dissident groups into extremism and violence to achieve their ends. Most important of all, however, the ideological consensus provides an umbrella which makes possible a two-party system of the American kind. The parties have important electoral and organizational roles to play, but they are not in any sense tied to nicely wrapped-up packages of political policies. They can divide on organizational and electoral matters (and as we have seen in that sphere there are important pressures towards a two-party system), without their organization being disrupted by policy questions. On policy questions, as we shall see, the divisions within the parties may be as great as the divisions between them, but this becomes tolerable in the American context in a way which is inconceivable in Europe. Thus the ideological framework allows the two-party system to evolve and to operate.

LIBERALISM AND CONSERVATISM

To many Europeans, America in recent years has come to mean a bulwark of conservatism in the world, a powerful force against revolutionary change. And yet America of all countries in the world has been the most liberal, if by that word we mean a readiness to accept change. As Daniel Bell has put it, America was perhaps the first large-scale society in the world to have change and innovation 'built into' its culture. American thought has always been dominated by the desire to *create* a new society, to *develop* its economy, to *move* to higher standards of living and a better life. It is this commitment to the very idea of change which has made American society so distinct from that of Europe, because there were no real conservatives in America to react against.

Indeed the very word 'conservative' was until quite recently a term of abuse, suggesting a lack of faith in America's ability to progress. Nevertheless Americans have been consistently conservative in one important respect: their veneration of the Constitution and their resistance to changing the system of government. The Constitution became the unchanging basis of a society which welcomed change. Peter Viereck has described the relation between liberalism and conservatism in America in these terms: American conservatism, he writes, 'has little real tradition to conserve except that of liberalism – which then turns out to be a relatively conservative liberalism'.

In recent years, however, the words 'liberal' and 'conservative' have taken on a rather different connotation in the hurly-burly of political life. They have come to be slogans used in the political battle without much reference to the way in which they were formerly used. 'Liberal' is now a term of abuse used by right-wing groups to mean anyone who is 'soft on Communists', or who is too concerned with asserting the rights of Negroes, or of other underprivileged groups. At the same time the label 'conservative' is now sought after as a badge of respectability by two quite different groups. On the one hand it is a label claimed by those intellectuals who wish to emphasize a spirit of progressive conservatism which they believe to be solidly within the American tradition, a conservatism which would have as a central concern the defence of individual rights without discrimination on the grounds of race, religion, or colour. Clinton Rossiter's *Conservatism in America* is a good example of the attitudes of the 'New Conservatives'. At the same time the title of conservative has been appropriated by groups on the extreme right of American politics, who are really not conservative at all. Groups such as the John Birch Society really consist of right-wing radicals who wish to change society fundamentally, not maintain its present form, or who wish to use methods in politics which are so far outside the American tradition as to be anything but 'conservative' of American values. These groups have been described as the 'pseudo-conservatives' of the present age, falling outside the consensual framework of the American ideology, although claiming loudly to be the only true Americans.

There are, of course, many people in the United States who may fairly claim to be conservatives, although in most cases they tend to be conservative only on some issues, as is the case with many Southern whites, or with President Eisenhower, who said : 'I am a conservative when it comes to economic problems but liberal when it comes to human problems.' Senator Barry Goldwater ran for the Presidency on the Republican ticket in 1964 on the assumption that 'America is fundamentally a conservative nation', although some of his views sounded so radical that he won the support of the John Birchers and the super-patriots. Yet when it came to a vote it seems that Goldwater's brand of conservatism was not popular, even in traditionally Republican areas. In rock-ribbed Maine, in 'conservative' New England, only 31·2 per cent of the voters chose Goldwater, and many of these voted out of loyalty to the Republican Party rather than positively for Goldwater's more ideological brand of politics.

EXTREMISM AND VIOLENCE

The diversity of the origins and interests of Americans has, over the whole course of their history, given rise to severe tensions within their society. The insistence upon conformity to the norms of the American ideology has been one means of controlling the potential conflicts in such a society, but it has also had the result of driving those with more intense feelings into using extra-constitutional channels to achieve their aims. Given the nature of the American experience it is not surprising that many of the more extreme movements have been generated by the concern of certain groups to assert an equality of status with other Americans or to insist upon their patriotism or 'American-ness'. Other extremist movements have represented an inability to cope with the complexity of the modern world : a desire to opt out of foreign involvement or to find simple, direct solutions for the enormously complex problems which face the United States. Ethnic politics provides endless possibilities for waves of extremism to sweep over certain elements in the population. Catholics, Jews and Negroes have all been the subject of attack by extremists who have been ready to make use of violence to give expression to their hatred and fear of what they considered to be alien elements in the community. Yet the groups that have themselves been the subject of violent attack may turn to this very same political weapon as a means of asserting themselves in the community. Thus in the 1850s Catholics and immigrants came under attack by the Know Nothing or American Party, which was able to achieve twenty-five per cent of the vote in the presidential election of 1856, and the Ku Klux Klan, although notorious for its efforts on behalf of white supremacy, has also been actively anti-Catholic. By the 1930s, however, many Catholics in their turn were giving strong support to the anti-semitic movement led by Father Charles Coughlin which ended up with the expression of outright support for Hitler. By the 1950s the emphasis had changed again, and although the attacks upon communism of Senator Joseph McCarthy drew strong support from Irish and Italian Catholics, McCarthy avoided attacking Jews and other ethnic minorities.

The greatest source of ethnic conflict in the 1960s was of course the battle by the Negro for equality, and the resultant explosions of violence in Northern cities as well as in the Southern States. The problem of the status of the Negro community is one which the normal political machinery has failed to solve. It represents a classic example of the way in which the American political machinery can be used to prevent a solution from emerging, so that the problem becomes progressively more and more difficult until only a violent solution seems open to the group that feels its demands are not being registered through the normal channels. The demand for 'black power' is the demand for action which will short-circuit the ponderous and complicated constitutional system with all its built-in checks and balances. In the Southern States the Ku Klux Klan have been blamed for murders, beatings, bombings and church burnings, and Klan members have been put on trial for the murder of Negroes and civil rights workers. As a natural reaction Negroes in Southern States have formed themselves into armed organizations to defend themselves. The Deacons for Defence and Justice was formed in Louisiana and spread into Mississippi and other

Southern States to give Negroes the protection which they felt they could not depend upon from the normal law-enforcement agencies.

Other manifestations of extremism have little to do with ethnic problems, on the surface at least. The John Birch Society, the Minutemen, and the fundamentalist movements of the Reverend Dr Schwartz and the Reverend Billy Hargis found their targets in the Communist influences that they saw everywhere in American public life. The Minutemen, a group formed to train for armed guerilla warfare against Communism, and the John Birch Society, advocated the use of Communist tactics to fight the agents of Communism who they believed to have taken over churches, schools, universities and business corporations alike. Robert Welch, the leader of the John Birch Society described President Eisenhower as 'a dedicated, conscious agent of the Communist conspiracy', and named the President's brother Milton as his superior in the Party, from whom he took his orders. The Society also believed that John F. Kennedy fed the Communist point of view to the American public. Unlike earlier extremist groups the John Birch Society drew support from well-to-do sections of the community, and from the better-educated.

However, extremism is not a right-wing monopoly. The later years of the Vietnam war saw the rise of militant left-wing movements, particularly among students. The New Left sprouted its crop of organizations demanding radical changes in the structure of American society, and in the political system, geared as it is to producing compromise solutions, or to shelving difficult problems for which no easy compromise solution is possible. The Black Liberation Front, the Young Socialist Alliance, the W.E.B. Dubois Clubs and the Progressive Labor Movement were some of the movements which focused discontent over racial discrimination, and anger over the American involvement in Vietnam, into a general attack on the values of American society. However, the ending of the Vietnam war seems, for the time being at least, to have taken the steam out of the protest movement and returned the United States to a more 'normal' political atmosphere.

Violence as a political weapon is no newcomer or stranger to the American scene. Whether in the hands of the white supremacist, the advocate of black power, the anti-Castro guerilla or the left-wing advocates of violent revolution, it seems a simple direct solution to intolerably complex problems, in an intolerably complex system of government. America, with its traditions of frontier life, with its insistence upon the right of the individual to bear arms in his own defence, is a society in which violence has always simmered below the surface, ready to break out when a particularly difficult problem resisted solution through the normal channels. The assassination of President Kennedy was simply the most recent and most shocking of a long line of assassinations and attempted assassinations of American Presidents. Nevertheless, too much emphasis should not be placed upon these aspects of the political situation, although naturally enough it is these which hit the newspaper headlines. In a sense it is the extraordinary success of the American political system in solving the vast majority of its problems which highlights the extremism generated by its failures. The fact that the system has worked, and continues to work, is a matter for wonder when the enormity of the problems it has faced is appreciated.

THE CLASH ON ISSUES

The major American political parties, Republicans and Democrats, are, then, not ideologically differentiated parties; ideology is important in American politics, but it is not the distinguishing factor between the major parties, rather it distinguishes them from the more peripheral political organizations. Nevertheless, this does not mean that Democrats and Republicans are as indistinguishable as Tweedledum and Tweedledee, nor that American politics is devoid of vital and significant issues. The popular images of the two parties differ quite considerably. The Democratic Party is often described as the party of the working-man whereas the Republicans are seen often as the party of big business, more favourable to the rich than to the poor. This characterization of the parties is largely fashioned by their policies since 1932, by the New Deal/Fair Deal/Great Society complex of ideas which the Democrats have fostered and which the Republicans have been lukewarm about, or have forcibly opposed. In particular the Republicans have in general been opposed to expanding the role of government, especially the Federal government, in economic and social matters, whereas the Democrats have been in favour of more positive government action to promote social welfare and to regulate business activity. Nevertheless, in all occupational groups large numbers of Americans see no real differences between the two major parties. Significantly a Gallup Survey of 1959 showed that of the white-collar group thirty-four per cent believed that the Republican Party best represented their interest, thirty-two per cent thought the Democrats favourable to their interest, and twenty-three per cent saw no difference between the parties, whilst eleven per cent had no opinion on the matter.

Thus although the parties tend to take different stances on different issues, there is no real ideological coherence in the bundle of issues which one party supports, and that the other opposes. Furthermore, neither party is ever wholly united against the other. Always there are members of one party who, on a particular issue, feel more in sympathy with the majority view in the opposing party. The intra-party divisions can be just as deep and just as bitter as the inter-party divisions. And there are issues enough to be bitter about, for the problems facing the United States, in domestic and in foreign affairs, are real enough. The problems of civil rights for Negroes, the integration of the schools, the war on poverty, the provision of medical care, the role of the Federal Government in education, the problems of urban renewal, the attitude of the United States towards Latin America, and above all the war in Vietnam : these are just a few of the tortuously complex problems that have faced policy-makers in recent years. Thus the content of American politics is by no means dull or uneventful. The politics of consensus does not result in a shortage of issues. Furthermore, the role of government in American life is much greater than many people outside the United States imagine. The view of the United States as an extreme *laissez-faire* capitalist society is very far from the truth. Regulation of labour and industry, and government intervention in economic life, have in many respects gone much further than in European countries; governmental expenditure on social welfare constitutes a larger proportion of the national income of the United States than in 'socialistic' Britain; the demand for government action to solve social problems has been a characteristic of American society throughout its history. America is a much-governed country, for regulatory activities and welfare services are the active concern of three levels of government, in part competing with each other, in part co-operating.

*

The explanation of the two-party system lies therefore in the complex inter-relationships between the constitutional structure, party organization, ideology, and the issues which face American politicians. The Constitution provides a stable framework within which political forces can form and re-form over individual issues and create coalitions, some relatively stable, others quite transient. The Constitution does not demand of President and Congress a degree of unified, coherent action, which they probably could not sustain in view of the latent multi-party tendencies in the political system, but the Presidency provides an institutional focus for politics which tends to polarize the political system around two great party organizations. The basic ideological consensus allows this organizational tendency towards two parties to evolve without its being disrupted, except at the periphery, by strong commitments to particular principles or programmes; it enables the two major parties to develop a different emphasis towards the role of government in society without coming into a head-on collision; and it makes it possible for each issue to be considered almost in isolation and a judgement to be made in pragmatic terms. The advantages of this system in a diverse society like the United States are obvious, for it damps down potentially serious divisive tendencies; but there are, of course, disadvantages as well. It makes it virtually impossible to achieve a planned, coherent set of policies to deal with related problems, for the criteria applied to the solution of each problem are as diverse as American society itself. It makes for the application of governmental power in a spasmodic and uncoordinated fashion. This is probably what the Founding Fathers wished to achieve in 1787, but they could hardly have foreseen the sort of problems that would face America in the mid twentieth century. But the disadvantages of this form of politics viewed from both inside and outside the United States can hardly be attributed simply to the governmental structure which they created, for this structure reflects deep divisions within the American community. The consensus politics of the United States is in a sense a false consensus, for it may often reflect more of a general agreement not to try to solve a problem, rather than a general acceptance of what should be done in a positive sense.

Politics and Elections

4

The structure of the American party system reflects the decentralization of authority under the Constitution, and the sectional diversity of American society: it reflects also the problems of political organization in the most election-conscious nation in the world. There are approximately one million elective offices to be filled in the United States, and in any one year there may be 120,000 or 130,000 elections held, most of them for local school boards. Inevitably the electoral system which regulates the filling of these offices is one of the structures which most faithfully reflects the geographical factors in American political life because constituencies are based upon geographical areas, but it has other important dimensions as well. The complex election machinery makes full allowance for the expression of the individualistic and personal elements in the American electorate, and among candidates for office. It gives to the individual elector almost embarrassingly rich opportunities to express his views on the personalities of the candidates, and to enter fully into the processes of choosing the men who will govern him. Party organization, already fragmented by the effects of federalism and the separation of powers, is subjected to further disintegrating forces by the introduction of primary elections, by the use of the long ballot, and by the opportunities for split-ticket voting. The complexity of the electoral system is in large part due to the fact that the electoral law, whether it relates to Federal, State or local elections, is almost wholly a matter of State law, with wide variations in practice among the fifty States.

The provisions of the United States Constitution deeply affect the way in which politics are carried on in America. The fact that the major American elections take place at fixed intervals structures the whole programme of political life. The exact dates

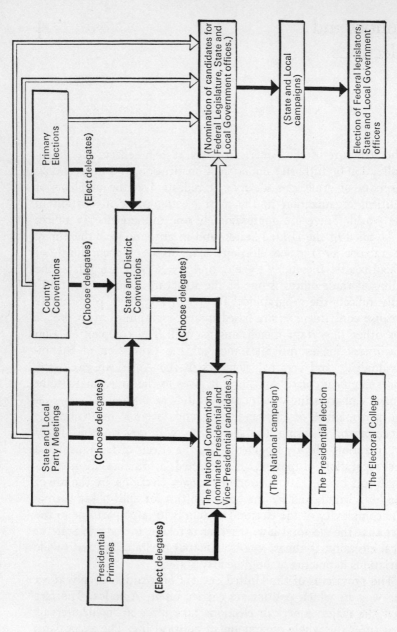

The Electoral Process

of future elections are known, so that there is a long process of electioneering, building up over a two-year period to the climax of the Presidential campaign every four years. Indeed, in a sense, the jockeying for position in the next Presidential election takes place almost as soon as the polls close. The fact that the elections take place upon the appointed day, regardless of the movement of world events or the complexities of domestic issues, means that elections are determined by the circumstances of the time, rather than as in a parliamentary system, where they are part of the machinery available to the Government to try to influence the course of events.

Elections to the Senate and the House of Representatives take place every two years, one third of the Senate and the whole of the House standing for election. Thus we have the phenomenon of 'off-year' elections, that is the election of 435 Representatives and some thirty-two or more Senators half-way through the term of office of the incumbent President, an arrangement which can result in some strange political situations, and which provides considerable difficulties for political strategists. The fact that the President cannot dissolve Congress, no matter how intransigent it becomes, and that he himself remains in office for four years, whether or not his policies receive the support of Congress, gives to each branch of the Government a degree of mutual independence which is clearly reflected in the behaviour of Presidential and Congressional candidates at election time. There are four major steps in an American Presidential election: the primaries, the conventions, the campaign culminating in the election, and the vote in the Electoral College. Let us trace the process through each of these stages.

PRIMARY ELECTIONS

At the end of the nineteenth century America saw the development, at county and city level, of some of the most formidable and cohesive political organizations that have ever evolved in a democratic system of government. Yet for the most part American elections are not fought between rival highly organized parties. Much of the vital stuff of American politics consists of battles between different groups *within* a particular party, often between the official party organization and other groups or factions who oppose it. The official party organization can be attacked, and at times defeated, by other groups within the party, bitterly divided from it on grounds of personalities or policies. Fratricidal strife is the hallmark of American political life with the most bitter battles being fought within as well as between the parties. This fratricidal strife has been institutionalized by the adoption of the device of the primary election.

The electoral process must begin with the selection of candidates for office and their nomination. It is at this first stage, rather than in the election proper, that the really decisive choices may be made, for it is the selection of the people who will at a later stage be the representatives and leaders of the party that determines its true character. The selection of party candidates may be achieved in a number of ways: by a group of party leaders in caucus, or by delegates at a party meeting or convention; they may be elected by the members of the party; or a combination of these methods may be used. Elections in which party members choose their candidates prior to the general election are called *primary elections*. The caucus system was the earliest method adopted for choosing candidates for elective office, but the result of this method was to entrench the power of party leaders and to perpetuate their control over the party. The development of conventions of delegates in which candidates were nominated was the result of dissatisfaction with the oligarchic character of the caucus system, and represented an attempt to associate the mass of party members, indirectly at least, with the choice of candidates. The primary election goes a step further, by giving party members a *direct* voice in the choice of the party representatives through the medium of an open, State-controlled election, in which any member of the party can stand as a candidate and all members can vote. Primaries are intended to make the instruments of mass democracy, the political parties, themselves democratically controlled. The primary elections used in the United States are in principle extremely democratic, for the definition of 'party member' which qualifies the elector to vote in a primary is extremely widely drawn. Party membership does not entail fee-paying or card-holding membership in an organization. It means nothing more than the declaration by the ordinary member of the electorate, when he registers as a voter, that he has voted for a particular party in the past, or intends to do so in the future, without of course in anyway committing him to the support of a particular party at the forthcoming election. Thus a 'registered Democrat' may vote in the Democratic primary to choose the candidates for that party in the general election, but when election day comes he is quite free to change his mind and to vote for the Republican candidate. In a few States the democratic principles is taken to the ultimate extreme, for in the so-called 'open primaries' voters are allowed to vote in whichever primary they choose, without restricting their choice at the time of registration. Potentially such a system is totally disruptive of party organization.

As the result of a wave of reform sentiment at the beginning of the present century the States began to adopt primary elections as a means of breaking the power of the regular party organizations over the nominating process. During the nineteenth century party conventions had become the standard method of selecting candidates at county, State and national levels. But the belief in the democratic character of the convention system proved illusory. Conventions could be managed by party leaders so that they became a mere façade for oligarchic control by professional politicians. As part of the revulsion against 'bossism' and all that it entailed, the primaries were introduced in order to break up the oligarchies of city and county machines. Gradually the primary spread throughout the country as the general method of selecting candidates for all offices other than the Presidency and the Vice-Presidency. For these, the most exalted offices in the United States, the selection of candidates still rests with national conventions of the parties; however, primary elections do play an important part also in the selection of presidential candidates. In thirty-three States and the District of Columbia, beginning with New Hampshire in March, 'Presidential primaries' are held in which delegates are chosen for the national conventions, or in which the preference of the voters for a particular prospective nominee for the Presidency is declared. The expression of such a preference may, or may not, bind the delegates from that State to support the candidate who was successful in the primary, but it may be a powerful influence in convincing delegates to the convention of the vote-catching power of rival candidates for the nomination.

Primaries are, therefore, in a sense a party matter, although carried on in the full glare of publicity, but they are by no means discreetly conducted internal affairs. They are usually fought out with as much publicity, effort and bitterness as the elections proper for which they are in theory only the preliminary round. Rival candidates for the party's nomination conduct public campaigns, and engage in every electoral tactic, including sometimes extreme attempts to discredit their opponents. Primaries are often a battle between the chosen candidates of the established party organization and challengers to their authority who create their own organization to contest the primary. In Massachusetts this internecine strife is even further institutionalized by the holding of a 'pre-primary convention' at which the party delegates endorse a list of the contenders for nomination for various offices as the 'official candidates' in the primary. Yet the 'official' candidates may subsequently be defeated in the primary, and replaced by their successful opponents as the party's official representatives at the general election. In those areas where only one party has any hope of winning at the general election the primaries then become the true battleground for office, where factions within the party fight out the contest for power, and where success in the primary is tantamount to election.

The bitterness of the primary contests extends to the highest level of the political system, the nominations for the Presidency of the United States, for here is the most to be gained and the most to be lost. The presidential primaries may become the forum for bitter personal battles between the foremost leaders of the same political party, carried on in the full glare of publicity before the eyes of the whole country, indeed of the world. The 1964 Republican primaries in which Senator Goldwater and Governor Rockefeller contended for the party's Presidential nomination were savage battles. When the battles were over, Theodore H. White has remarked, 'the Republican Party was so

wounded that its leaders were fitter candidates for political hos-
pitalization than for governmental responsibility'. Equally important may be the internal political divisions in the State where
a Presidential primary is being held. Candidates for the presidential nomination inevitably become involved in the factional
fights at State and local level, for each aspiring President will
have his supporters in the State who will hope to gain in their
local political struggles by the success of their champion at the
national level. However, the result of these cross-currents of
national and State politics may be very serious for contenders for
the Presidential office. If the dominant leadership of the State
party is opposed strongly to a leading contender in the Presidential primary in the State, the State party might be torn apart in
the ensuing campaign, deepening personal animosities within
the party and weakening its organization and morale. The resulting divisions within the party might have a considerable impact
upon the Presidential election itself, and indeed upon the politics of the Presidency for many years. The danger of such a situation arising may decide contenders for the nomination not to
enter for a particular primary.

Whether or not to enter for the primaries is a difficult decision
for the Presidential aspirant. The primary trail to the national
convention, taking up the spring months of a Presidential year,
is an expensive and exhausting process. Primary elections follow
hard upon each other across the country; New Hampshire,
Wisconsin, West Virginia, Oregon, California. Few candidates
would wish to fight them all, and it becomes a matter of tactics to
decide which, if any, to contest. In 1960 John F. Kennedy chose
the primaries as his route to the nomination, unlike the candidates who were more favoured by the professional politicians in
the party, and who chose to remain in the background. Kennedy
had to demonstrate his popular appeal, and in particular to prove
that a Catholic could win votes in Protestant areas. His victory
over Hubert Humphrey in West Virginia, a State with an overwhelmingly Protestant population, was a major factor in his
successful bid for the nomination. In the election of 1968 the
profound impact of the early primary victories of Senator Eugene
McCarthy upon the political fortunes of President Johnson in-

dicated the importance which the primaries can attain in the era
of televised politics, but at the same time the fact that the Democratic National Convention accepted both President Johnson's
nominee, and his policy, reflected the power of the politicians
over the convention. What the outcome would have been if
Senator Robert Kennedy had not been assassinated no one can
say. The primaries are also a great risk. Defeat in the primaries
can kill a candidacy long before the convention meets, and some
contenders for the nomination prefer to remain aloof from the
primary battle, hoping that those who do enter will kill each
other off, leaving the field clear for political manoeuvring at the
convention. Equally, success in the primaries is no guarantee of
victory at the convention – in 1952 Senator Kefauver had great
success in the primaries but failed to gain the nomination.

The primaries exhibit some of the most individualistic elements in American politics. It is possible, though not very
common, for an almost unknown candidate to win a victory over
the established party organization, and primaries also provide
opportunities for the voters to express their views and preferences, even for candidates who are not technically up for election.
Many primary laws allow the voter to 'write-in' the name of a
candidate, and so to cast his vote for a man whose name does not
appear on the ballot. Of course, the likelihood of such write-in
votes constituting a majority of votes cast is small, and yet
strange things do happen in American politics. In the 1964 New
Hampshire Presidential primary, Goldwater and Rockefeller were
the names on the ballot-papers and yet the winner of the primary
was Henry Cabot Lodge, Ambassador to Vietnam, who had not
even campaigned, and who at the time of the election was many
thousands of miles away. A small group of enthusiastic supporters urged the New Hampshire voters to write in Lodge's
name.

Thus primary elections introduce many complications into
the rich complexity of the American political scene. Introduced
as a challenge to the power of the professional politicians they
have certainly made life more difficult for that hardy breed, and
they have certainly aided the tendency towards weaker party
organization which has been under way during the present cen-

tury. Primaries have not, of course, completely democratized the political parties, and to the extent that they have done so, they highlight the dilemma of the reformer in this field. How does one break the power of an oligarchy without destroying altogether the basis of strong leadership? If the parties were strongly ideologically-oriented, then party allegiance might be a substitute for organizational power, as a basis for the exercise of leadership; but they are not. Another alternative might be the cohesive force of spoils and corruption; but although American politics are not free from these things, they have declined considerably in importance in the present century. The power of the professional politician has not evaporated. But he has had to adapt himself to new techniques and learn how to live with the primaries. In the field of Presidential nominating politics, however, the democratization process has made even less headway. The national conventions are still the arenas in which decisions are made about nominations, and in spite of the development of Presidential primaries in almost a third of the States, they remain a forum for the traditional behind-the-scenes manipulations of professional party politicians.

THE NATIONAL CONVENTIONS

American political parties are great coalitions of sectional, class and pluralistic interests which coalesce for certain purposes, the most important being to contest the election of the President of the United States. It is in the national conventions of the parties that their most difficult task is performed; the choice of candidates for the Presidency. The peculiarities of the national conventions can be understood only if they are seen as arenas in which political parties composed of very diverse economic and social interests, embracing groups with very different views on domestic and foreign policy, are forced to choose *one man* as their representative, to lead them in the forthcoming election, and thereafter perhaps to wield the power of the Presidency. Thus the Democratic Party is composed of Southern segregationists and Northern Negroes, of automobile workers from Detroit and small-businessmen from California, of Irish-

American truck drivers from Massachusetts and Spanish-speaking Puerto Ricans, together with millions of other Americans across the continent. Yet only one person can be the standard-bearer of the party, and of what it shall stand for in the following years, at the Presidential level at least.

It is hardly surprising, then, that outwardly the national conventions present a picture of bombast and ballyhoo, in which brass bands raucously puncture the proceedings, processions of banner-waving supporters and attractive drum-majorettes take over the floor of the convention hall in a well-organized chaos, and speakers make vague appeals for party unity based upon historical and emotional considerations rather than upon future policy. Clearly the problem which they are there to resolve is not one which can be dealt with simply by calm reasoning and persuasive argument from the rostrum : it is the much more emotional problem of settling upon a leader whom the vast majority of the party are prepared to follow. Behind the ballyhoo, however, lies a long period of careful preparation for the convention, the effort by candidates to gain the support of important figures, the making of bargains and concessions to waverers, the hardheaded political bargaining which alone can bring order out of chaos.

National conventions are enormous affairs. In 1964 in Atlantic City there were over 2,900 delegates and 2,200 alternates at the Democratic convention, as well as a host of reporters, television men and spectators. The delegates are chosen in a variety of ways. Some are chosen in the presidential primaries and are committed in some degree to the winner of the primary in their State. The majority of the delegates to the national convention are chosen in State and district conventions across the country, the members of which are, in their turn, chosen in a number of different ways. The delegates to this lower level of conventions may be elected in primaries, or selected by conventions at county level or by ad hoc meetings of party members. This pattern of indirect election through several stages provides the perfect set-up for the political manipulations which precede the convention. To gain the nomination a candidate must win an absolute majority of the votes in the convention, and balloting will continue until a candidate gets more than fifty per cent of delegate votes. Thus in the months before the convention, candidates must try to get as many of the delegates as possible committed to their support, in the hope that when the convention opens, they will either have sufficient support to win outright on the first ballot, or will at least have enough committed votes to convince waverers that they are in a position eventually to win the nomination.

The factors which determine the way in which delegates cast their votes determine the candidates' strategies. In some States the delegates may be under the control of a local political leader, the State Governor, a county chairman or other important political figure. Those who seek the nomination must seek his support, particularly for those States which cast their votes as a block in the Democratic convention. For the rest, however, the individual delegate may be free to dispose of his vote, or sometimes half a vote, as he pleases. At this level the arithmetic of convention politics becomes complicated indeed. Candidates with the organization and finance can attempt to establish direct contacts with a large proportion of the delegates in order to predispose them to their cause, if not to obtain an outright commitment of support. Or they may try to influence State or county conventions to choose their supporters as delegates to the national convention. Thus local political figures without any national stature become the object of the attentions of the great men of the land who flatteringly seek their support. Card indexes of delegates listing their leanings and characteristics, files filled with the details of local politics and personalities, visits of the candidate or his emissaries to impress and to persuade, these are the methods and instruments of nominating politics. To do this effectively, as the Kennedy organization did in the months and years preceding the national convention in 1960, takes careful organization and money. It also demands a very clear awareness of the fact that to become President of the United States it is necessary to interest oneself in the politics of small towns and big cities across the whole continent.

Not all the prospective candidates for the nomination have the money, the popular appeal, or the organization which would enable them to win primary elections, or conduct an extensive campaign among delegates, or at the level of State and county conventions. Lacking these advantages in some degree, they must follow a different strategy. Their hope is to cultivate the good will of important figures in the party, Senators, State Governors, Congressmen, important City Mayors, in the hope that the more active and public contenders for the nomination will produce a deadlock at the convention. In such a situation the influence of a relatively few important men behind a candidate who is 'available' may be decisive. An available candidate is one who has not by his past record antagonized a large section of the party, or so publicly committed himself to certain points of view that he is likely to be objected to by delegates who cannot accept his views. The danger of publicly entering the race for the Presidency too soon is that the candidate may be forced to expound his views and to reveal the strength of his support, and in so doing to build up against himself a large body of opposition. It is largely for this reason that a man who desperately wishes to be President will coyly hang back, refusing to announce his candidacy, even denying his presidential ambitions, in the hope that a movement will begin in his support which will eventually sweep him through the convention. The danger of such a strategy is that a brasher candidate who enters the public arena at an early stage will set a popular movement in motion, and will not eliminate himself by his activities, but rather will succeed in establishing a powerful position well before the convention begins.

By the time the convention meets, in July or August, a number of candidates will have delegates committed to their support, with a proportion of the delegates uncommitted or whose views are unknown. Some delegations will be pledged to support the State's 'favourite son', usually the State Governor or a Senator, who may entertain hopes of emerging as a compromise candidate. Usually, however, the favourite son will release his delegates to the support of one or other of the major candidates whenever it seems politic to do so, that is when it seems likely that a particular candidate has a good chance of winning. Delegates who have no strong commitment to one candidate or another naturally wish to be on the winning side, for successful presidential candidates have largesse to distribute and notoriously long memories. If no candidate has an absolute majority on the first ballot, the balloting continues until one is attained.

The balloting at the Democratic national convention in 1952 illustrates the sort of situation which can develop when no candidate is in a dominant position at the opening of the convention. There were four major candidates, Adlai Stevenson, Governor of Illinois, who had neither entered the primaries nor conducted a pre-convention campaign; Senator Estes Kefauver of Tennessee, who had attracted national attention by his televised hearings on crime, and who conducted very successful primary campaigns in a number of States; Senator Richard B. Russell of Georgia who beat Kefauver in the Florida primary and was solidly supported by the Southern States; and Averell Harriman, former Governor of New York, who won overwhelmingly the primary election in the District of Columbia. There were a number of other candidates including favourite sons from Massachusetts, Arkansas and Michigan, as well as a number of candidates who appeared as a result largely of the political situations in their home States. On the first ballot, votes were cast for no fewer than sixteen candidates, with Kefauver getting 340, Stevenson 273, Russell 268, and Harriman 123½. The number of votes needed to win the nomination was 616. On the second ballot the supporters of some of the minor candidates shifted over to the major figures in the contest. Kefauver retained the lead on the second ballot, but improved his position only marginally, going up to 362½ votes. Harriman lost a few votes, and Russell gained a few, but the biggest advance was made by Stevenson, who now had 324½. It had become clear that there was little hope of either Kefauver, Harriman or Russell improving their positions, and the leaders of the New York delegation were having difficulty in keeping their delegates behind Harriman. The latter then withdrew in favour of Stevenson, and the labour leaders who had formerly favoured Kefauver began to see Stevenson as the only possible successful candidate who would be acceptable to them. A third ballot was held, and Stevenson shot up to 613 votes, just a few short of the number required. Immediately the Utah delegation announced that it wished to give all of its twelve votes to Stevenson, having given him only seven

and a half on the third ballot. With the nomination assured
to Stevenson, the Minnesota delegation proposed that the nomination be made unanimous and the convention agreed.

Thus it is quite possible for a candidate to secure the nomination although not having the most votes on the first ballot. In
1940 Wendell Willkie won the Republican nomination on the
sixth ballot, although on the first he had only 105 votes compared with 360 for Thomas E. Dewey and 189 for Senator Taft.
In recent years, however, the tendency has been for conventions
to reach a decision after very few ballots; when one candidate
seems to be in a strong position early on in the first ballot, delegations may switch their support to enable a decision to be made
without further balloting. When an incumbent President is seeking the nomination he is usually in a very powerful position,
almost immune to a serious challenge, for to replace him would
be to repudiate the party's leader while he was still President of
the United States, and to condemn the party's record over the
previous years. President Johnson was nominated by acclamation
in Atlantic City in 1964. But it is possible for a challenge to be
made to an incumbent President, forcing the convention to hold a
ballot. Contested ballots were held when President Truman sought
the nomination in 1948 and when President Roosevelt asked for
his fourth term in 1944. But even in 1948 when the President's
prestige was at a very low ebb the challenge was weak and had
little hope of success, and in 1944 it was trivial. In the nineteenth
century a number of incumbent Presidents were unsuccessful in
seeking a nomination for a further term of office, but all but one
of them, Franklin Pierce, were former Vice-Presidents who had
succeeded to the Presidency on the death of their predecessors.
No incumbent President who sought the nomination has been
rejected since 1884, and until 1968 even former Vice-Presidents
seemed to be in an impregnable position, as Truman suggested
twenty years earlier when he said that 'a President in the White
House always controlled the National Convention'. President
Johnson's withdrawal from the contest for the nomination in
1968 represents a rather special case, for he preferred not to wait
for the convention and a possible trial of strength with his opponents.

When a decision has been reached the nominee makes an acceptance speech to the convention and receives its homage as the party's leader in the forthcoming battle; for the man who a few hours before was just another politician wooing the delegates has suddenly become a man who may be the next President of the United States. Once the nomination has been made the intra-party battle, which has largely dominated the political scene for months, must give way to the contest between the parties, and self-inflicted wounds must be sewn up in order to present, as far as possible, a united front to the enemy. This switch from the bitterness of internal conflict to the competition between parties for office, whether at the level of the Presidency or for State and local office, is one of the perennial wonders of the American political scene. The transition from defeated candidates for the nomination to loyal supporters of the party's chosen leader is often made to seem as complete and as beautiful as the transformation from caterpillar to butterfly. In 1960 Lyndon Johnson was the strongest opponent of John F. Kennedy for the Democratic nomination for the Presidency, yet overnight he became Kennedy's 'running-mate' as Vice-Presidential candidate, working hard to bring the Southern States solidly behind the Kennedy-Johnson ticket. However, the battles for the nomination in primaries and conventions, reflecting as they do real divisions within the parties, may have a lasting effect on party unity. Sometimes even a pretence of papering over differences of policy or personality is not made. Defeated chieftains may refuse to make their peace with the candidate, and State and local leaders may campaign vigorously under the party banner in their own bailiwicks, pointedly ignoring the party's national leader, as many Southern Democrats ignored John F. Kennedy in 1960, or indeed openly opposed him. At the extreme a defeated faction may openly dissociate themselves from the party's candidate and nominate their own. In 1948 the Southern wing of the Democratic party, disgusted with the nomination of President Truman on a civil rights programme, bolted the party and campaigned for Governor Strom Thurmond of South Carolina under the banner of the States Rights Party. The decentralization of the American party system allows dissatisfied local politicians to make the best of a bad job. As the 1964 campaign drew to its close and it became increasingly clear to Republican politicians that Goldwater's bid for the Presidency was lost, many of them withdrew into their local political battles, and left the national candidate to fight on virtually alone.

The national convention has two other major functions to perform: to formulate the party platform and to nominate the Vice-Presidential candidate. Before the convention meets, a Resolutions Committee or Platform Committee is appointed to consider the content of the party's programme and to report to the convention. Often party platforms are dull documents, phrased in vague and general terms in order not to offend important sections of the party, yet this is not always the case. It was the strong civil rights proposals contained in the 1948 Democratic programme that provoked the defection of the Dixiecrats, and in 1960 the content of the Republican platform became a major point of dispute between Richard Nixon and Governor Rockefeller when the latter, finding the draft programme vague and inadequate, threatened to fight it on the floor of the convention if alterations were not made. In general, however, given the nature of American party politics, it is impossible for the party programme to be a bold, exciting document, and as it is drawn up before the Presidential candidate has been nominated he cannot be closely bound by what it contains.

The nomination of the Vice-Presidential candidate follows the balloting for the Presidential nomination. Throughout much of its history the office of Vice-President has been insignificant, and as a consequence the nomination of a Vice-Presidential candidate was not considered a matter of great consequence, particularly as it comes at the end of the convention when delegates are tired and wish to get away. The position came to be used as a sop to the unsuccessful faction at the convention, so giving balance to the ticket, by drawing the Vice-Presidential nominee from a region of the country different from that of the Presidential candidate. In recent years, however, the stature of the Vice-Presidency has been growing and consequently a rather different attitude towards the nomination of Vice-Presidential candidates has been perceptible. In 1940 President Roosevelt threatened that he would not run for a third term if Henry Wallace was not nominated for the Vice-Presidency. Wallace, and later Richard Nixon, were both active and important Vice-Presidents. The assassination of President Kennedy dramatized, as no other event could, the potential importance of the man holding the Vice-Presidential office. It is likely, therefore, that a rather different attitude may be adopted in future to nominations for this office. In 1964, partly because there was no contest for the Presidential nomination in the Democratic party, there developed a distinct campaign on behalf of Hubert Humphrey for the Vice-Presidential nomination, and in an unprecedented move President Johnson appeared on the rostrum at the convention and put Humphrey's name before the delegates. However, the experience of the election of 1968, and in particular the way in which Mr Nixon selected Spiro Agnew as his Vice-Presidential candidate, suggests that the tendency to underplay the potential importance of this office is by no means a thing of the past.

THE CAMPAIGN AND THE ELECTORAL COLLEGE

The dispersal of the national conventions brings to an end the long and exhausting process of selection for which the candidates have been planning, working and campaigning for months, even for years. After a short pause the election proper begins, with its even more intensive and exhausting campaign, building up over eight or nine weeks to the climax of election day itself, on the first Tuesday after the first Monday in November. The American people will then give their final verdict upon those who aspire to the Presidency, yet the way in which the campaign is conducted, and the very nature of the institution of the Presidency itself, depends upon the electoral machinery devised by the Founding Fathers in 1787. For just as the strategy of Presidential nominating politics is determined by the need to obtain an absolute majority of the votes at the convention, so the strategy of the Presidential campaign is determined by the need to obtain an absolute majority of votes in the Electoral College. Although Americans vote for their President early in November, and a

few hours after the polls close the result of the election is common knowledge, it is not until a month has passed that the election of the President actually takes place, when the members of
the Electoral College cast *their* votes. Although in itself this
procedure is usually a formality, hardly noticed by the world, it
is, nevertheless, a procedure which has a profound effect upon
the way in which Presidential elections are conducted, upon the
strategy of the candidates' campaign managers, and upon the
type of candidate who is chosen for the Presidency.

At the end of the eighteenth century the Fathers of the Constitution wished to isolate the election of the President from the
turbulence of 'mob politics', for they were creating an elective
Head of State at a time when democratic government was virtually untried – in France Louis XVI was still on the throne,
Hohenzollern and Hapsburg dominated Europe, and even in England a hereditary aristocracy ruled in collaboration with a still
influential King and a corrupt and unrepresentative House of
Commons. The Americans were embarking upon a great adven-
turous experiment but they wished to be cautious also, and not
to give this potentially powerful office over to demagogues. They
provided, therefore, for a system of *indirect* election for the Presidency. They created an Electoral College in which each State was
to have a number of votes equal to the number of Senators and
Representatives to which it was entitled in Congress. The State
legislatures would determine how the Electors were to be chosen,
and the Electors would then choose a President from among the
men most suited for the position, remote from the white heat of
a popular election. Today the Electors are chosen by popular vote
in November, but in law it is still the Electoral College which
makes the final decision in December. Strictly speaking, when an
American casts his vote for President he is really choosing between competing lists, or 'slates', of Electoral College candidates,
although today the names of the candidates for the Presidential
office appear on the ballot-papers.

Of course the idea that the members of the Electoral College
could quietly and calmly choose a President according to their
best judgement, and perhaps fly in the face of the popular will,
was a delusion. The mechanisms of organized politics soon

entered into the process, and the candidates for the Electoral College soon became pledged to cast their votes for one of the contenders for the Presidency. The members of the Electoral College thus ceased to exercise any individual judgement and merely registered the decision of the voters in their State. The Electoral College does not even meet to deliberate as a body – the members meet in the State capitals and their votes are carried to Washington. It is true that the operation of the Electoral College is not yet quite a formality. Occasionally individual Electors have changed their minds after the November election and refused to cast their votes for the candidate to whom they were pledged. In 1948 a Tennessee Elector refused to cast his vote for President Truman, although the latter had carried the State, and cast his vote instead for the States Rights candidate. In 1956 an Alabama Elector refused to vote for Stevenson, to whom he had been committed, and in 1960 an Elector in Oklahoma pledged to support Richard Nixon cast his vote for Senator Byrd. In 1968 a North Carolina Elector switched his vote from Nixon to George Wallace. These minor deviations from the normal practice have made no difference to the working of the Electoral College, but a recent strategy in certain Southern States has potentially a more important effect. In 1960, as an alternative to setting up a dissident third party, Democrats in Alabama and Mississippi who were opposed to the official candidate, John F. Kennedy, put up an 'unpledged slate' for the Electoral College. This was in a sense a reversion to the earlier ideas of the Founding Fathers, for it was intended that these Electors should not be committed to one candidate or another, but should be free to choose according to the outcome of the election in other States. If it was a very close election in terms of Electoral votes these uncommitted Electors could tip the balance in favour of one candidate or another in return for concessions to the Southern point of view, or else they could throw the election into the House of Representatives. Although it was a close election in terms of the popular vote, Kennedy had a good margin of Electoral votes and the unpledged slate which won in Mississippi cast their votes for Senator Harry F. Byrd along with some of the unpledged Electors from Alabama.

The Electoral College, therefore, would seem at first sight to be merely a rather complicated mechanism for the indirect registration of 'the people's will'. Yet that is not the case at all. To understand why the structure of the Electoral College is so important it is necessary to examine the way in which, purely by convention, the States have come to operate the machinery of the College. The Constitution simply laid down that 'The Electors shall meet in their respective States, and vote by ballot for President and Vice-president ...', but it does not stipulate the manner in which balloting shall take place. The most obvious way to conduct the balloting might be to allocate the Electoral votes among the candidates proportionately to the number of votes they received in the popular election. Thus in 1960 New York State *could* have divided her forty-five Electoral votes between Kennedy and Nixon in the following way:

	Proportion of popular vote	Electoral votes
Kennedy	52·5%	24
Nixon	47·3%	21

This would seem surely to be the fairest way to express the views of the seven million New Yorkers who voted in the election. In fact the States do not allocate Electoral votes in this way. By convention *all* the Electoral votes of a State are given to the candidate who attains a plurality, that is a simple majority, of the popular vote in the State. Thus in the example given above all of New York's forty-five Electoral votes went to Kennedy.

The effect of this method of casting the Electoral College votes is to increase enormously the effects of sectional and geographical factors on the selection and election of Presidential candidates. The significance of the more populous states becomes disproportionately great. To succeed in an election a candidate must get an absolute majority in the Electoral College, and the votes of a relatively small number of large States will put him well on the way to achieving this aim. In 1968 the number of votes required for election was 270 out of the total of 538 Electoral votes. When aiming at this figure the big votes of New York (forty-three votes), California (forty votes), Pennsylvania (twenty-nine votes), Illinois and Ohio (twenty-six votes each), and Texas (twenty-five votes), become critically important. Each candidate must hope to capture most of these large States with enough of the middle group, like Massachusetts (fourteen votes), New Jersey (seventeen votes), or Virginia (twelve votes), and of the smaller States to reach the magic figure. Thus the large urbanized States play a disproportionately large part in electing the President, in influencing Presidential politics, and consequently in widening the gap between congressional and Presidential politics. It has been shown that a vote cast by an individual member of the electorate in the States of the North East and North Central areas is potentially worth more than a vote cast in the Western States, so that naturally enough Presidential candidates concentrate their attention on these areas, and are more sensitive and responsive to their interests. Similarly the political parties tend to choose their candidates from these areas in order to make the greatest appeal to them. Thus the Electoral College usually exaggerates the margin of victory gained by the successful candidate – in 1960 John Kennedy had a popular vote majority of only 0.1 per cent over Nixon, but he finished up with sixty-two per cent of the Electoral vote to Nixon's thirty-six per cent. In 1964 President Johnson's sixty-one per cent of the popular vote turned into ninety per cent of the Electoral vote. On the other hand it is possible for a candidate to be elected with fewer popular votes than his rival, as happened in 1876 and 1888, and could well have happened in 1960.

The most dramatic result of this eighteenth-century method of electing the President occurs if no candidate succeeds in obtaining an overall majority of the vote in the Electoral College. In this case the election is decided by the House of Representatives, by a rather extraordinary procedure. The House chooses a President from the three top names in the Electoral College ballot, *each State delegation exercising one vote*, irrespective of the number of members in the delegation, or of the population of the State. Thus the State of New York would have the same voting power as Nevada or New Mexico. Each State delegation determines how to cast its vote by a majority vote within the delegation. As the delegation would usually be divided between the two parties, voting within delegations might go along party lines, but in some situations the Members of the House might vote across party lines to choose a compromise candidate, or even in order to reject a candidate of their own party to whom they objected. The outcome of such a vote in the House could be a most extraordinary choice, in which the expression of the popular will would be ignored. Other even more bizarre possibilities exist. The Constitution provides that to be elected a candidate must receive an absolute majority of votes in the House, as in the Electoral College, but the former can go on, ballot after ballot, until a result is reached, whereas there is only a single ballot in the College. However, suppose that a deadlock ensues, and no President is elected! The Constitution provides that in such a situation, if no President has been elected by the date on which the new President should take office, then the Vice-President-elect shall act as President. Of course if the Electoral College failed to elect a President they might also fail to provide an absolute majority for any vice-presidential candidate. In such a case the Senate chooses the Vice-President from the two top candidates, and one glimpses the extraordinary, though fortunately extremely unlikely, possibility that the vice-presidential candidate of a party with a minority of the popular vote might become Vice-President, and then act for a time as President.

Such an extreme situation has not occurred, but on two occasions the election has been thrown into the House of Representatives – the presidential elections of 1800 and 1824. In the former case Thomas Jefferson was elected only after thirty-six ballots in the House. On the second occasion the election of John Quincy Adams turned upon the vote of one member of the New York delegation, General Stephen Van Renssalaer, whose decision to vote for Adams seems to have been arrived at in a rather strange fashion. As Van Renssalaer sat in the House deliberating upon how to cast his vote he bowed his head in prayer, only to see on the floor a piece of paper with Adams' name written on it. He picked it up and cast the vote which decided the issue. In the election of 1968 the possibility of a deadlock occurring seemed very real. The intervention of a third party candidate with wide support, Governor George Wallace of the American Indepen-

dent Party, might have prevented either of the major party
candidates from achieving an overall majority in the Electoral
College. Wallace hoped that if this were to happen he could use
his position to bargain for policy concessions on civil rights from
the other two candidates. If the election had been thrown into
the House the Southern States might have been able to cause a
deadlock there, possibly with disastrous consequences for the
political system.

These complications in the Electoral College system have led
to many proposals for its reform or abolition, but perhaps the
greatest criticism of the system is that it turns the only really
national event in the American political calendar into a process of sectional coalition-building. It is within this context that
the Presidential campaign is conducted. Students of voting behaviour have suggested that election campaigns are little more
than ritualistic performances through which the candidates must
go, although their influence on the result of the election is very
small, and usually nowhere near as significant as the amount of
time, energy and money that is spent on them would suggest.
Yet no politician dare make such an assumption; certainly in a
close race like that of 1960 almost any aspect of the campaign
might have been 'decisive' – Kennedy's telegram of support to the
jailed Negro leader Martin Luther King, or even the fact that
Nixon perspired freely on television. Yet although the campaign
allows the electorate to see and choose between rival candidates it
also fulfils a deeper function in the political system. It is the first
step by which the future President establishes himself as the
leader of the nation and seeks to establish a basis for the exercise
of his authority. Every President has in some degree to establish
a charismatic authority over this diverse and individualistic
nation, for, as we shall see later, it is in his ability to claim the
status of national leader that the main strength of the President lies. The powers of the Presidency are great, but the constitutional machinery is so complex, with so many barriers to the
effective exercise of power, that a President has to impose his
views on the machine by sheer force of will, and to do this successfully he must have popular support. With the exception of a
man like General Eisenhower, few of the men who enter for the

presidential race have a truly national reputation and following, when they first make a bid for office.

With the coming of television and the aeroplane the means are at hand with which the candidates can attempt to impress their personality upon a nation of two hundred million people spread over thousands of miles. The discussion of policies *may* be important in the campaign, according to the circumstances of the time, but essentially the campaign is a battle of personalities. It is perhaps in the very nature of this democratic system that in attempting to create a position of authority the candidates must submit to a process which is almost lethal in the demands it makes upon them, and which will almost certainly involve them in embarrassing, even humiliating situations. In the course of the campaign a candidate may travel 50,000 miles, making speeches on both sides of the Continent in a single day. He will address great rallies and speak to a handful of voters at a street corner. He will shake as many hands as is humanly possible. He may be photographed wearing the comic headgear of this or that association, or like the President of the United States campaigning for re-election in 1964, give cowboy whoops from the saddle of a horse whilst his audience laugh and clap in appreciation. The man who wishes to be President has at one and the same time to convince the electors that he is an ordinary fellow who understands the problems of everyday living, and that he is capable of dealing with complex questions involving war and peace and of daily making decisions that deeply affect the welfare of all Americans.

HOUSE AND SENATE ELECTIONS

The election of the President takes place every four years, but elections for one third of the Senate and the whole of the House of Representatives take place every two years. Thus when the President is in the middle of his term of office, just beginning the climb up to the next test of strength at the Presidential election two years hence, a large proportion of the legislators come up for re-election. These mid-term elections differ in many respects from elections in presidential years, and their results can be of critical importance to the incumbent President. At the extreme, these mid-term elections can result in a change of control, so that one party controls the Presidency, and the other party controls either the House or the Senate, or both Houses. For the remaining two years of his Presidency a Democratic President may have to cope with a Republican Congress, or vice versa. Thus President Truman in 1946 and President Eisenhower in 1954 were faced with a House and Senate containing a majority of the opposing party. Indeed the second Administration of President Eisenhower illustrates the extreme possibilities implicit in the constitutional gulf set between Congress and Presidency. In the election of 1956 the American people returned Republican President Eisenhower to power with a huge popular majority, but elected a Democratic majority to the Senate and House of Representatives. However, the system of government did not crumble, for enough Democrats were prepared to go along with the Republican President to make the system workable. The elections of 1968 and 1972 almost suggest that this has now become the norm.

Regularly at the mid-term elections the President's party loses support, and sometimes the shift of party strength may be considerable. In 1966 in the middle of President Johnson's term of office the Democrats lost forty-seven seats in the House to the Republicans. Partly this loss of support is a reflection of the normal disillusionment with the party in power, partly it is because local issues tend to be more important at mid-term than in presidential years. At mid term, therefore, the President is faced with a difficult tactical problem – to what extent should he and members of his Administration campaign in support of his party in the Congressional elections? There are dangers both in giving only lukewarm support and in wholehearted involvement. If the President actively commits himself to ensuring a victory for his party, then an ensuing defeat for them is a defeat for him. His prestige will suffer a serious blow and the result will be doubly damaging to his hopes of legislative support for his policies in the last two years of his Administration. Furthermore, if the President conducts a hard-hitting campaign on behalf of the congressional party he will to some extent antagonize those members of the other party in Congress who have been sympathetic to his aims and on whose support he may need to depend in the future. On the other hand if he remains aloof from the battles in which the members of his party are engaged, he may endanger morale in his own party and antagonize members of Congress who feel that they have a claim to his support. The dilemma is compounded by the fact that some of the bitterest enemies of his policies will be found among the ranks of Senators and Congressmen of his own party, and the President will not be keen to see them back again in the next Congress. A possible solution to the problem is for the President to give selective support at mid term to those members of his party in Congress who have supported his policies, but this is a tricky strategy, which will embitter the President's opponents within his party and may well not be particularly successful anyway in the morass of State and local politics at mid term. To try to eliminate this problem and to bring Congress into closer harmony with the Presidency, President Johnson proposed an amendment to the Constitution which would give Congressmen a four-year term to coincide with that of the President.

However, the exact nature of the relationship between the forces affecting the election of the President and those influencing congressional elections is not very clear, even in Presidential election years. The fortunes of a political party usually show a very close relationship in Presidential and Congressional elections, but how far does the character and popularity of a Presidential candidate affect the results of House and Senate elections? Does the successful Presidential candidate carry the members of his party into office riding upon his coat-tails? And what about the relatively uninspiring candidate for the Presidency; does he hurt the chances of election of his party colleagues? In 1952 the Republicans won control of both Senate and House together for the first time since 1928. Was this not the 'coat-tails effect' in operation, in which the Republicans were swept into power by the magic of Eisenhower's name? And yet four years later Eisenhower was re-elected with an even greater percentage of the poll, but, incredibly, the Democrats retained the control of House and Senate that they had won in the mid-term elections of 1954. The lustre of Eisenhower's name seemed to do Republican candidates little good on that occasion. Because John Kennedy

performed less well as a vote-getter than his party as a whole in
1960, does this mean that *he* rode into office on the coat-tails of
his party, or perhaps that congressional Democrats did less well
because of his candidacy than they might otherwise have done?
There are no clear answers to these questions, for the so-called
'coat-tails effect' provides one of the enigmas of American politics. The evidence suggests that a popular presidential candidate
may have a considerable effect upon the turnout of voters at the
elections, but probably does not have much effect upon the way
in which the electorate cast their votes in congressional contests.
Voters' reactions to congressional candidates seem to depend
much more upon local factors than upon the influence of the
national leader of the party. If this is the case it is of the greatest
importance for the working of American politics, for it is the
Congressman's or Senator's perception of his constituents'
attitudes which will determine the extent to which he supports
Presidential policies in Congress. If he feels that his re-election
depends more upon local issues and attitudes than upon the
appeal of the Presidential candidate to the voters, then he will
react accordingly in the legislature, giving the President support
when, and only when, he feels that this is what his constituents
want.

Thus the gulf between Presidential and congressional politics
which was created by the makers of the Constitution in 1787 has
been widened in a number of ways. There is one other important
way in which the tensions in the American political system
between Congress and President have been aggravated over the
years – the impact of gerrymandering and the malapportionment
of congressional constituencies. Gerrymandering is the practice
of drawing constituency boundaries in such a way that an unfair
advantage is gained by one political party over the other. Congressional district boundaries are drawn up by the State legislatures, and they can be drawn in an irregular way so that pockets
of strength can be linked together in one constituency. Alter-
natively boundaries can be drawn so that the concentration of
the supporters of one party in a few constituencies where it will
receive large majorities, will enable the other party to take a
relatively large number of constituencies with small majorities.

Another way of giving one party an unfair advantage over the other is to provide for constituencies of very different sizes, so that the congressional districts are malapportioned among the population. This can be done by deliberately drawing boundaries in such a way that one constituency may have two or three times as many voters as another; or it may be done simply by ignoring movements of population, usually movements into the city. Until recently the malapportionment of State legislatures and of congressional districts was one of the major reasons for the difference in emphasis between congressional and presidential politics. The fact that the election of the President depended so greatly on the large urbanized States contrasted strangely with the electoral base of Congress. State legislatures were mostly dominated by rural interests, a domination maintained by malapportionment. In their turn the State legislatures provided congressional districts which over-represented rural interests. In Texas in 1962 the largest congressional district contained 951,527 people whilst the smallest had only 216,371. Thus the different constituencies of President and Congress emphasized strongly differing interests.

In 1962, however, the Supreme Court of the United States handed down a judicial decision with endless political ramifications. In the case of *Baker v. Carr* the Court decided that it was unconstitutional for a State to retain a malapportioned legislature, and the American courts set about re-shaping the American legislatures. In 1964 the Supreme Court applied the same principle to Congressional districts, stating that 'as nearly as is practicable, one man's vote in a Congressional election is to be worth as much as another's.' How far will the application of the Court's ruling affect the balance of interests between the different sections of the community? It used to be the case that rural interests were much over-represented compared with the cities, and the assumption was that a 'fair' system of apportionment would increase the number of liberal Democrats in Congress. But the situation is rather more complex than this. Recent large-scale movements of population have been *away* from the city centres into the suburban areas. It is probably the suburbs which suffer most from under-representation today, and as we have seen, the future effect of suburbia on American politics is difficult to estimate. An increase in the number of Representatives from suburban districts would presumably be to increase the number of independent-minded members of Congress, so that although there might be some change in the nature of the relationship between President and Congress it would not necessarily be in the direction of making that relationship more harmonious.

ELECTIONS AND THE STATES

Each of the fifty States elects its Governor, State legislators, and State and local officials, often on the same day and on the same ballot as Presidential and Congressional elections, although many cities, townships, school districts and other elective bodies have elections at other times of the year. It is difficult to generalize about this enormous array of elections and the way in which they are conducted. The Governorship of a great State, like New York or California, Pennsylvania or Illinois, is an office to be coveted, both for its own sake and because it may form that essential basis of State political power which a man needs in order to make a bid for the Presidency itself. At the other end of the political spectrum, it may be the height of a man's political ambition to become one of the Selectmen of a New England town of a few hundred people. The movement of the great tides of national politics may affect the outcome of some of the State and local contests, and equally the politics of the Presidency itself may be dependent upon the outcome of local political battles. State politics are not autonomous and distinct from national politics, but neither are they wholly dependent upon and subservient to national trends. Indeed the candidacy of a well-known and popular figure for a State Governorship may well have a considerable effect upon voter turnout for Congressional elections, as was the case when Nelson Rockefeller ran for Governor of New York in 1958.

Political campaigns at State and local level differ widely – in some areas the 'lone-wolf' campaign is the norm, in which each candidate runs for office on his own, creating his own organization as he goes along. Elsewhere the parties are highly organized and in control of local politics. Similarly the finance for campaigns may be run on a shoe-string, or involve millions of dollars in a State-wide campaign for the Governorship. Electoral tactics are as varied and ingenious as the American imagination: in 1958 Senator Kuchel, campaigning for the Governorship of California, staged a 'telethon' in which he appeared before the television cameras in Los Angeles in a programme lasting for over twenty hours. Constituents were able to telephone the Senator and ask him questions, he discussed campaign issues and had voters in to meet him before the cameras. Vice-President Nixon used a carefully staged telethon in the 1960 Presidential campaign.

Perhaps the most important aspect of the variety of political styles in the States is the fact that it is the States themselves that control the machinery of election for all elective offices, and that in the past this control of the election machinery has been used as a weapon in the political battle rather than as a piece of neutral machinery of representative government. The electoral law has been used to prevent Negroes, poor whites, or immigrants from exercising the vote. Poll taxes, literacy tests, residence requirements, and making primary elections open only to white voters, have all been used in the past to discriminate against 'undesirable elements'. In recent years this form of electoral discrimination has been attacked by the courts and by Congress. The 'white primary' was finally declared unconstitutional by the Supreme Court in 1944; in 1957 and 1960 Congress passed Civil Rights Acts providing Federal machinery to aid Negroes who had been improperly deprived of the right to register as voters; in 1964 a further Civil Rights Act strengthened the power of the U.S. Attorney-General to supervise voting registration, and regulated the administration of literacy tests by the States; in the same year the Twenty-Fourth Amendment to the Constitution was ratified, which outlawed the use of the poll tax as a prerequisite for voting in Federal elections. As a result of these measures, and of the 'registration drives' by civil rights workers on behalf of Negroes, Negro registrations in the Southern States had risen in 1964 to over two million, giving rise to the situation long feared by Southern whites where in a number of States the outcome of elections could depend upon the Negro vote. In spite of these advances, however, the fact remains that the *administration* of the electoral laws is in the hands of State and local officials, and that the machinery for the enforcement of Federal legislation is cumbersome and cannot possibly be brought to bear upon all the innumerable points where a citizen may be deprived of his rights.

The form of the ballot is also a matter of State law, and it is difficult to assess the importance of differing practices upon the working of the electoral system. The 'long ballot' results from the great number of State and local offices to be filled. Ballot-papers can reach ludicrous proportions – at the extreme they can be six feet long and contain a thousand names. The way in which the ballot is set out can favour or hamper the tendency to split-ticket voting. The use of voting machines has spread in urban areas, and has cut down the use of corrupt practices at election time, but even these machines can be rigged if election officials are corrupt, and there then remain no ballot-papers to be checked. The introduction of the machines has greatly speeded up the counting of the votes, and, together with the introduction of computers, has created an election problem possibly unique to the United States. The polls close at 7 p.m. in Connecticut, on America's Eastern seaboard, but because of the time difference it is then only 4 p.m. in California. Within a short time of the end of voting in the East the television sets across the nation are giving out the computer's predictions of the election result, and yet there are millions of people still to vote in the Western States. How does this affect their behaviour? Do the supporters of the candidate whose defeat has just been predicted lose heart and ensure that defeat, or are his party workers spurred to new efforts, whilst the supporters of the apparent victor become over-confident and lethargic as they have presumably already won?

*

It can now be seen just how far the electoral machinery in the United States emphasizes the geographical and sectional influences in her politics. In all Western democracies the adoption of geographical constituencies provides a built-in tendency to stress regional differences of interest rather than class or pluralistic factors. In the United States this tendency is powerfully reinforced by the constitutional provisions which decentralize power and authority. In other countries ideological and organizational forces have modified, sometimes almost obliterated, the built-in emphasis upon geography in the electoral system, but in the United States the party system and the electoral system have tended to reinforce each other's decentralizing tendencies. Only the Presidency acts as a centralizing force, and the selection and election of Presidents is by no means free of sectional influences. Thus the party system and the electoral system discharge one vital function: they select the men to fill political office. But because of their sectional nature they are relatively poor at performing another function vital to the political system – the formulation of policies. The job of partly filling this gap is performed by the next set of political structures to which we shall turn our attention – the interest groups.

Pressure Politics

5

GROUP PLURALISM

Political decisions are arrived at by complex processes which vary according to the issues involved, the circumstances at the time they are being taken, and many other institutional and personal factors; yet we might distinguish three overlapping major sources from which the eventual solutions to problems are generated – the institutional machinery of government itself, the party system, and interested groups. Of course most decisions will involve all three of these structures in some degree or another, but we have already seen that the machinery of party, *outside* of Congress and Presidency, is relatively weak in terms of policy formation, and a vacuum is created to be filled by the complex structure of interest groups. This relative separation of the functions of selecting leaders and of initiating and influencing policy gives to the American political system its peculiar flavour and complexity, which will become fully apparent only when we look at the behaviour of Congressmen and Senators and their relationship with the President and his Administration. Party politics and pressure politics criss-cross and merge together to produce an ever-changing pattern of legislative and executive behaviour.

But how do we distinguish between the party system and the structure of interest groups? After all, many of the persons involved in one of these patterns of behaviour will be involved in the other as well. Formally the difference between political party and interest groups is that the former organization nominates candidates for public office, and the latter do not. If a group attempts to put up its own candidates for election it becomes a political party and subject to all the legal provisions which in the United States regulate the operations of political parties. Yet this relatively straightforward distinction does not mean that in

practice a sharp, clear line can be drawn between the two forms
of political organization. Holders of elective office, wearing a
party label, may be very closely associated with particular interest groups, and although such groups do not formally nominate candidates they may publicly endorse a particular party or
its candidate, contribute to campaign funds, and either secretly
or openly work to elect or defeat particular individuals. The
membership of party and group may overlap to the point where
a particular group may be little more than one 'wing' of a political party, or, on the other hand, a group may be at pains to
remain aloof from both parties in order to be able to appeal to
them both on an equal basis. Thus interest groups may be seen
either as alternatives to the political parties or as complementary
to them. The complexity of the American party system gives
added significance to this characteristic of interest groups, for a
particular group may be identified more closely with a political
party at State or local level than at the Federal level, or have a
closer relationship to the Presidential party than to the congressional party, so that a group of individuals may emerge and re-
emerge in different guises at different times, as the occasion
demands. Thus although for analytical purposes it is useful to
describe the party system and the structure of interest groups as
if they were quite distinct entities, the realities of political life
are more complex.

This blurring of the distinction between parties and interest
groups is paralleled at the other end of the spectrum by the way
in which the structure of interest groups merges into the
machinery of government itself. Thus some groups, like the
Farm Bureau Federation, for instance, have achieved a position
which makes them almost an essential party to any government
action affecting their interests, so that groups formally outside
the government become appendages to it. In the same way, parts
of the government machine itself may behave like interest
groups in order to safeguard their own position. Thus for many
years the Air Force was a powerful interest group exercising influence on Congressmen in opposition to the policy of the Defense Department and other branches of the armed services. The
National Guard, a part-time reserve military organization, was

extremely successful in obtaining its aims through traditional interest-group methods, particularly through the efforts of the National Guard Association.

Bearing these complexities in mind it is true to say that the importance of interest groups in the American political system has given rise to a theory of politics in which the interaction of groups becomes the essence of democratic government. Group pluralism is perhaps *the* American theory of politics, finding its roots in James Madison's theory of the Constitution in 1787, and providing an alternative both to the Marxist class theory of politics and to the nineteenth-century individualistic theories of democracy. This theory of government is based upon the assumption that the individual as such can have little or no impact upon the way in which decisions are taken. The group is the significant unit of the political system. In a free society innumerable groups will form and reform to express the diverse and changing interests of their members. Such groups are not a threat to the traditional channels of government action but a necessary complement to them. The groups perform the functions of supplying information about the enormous range of complex activities in which government becomes involved, and of giving expression to a range of opinions of far greater diversity than the normal representative machinery of government could cope with.

Two things are necessary for the successful operation of this type of political system. First, there must be a broad consensus of agreement about the basis and aims of the society so that no group will attempt to enforce its views upon the rest to the point where civil war might ensue. As we have seen, this consensus is one of the characteristic features of the American ideological scene. Second, there must be a set of political mechanisms through which inter-group bargaining can be conducted in such a way that some sort of equilibrium can be attained between the competing demands. Perhaps the first requirement of this system of government is that it should be flexible, for although the aim is to attain an equilibrium it cannot be the equilibrium of deadlock or stagnation. The pattern of demands is continually changing as new economic, social, and military developments take place, and a stable political system must be able to accommodate them. Changing group aspirations, such as those of the Negro today, will disturb the established distribution of authority or wealth, and a new position of equilibrium, a new compromise, must be attained, a new bargain struck. This flexibility, the ability to adapt to changing circumstances, is one of the outstanding characteristics of the American political system, in contradiction to the oft-laboured clichés about the inflexibility of the American Constitution.

This description of the working of the political system undoubtedly over-emphasizes the pluralistic features of American government, certainly failing to give sufficient weight to the policy-making functions of the Presidency. Nevertheless it is by no means negligible as an explanation of the general working of American politics. As we shall see, on many issues the Congress of the United States becomes something of a market-place in which the pressures of party, constituency and interested groups, including in the last category departments of the Federal Administration, are assessed, balanced and reconciled to produce legislative compromises which seem in the eyes of the members of the legislature to be as satisfactory as possible to the interests involved. Given the diversity of American society these interests can only be effectively represented by a wide variety of competing groups with overlapping membership. This last consideration, the way in which membership of different groups overlaps, is an important factor in the operation of group bargaining, making the processes of the reconciliation of competing demands far easier than if the groups concerned were ossified into completely distinct and separate sections of the community.

The flexibility of the political system flows to a considerable extent, therefore, from the way in which interest groups work the cumbrous machinery of American government. The constitutional devices of federalism and the separation of powers, which together serve to decentralize both the government and the parties geographically and to disintegrate them vertically, create the conditions in which interest groups can flourish and indeed become essential to the operation of government. Interest groups, unlike political parties, are not bound to particular geographical constituencies. They can organize themselves across

States or sections, or across the whole nation. They can adopt a unitary or a federal structure as circumstances seem to demand. A retail drug-store owner in a small Southern town can ally himself with fellow drug-store owners in New York City or Los Angeles to achieve common aims even if his views on all matters other than retail prices are completely at odds with those of other members of his profession. Interest groups thrive upon the fragmented character of the government system. A group which is frustrated at one level or in one department of the government can quickly switch its efforts to another level, or to another point of access, in order to try to get its views adopted. Thus it could well be argued that it is interest groups rather than political parties which bring into some sort of coordinated relationship the various branches of the government, Federal, State and local – although it could also be argued, with equal justification, that it is the conflicting demands of interest groups operating through different levels and branches of the government that generate the sharp conflicts which do arise between the parts of the government machine.

However, the above discussion does not give full expression to the complexity of group politics. It suggests that there are clearly identifiable groups in the population each with its common interest, but this is not really the case. How does one define or designate an 'interest'? The Negro community might seem to be a group with an obvious interest in common, and yet the Negro community is represented by a wide range of organizations, some more militant than others, with different aims, varying from the desire to integrate the Negro fully into American life to the proposal to set up a separate Black State or States. Similarly there are sharp divisions of opinion within the business community or between labour unions, or within a group of professional people such as schoolteachers, about the way in which their aims should be pursued. Thus we must turn our attention from the existence of different groups of people in the community at large who can be labelled as economically, racially, or socially similar in 'interest', to the actual organizations, in their enormous number and variety, which figure on the political scene.

We have seen that the existence of a distinct group in the electorate, such as the Negro community, may be an important factor in the outcome of political battles at election time. But politics is a continuing process, in which interested groups may wish to be involved at every stage of government activity, and in order to achieve this they must be organized. Thus the importance of the Negro community does not lie simply in its potential voting power, but also in the numerous organizations which capitalize upon that potential by bringing pressure to bear upon government agencies to further the Negro interest as they see it. The associations and organizations which come into existence to express new demands or to defend old positions vary considerably in the form and durability of their organizational life. Some are ephemeral operations which come into existence in response to a particular stimulus, say the threat of government regulation of the affairs of a particular section of the community, and which expire as soon as a decision has been taken or a problem solved. At the other extreme there are those organizations which exhibit a formidable degree of stability, homogeneity of purpose, and expertise, which makes them more significant elements in the process of policy-making than the great political parties. Trade associations, the National Association for the Advancement of Colored People, the American Medical Association, are examples of such organizations, and are continually involved in political situations. Between these extremes there is a bewildering variety of organizations with differing aims which may from time to time become involved in political decisions and which are potentially part of the political process.

The list of such organizations is endless, and their concerns are equally various. Many of them are to be identified with an 'interest' only in the very broadest sense, for example, the League of Women Voters or the National Federation of Business and Professional Women's Clubs. Nor do groups have to be associated with economic interests in order to be effective, as the Marxist analysis would suggest. Perhaps the most famous of all interest groups was the Anti-Saloon League which played an important part in bringing about the passage of the Eighteenth Amendment prohibiting the manufacture or sale of alcohol in the United States. Religious denominations, some with representatives in Washington, maintain organizations to keep an eye upon governmental affairs which interest them; such are the National Council of Churches of Christ, the Board of Temperance of the Methodist Church, or the National Catholic Welfare Conference. The Zionist Organization of America naturally concerns itself with American policy in the Middle East. Associations of ex-servicemen such as the American Legion or the Veterans of Foreign Wars concern themselves both with pensions and with wider political issues such as the activities of the United Nations and its impact upon American interests. Professional associations such as the American Medical Association and the American Bar Association exercise very considerable influence over the areas of government action in which they can claim a special expertise: the activities of the A.M.A. in combating proposals for State-operated medical insurance schemes, or 'socialized medicine', represents perhaps the best known interest-group campaign of recent times, in which the A.M.A. used every tactic available to a highly organized interest group to influence public opinion and members of Congress in their favour. Other professional bodies, such as the American Federation of Teachers, represent the concern of their members with salaries and conditions of work. In the field of Civil Rights there is a bewildering variety of groups ranging from the N.A.A.C.P. and the Congress of Racial Equality, to the Black Muslims representative of black nationalism. And then, almost as appendages of the great political parties, there are those groups whose 'interest' is ideological rather than economic or social, the Americans for Democratic Action on the one hand, or the John Birch Society on the other. There is thus a great spectrum of groups with differing degrees of political involvement, with different organizational bias, and using different techniques in the search for 'influence' upon government. But there are three major complexes of interest groups which demand greater attention – those representative of business, labour and agriculture.

Business and politics are inextricably interwoven. Great decisions of national policy on matters of foreign affairs or defence will have an immediate effect upon the business community, and in the mid twentieth century the decisions of the Federal Government on space programmes, aircraft production, and the methods of prosecuting foreign aid programmes or military operations may involve the expenditure of thousands of millions of dollars on contracts with American firms. The tax policy of Federal and State governments is of immediate interest to every business corporation in the country as well as to a host of small businessmen. Business interests may seek to promote or to prevent government action, to gain a competitive advantage over other businesses, or to defend themselves against legislation promoted by labour unions to improve wage-rates or working conditions. The United States at the end of the nineteenth century pioneered attempts to deal with the monopolistic tendencies of modern industry and to legislate against restrictive pricing agreements. The Wagner and Taft-Hartley Acts embody a comprehensive scheme of government control of collective bargaining, and the Federal Government sets a minimum wage and maximum working hours for all workers engaged in interstate commerce (a definition which has been expanded by the Supreme Court to include a high percentage of all American workers). An impressive range of Federal agencies, the independent regulatory commissions, operate legislation regulating many areas of business activity: the Federal Trade Commission is charged with the promotion of free and fair competition by controlling false and misleading advertising and other business practices; as early as 1887 the Interstate Commerce Commission was established to regulate the rates and operations of railroads and motorways and later to take over the regulation of interstate trucking companies. The Securities and Exchange Commission, the Federal Communications Commission, the Federal Power Commission, the Civil Aeronautics Board, all exercise extensive authority over businesses engaged in their field of interest, and there are many other Federal agencies engaged in regulation of business activity. The fifty States also have a wide variety of regulatory functions, and the concentration of some types of business in a few States, for example the insurance business in the North East, renders the activities of these States particularly important in certain fields. State and local regulation of road hauliers has been of particular importance in the past because of the great variety of State laws concerning the taxation of road transport and the standards which hauliers must meet in the construction and operation of their vehicles. Local businesses are subjected to an enormous variety of State and local regulations covering, for instance, health regulations on the production of milk.

There is, therefore, enormous scope for business groups to interest themselves in, and to become involved in, the legislative and administrative operations of government. Furthermore, the large volume of legislation on the statute books which involves business operations, in a country where legislation is subject to judicial review by the courts in order to test its constitutional validity, means that businesses are quite frequently involved in litigation to determine the extent of their rights and obligations under the law, right up to the level of the Supreme Court of the United States. The size and power of some of the corporations which thus come into contact with the government is awesome – a few of them seem even to rival the government itself in the size of their operations and the extent of their influence. Giants such as General Motors or the American Telephone and Telegraph Company conduct their own relations with government, using all the paraphernalia of modern public relations techniques. But the business community in general is represented in its contact with government agencies by associations which specialize in representing their members' interests. A few of these, in particular the National Association of Manufacturers and the Chamber of Commerce of the United States, are nation-wide organizations claiming to speak for the business community as a whole. But each branch of industry and commerce has its own trade association to represent its interest. In 1961 there were estimated to be 1,800 national trade associations in the United States, 11,000 State, regional and local associations, and 5,000 local chambers of commerce. The more inclusive an association attempts to be, the less likely it is to be able to develop clear policy positions, except on a very few matters of common interest, or to exercise leadership in business affairs, and when an association does take a stand on a matter of importance the views of the leadership may be quite unrepresentative of the membership of the association. Thus the larger and more inclusive the group becomes the more it is likely to suffer from the same disabilities as those that beset the political parties themselves.

The operation of inter-group bargaining and the divisions within the business community can perhaps be illustrated by the way in which the battles over resale price maintenance and the control over the production of natural gas were conducted. The group most interested in the continuation of resale price-maintenance legislation was the National Association of Retail Druggists, who over a long period fought off attempts by the Federal Administration, by the Courts, and by price-cutting competitors to outlaw price-fixing agreements. The N.A.R.D. was successful in getting legislation supporting their position adopted by the Federal Congress and by many State legislatures. In the 1930s, in their effort to obtain the passage of the Miller-Tydings Amendment, which exempted price-fixing agreements made under State law from the prohibitions of the anti-trust laws, the N.A.R.D. established 'contact committees' of local retailers in every Congressional district, choosing acquaintances and friends of Congressmen to staff them. The Amendment was passed over the opposition of the President and F.T.C. At the State level the Association was extremely successful in getting States to pass the necessary legislation, and the model law that it supported was passed by eleven States before a typographical error in the draft was noted. The success of the N.A.R.D. in these years, although resale price maintenance has succumbed to other forces since, illustrates one very important aspect of business in politics in the U.S. It is not only the giants of the 'military-industrial complex' which can successfully exercise pressure upon government: one of the most persistently successful interests in getting help from government has been the small business-man.

The battle over the regulation of the production and distribution of natural gas during the Eisenhower administration was illustrative of the way in which different business groups could line up against each other, using the different levels of Federal and State government to attempt to achieve their aims. Basically this was a dispute over whether the States or the Federal government should control the output and pricing policy of the natural gas industry. The producers were fearful of Federal control and formed a Natural Gas and Oil Resources Committee to keep control in the hands of the States. The local gas distributing companies, however, hoped for lower prices with Federal control, and allied with labour, municipal and consumer groups they fought to assert Federal power. A Council of Local Gas Companies allied with a committee of mayors pleaded for the consumer before Congress. The oil and gas industry was reported to have spent over $1·5 million to 'educate' Senators. The gas producers scored an initial success by getting the legislation that they wanted passed by Congress, but allegations of improper lobbying, in particular the revelation by Senator Case that a large sum of money had been paid into his campaign fund in connexion with the legislation, led President Eisenhower to veto the Bill.

LABOUR AND POLITICS

The paradoxical position of labour in the United States has been expressed by V. O. Key as 'a numerically great force in a society adhering to the doctrine of the rule of numbers, yet without proportionate durable political power as a class'. We have already seen some of the special factors in American history which have contributed to the spectacle of a highly-industrialized society in which socialism has been of negligible importance – the lack of any true feudal tradition, the open character of American society in the nineteenth century, the influence of the moving frontier of settlement. Yet although these factors help to explain the absence of any significant *socialist* party they only serve to explain in part the weakness of labour as a political force. Part of the explanation lies in the general dispersion of constitutional authority

and political power, which has militated against the growth of
any national political organization based upon an appeal to a
single principle or a single group in the population. Similarly
the diverse make-up of the American population, the great
variety of ethnic and religious elements, has tended to fragment
the labour force and to prevent the development of any cohesive
attitudes or organizations based upon a specifically *labour*
approach to politics. The lack of any ideological impulse on the
part of the working-class was reinforced by the absence of any
truly conservative attitudes at the other end of the social scale,
at least until the post-Second-World-War period. The acceptance of change was built into the American philosophy so that
there was no need for a political force based upon the demand
for change as an end in itself. All these factors helped to create a
situation in which labour became a series of interest groups
rather than a political party.

It is not only that labour has not wanted to become an independent political force, however, for American unionism has
also in one sense failed even as a movement with the aims of
improving wages and working conditions. In 1964 only 29·5 per
cent of the non-agricultural labour force was unionized, and in a
few States the proportion of workers in unions was very small
indeed – in South Carolina only 7·9 per cent and in North
Carolina only 6·7 per cent. The union movement has also failed
in other ways which have affected its political influence. Some
sections of the movement have been associated with racketeering
and criminal activities, which have brought organized labour
into disrepute, the extreme example being the Longshoremen's
Union in N.Y. and Jersey City which for many years was virtually run by racketeers, enforcing their authority by gangsterism,
and maintaining their position because of their connexions with
local political machines. Furthermore, the labour movement has
been riven by internal dissension and personal rivalries. The
American Federation of Labor (A.F.L.) was formed in 1886 as a
federation of unions largely organized upon a craft basis, and
for much of its history it was firmly opposed to the intervention
of government in labour matters. It favoured *laissez-faire*, and
was squarely capitalistic in philosophy. With the growth of mass-

production industries, however, and in particular the car industry, industrial unions became increasingly important, and resulted in the establishment of the Congress of Industrial Organizations (C.I.O.) in 1938.

The built-in conflict between the principle of craft and industrial unions naturally led to great hostility between A.F.L. and C.I.O., but they differed also in terms of their philosophy of government. The C.I.O., born of mass-production industry and the years of the Depression, was more dependent upon government support than the A.F.L. and consequently in favour of government intervention in labour affairs. In 1943 the C.I.O. established a Political Action Committee to provide for the organization of labour's political arm. Whereas the A.F.L. had avoided outright endorsement of presidential candidates, the C.I.O. executive endorsed Truman as the Democratic candidate in 1948, and four years later the A.F.L. followed with their endorsement of Adlai Stevenson.

The weakness of the labour movement as a political force was demonstrated in 1947 when Congress passed the Taft-Hartley Act with provisions restrictive of organized labour, including a clause which allowed State governments to outlaw the closed shop. The passage of the legislation, which was supported by the National Association of Manufacturers, emphasized the disruption of the Unions, for the A.F.L. and the C.I.O. were at odds about the strategy for opposing the Bill, and internal dissensions within the C.I.O. threatened that organization itself. In 1955 the two federations combined into the A.F.L.–C.I.O., but this remains a loose federation of craft and industrial unions each with autonomous powers. The new federation set up a Committee on Political Education which exerts itself on behalf of candidates who receive its endorsement, particularly by carrying out registration campaigns. It made a very considerable effort to obtain the nomination of Senator Estes Kefauver in 1960 by distribution of literature and telephone canvassing on his behalf.

The orientation of the unions towards Democratic presidential candidates in recent years is clear enough, but officially the A.F.L.–C.I.O. has a 'non-partisan' approach towards legislative elections, a policy which is described as rewarding labour's friends and punishing its enemies whatever their party label. In practice only very few Republican senatorial or House candidates receive union endorsement, compared with the large number of Democratic candidates who do so. However, endorsement by the unions is not an automatic matter for Democrats, and the views and record of the individual candidate become crucial. Similarly, the unions make large contributions to the campaign funds of Democratic candidates, but the *political* aims of the unions remain limited. They wish to further the interests of their members through political action and to defend themselves against attempts by business interests to attack their position, but they do not wish to govern, nor to bring about fundamental changes in American society. The American labour movement is not opposed to capitalism, it merely wishes to promote the interests of the workers within a capitalistic economy.

THE FARMERS AND THE GOVERNMENT

Agriculture in the United States provides an example of the way in which an important minority group can achieve political power out of all proportion to its numbers. The farm population is much less significant in numbers than the unions and less wealthy than the business community, yet it seems able to fight off all attacks upon government programmes and supports which have evolved to help the farming community as a result of earlier depressed conditions. Farm groups, allied with Congressmen and with the sections of the Administration which operate the farm programmes, seem to have created, in the words of one observer, a private system of government in which decisions on agricultural matters are taken exclusively by the agricultural interests themselves. Since the 1930s the power of the farmer has become institutionalized by the way in which agricultural organizations have become closely integrated with the government machine to the point where it is difficult to draw a line between public agency and private group. Much of their power, however, stems from the peculiar characteristics of the farm vote. The farm vote is, even in American terms, both highly independent and highly variable. Farmers tend to switch to the party which is currently supporting them more readily than is the case with other groups. Split-ticket voting is frequent, and the turnout of the farm vote is more changeable than in other sections of the population. This makes the farm vote an unpredictable and potentially very important factor in elections, as proved to be the case in 1948. Congress is, therefore, particularly sensitive to the reactions of the farmer.

However, the success of farm groups does not mean that agriculture is free of the divisive forces which fragment business and labour interests. The organizations representative of agriculture are very numerous. The variety of crops and products, many of them in competition with others, produces its own crop of associations to represent producers, for example, the American Dairy Association, the National Cotton Council of America, and the National Association of Wheat-growers. However, three major organizations claim to speak for agriculture as a whole, the National Grange, the American Farm Bureau Federation and the Farmers' Union, but each of them tends to be strongest in a particular area of the country, and they come into conflict with each other. The Farm Bureau Federation has maintained close contact with government agencies since the New Deal period, when it was associated with the creation of agricultural programmes to combat the depression. It has been said of the A.F.B.F. that its support is necessary for the success of any legislation relating to agriculture, and the Federation can if it wishes turn enormous pressure on Washington.

INTEREST GROUPS AT WORK

How do interest groups operate? The almost infinite flexibility of this type of political structure is reflected in the wide variety of the methods open to the interest group to try to achieve its aims. Groups can attempt to influence public opinion through all the media of communication available in modern society, through the press, television, and radio using all the modern techniques of the public relations industry. Or they can use even more direct methods of gaining the attention of the public, organizing protest marches or going to the extreme of the sit-down strike, or even, as with the Negro in recent years, the technique of the riot. When these extremes are reached, of course, the groups concerned are close to rejecting the whole basis of the equilibrium theory of democracy through group interaction in favour of a different type of politics, the politics of extremism. The basis of pluralist democracy is agreement on fundamentals and upon the necessity of using the 'normal channels' of the institutional machinery to achieve group aims. When a group feels that its minimum demands are unacceptable to the society in which it exists it may opt out of the system, cease to be an interest group, and attempt to become a revolutionary force. As with so many of the distinctions used in the analysis of political activity, it is not always possible, in practice, to draw hard and fast lines in order to label particular groups as part of the interest group structure or as placing themselves outside it. Many groups hover on the fringes of the equilibrium system of politics – the use of company police in the 1920s, the Minutemen, the advocates of 'black power' – and it is one of the characteristics of the American political system and of its ideological basis that there is a sizeable part of the population that is potentially ready to step outside the framework of compromise politics to further its 'interest' by violent means if necessary. Thus the same group of people may at one moment be behaving as an interest group and at another as a conspiracy. It is at this point that the government ceases to be merely the neutral mechanism through which competing group demands are reconciled and becomes again both the instrument of law and order and the instrument for the imposition of policy, whether at Little Rock or in Harlem.

The normal channels of group activity, of course, relate very closely to the institutional structures of government through which decisions are taken – groups may attempt to exert influence on elections, on the process of legislation, on the way in which government programmes are administered, or upon the courts. Groups may attempt to influence the selection of candidates for office at all levels of government, both in primary and general elections. Thus labour unions and other groups attempt to secure the election of candidates responsive to their demands. The Congress of Racial Equality in 1967 pledged itself to secure the return to Congress of Representative Adam Clayton Powell after his dismissal. In 1952 oil producing interests made clear to delegates at the Democratic National Convention that Adlai Stevenson's attitude towards State control of offshore oil deposits was hostile to their interests. Groups may contribute to party funds, help with canvassing, aid party organization, provide speakers and literature to help in a campaign. The effectiveness of such activities and the extent to which the interest groups benefit from the later behaviour of candidates who achieve office with their support varies, of course, from negligible to very considerable, but it is very difficult to give any precise indication of the results of 'pressure politics' at any stage of the governmental process. Congressmen who benefit from the support of a particular group at election times are probably predisposed towards their point of view in any case, and would normally assist them as far as seemed practicable in view of all the varying interests of their constituents. Perhaps the most that such groups can hope for, at Federal level at any rate, is to maintain close contact with legislators through their supporting activities and thereby to have easier access to the Congressman or Senator at critical times.

Interest groups attempt to influence the behaviour of the legislators in a number of ways. They may arrange to deluge him with letters and telegrams from constituents urging their point of view, or arrange for groups of electors to present their views to their representatives at the Capitol. Rather more subtly, and perhaps more effectively, they may prepare detailed briefs to deliver as evidence before Congressional committees or to convince individual members of the legislature of the rightness of their case. Many interest groups maintain permanent offices in Washington, or in State capitals, in order to maintain close personal contact with legislators and administrators; other groups use the services of a professional lobbyist who may represent a number of groups who cannot afford to maintain their own representative. The use of a lobbyist who will pursue a group's interest in the legislature is by no means new. In 1846 a certain A. J. Marshall was hired by the Baltimore and Ohio Railroad to obtain from the legislature of the State of Virginia the grant of a right of way through the State to the Ohio River.

When offering his services to the company Marshall emphasized
that he was not proposing to use corrupt methods in dealing
with legislators. 'My scheme is to surround the Legislature
with respectable and influential agents, whose persuasive arguments may influence the members to do you a naked act of
justice. That is all.' The modern lobbyist must be skilled in
producing 'persuasive arguments' and many are equipped with
staffs and research facilities to enable them to do this. They must
be capable of producing draft legislation which a sympathetic
Congressman or Senator will be prepared to introduce into the
legislature and to sponsor its passage. Much legislation of importance on the Statute books of the United States today originated in the offices of interest groups.

The importance of lobbying activities, and some past scandals,
led Congress in 1946 to pass the Regulation of Lobbying Act,
and a large number of State legislatures also have regulating
legislation on their books. The Federal Act requires persons or
organizations who engage in paid lobbying activities to register
and to file reports upon money spent in pursuance of attempts to
influence the passage or defeat of legislation in Congress. In 1956
over 600 lobbyists were registered under this legislation. Inevitably the activities of interest groups who wish to influence the
legislature will shade off from the purely laudable functions of
providing valuable information for Congressmen and channelling opinions to the legislature, to the outright use of bribery
and inducements. The incident referred to earlier in which a
large sum of money was paid into Senator Case's campaign fund
touched off a demand for investigation into lobbying practices;
but little of importance was revealed. Although scandals can be
dug up from earlier decades there seems to be very little evidence
of outright bribery today at the Federal level, although many
lobbying organizations provide lavish hospitality for legislators.
At the State level it is not so easy to absolve lobbyists and legislators from the suspicion of corrupt practices, and in a few
notorious States there is ample evidence of the way in which the
cooperation of legislators and officials is sometimes purchased.

The importance to interest groups of the decisions of the
legislature follows from the fact that, as will become clear later

on, the Congress of the United States exercises more effective
decision-making power than any other Western legislature. But
the concern of interest groups with government decisions does
not end with the legislature. Administrative agencies, and particularly the independent regulatory commissions, daily make
decisions of great importance, in some cases involving the fate of
commercial activities amounting to millions of dollars. On
the decision of a government agency depends the granting
of a licence for a television station, or to operate an airline, the
prices to be charged by companies producing electric power or
running a railroad, or the authority to make a large issue of
securities. Inevitably the groups interested in such decisions attempt to ensure that their interest is represented to the authority
concerned. Equally inevitable is the feeling that these agencies,
set up to regulate an industry, in practice become too closely
associated with it and too responsive to its needs rather than
those of the general public. In recent years charges have been
made of excessive entertaining of members of government commissions by companies with an interest in the decisions to be
made by these members, of the provision of free transport by airline companies, of gifts of colour-television sets by broadcasting
companies, and in one case at least of the payment of an outright bribe.

Finally interest groups must involve themselves in the activities
of the courts and represent their point of view as strongly,
although by using different techniques, to the judges as to
legislators or administrators. In the United States the courts
are a part of the political process in its widest sense, for the
courts make decisions which in other countries are usually made
by the elected or appointed officials of the other branches of
government, and because the application of the American Constitution has involved judges in every phase of American social,
economic and political life. Again at State and local level the
judges cannot be completely absolved from charges of corrupt
practices, but at the Federal level where the judiciary is of very
high calibre, the tactics of the interest group must be to argue
its case before the courts as persuasively as possible. If a group
fails to block undesired legislation in Congress it can fight it in

the Courts on various grounds, including its constitutionality. It is also possible to use the courts as a means of furthering positive political aims. The most striking use of this technique in recent years has been the success of the N.A.A.C.P. in using litigation as a long-term programme in the fight against segregation, both in State and Federal Courts. The Supreme Court of the U.S. allows the filing of briefs by *amici curiae*, 'friends of the court', who can support one or other side of the dispute before the Court. In this way organizations, as well as the U.S. or State governments, can lend their support to the individuals involved in a case to the extent, in the past, that cases before the court came sometimes to look like inter-group battles rather than a judicial dispute between individual antagonists.

In this way the pluralistic battles of American politics are initiated and fought through the machinery of government. Inevitably the emphasis upon the pressure politics of interest group interaction leads to an impression of confusion, almost of anarchy in American political life, to which are added overtones of corruption and the exercise of undue influence. Yet it must be recognized that the structure of interest groups performs an essential function in a diverse society. It provides for the representation and the expression of opinions and interests which the party system, any party system, would be incapable of providing. Alongside the political parties, interest groups articulate and channel demands to those elected and appointed officials who make the decisions which bear the imprint of the authority of government, whether Federal, State, or local. We must now turn to the working of the institutions of government itself, within the context of these forces.

Congressional Politics

The Congress of the United States is, without doubt, the most powerful representative assembly in the world today. This is not merely to reiterate the fact of the power and wealth of the United States – it is also a recognition of the fact that as a *legislature* Congress in the 1970s continues to exercise a degree of independent decision-making power far greater than that retained by the other legislatures of the Western democracies. It is true that, like all legislative bodies in the complex world of the twentieth century, its power has declined relative to that of the so-called 'executive' branch of government. Increasingly it is the President and his Administration who initiate policy and provide leadership in legislative affairs, but Congress still actively makes decisions upon domestic and foreign policy, upon the role of government in society and the way in which government activities will be financed. The President can initiate policy, and he can urge it upon Congress with all the resources at his command, but he cannot *determine* what legislation shall pass, when it will be passed, or in exactly what form it will pass. Once legislation has been introduced into the British House of Commons by the government it is virtually certain that it will be passed, but one can only *predict* what *might* happen to legislation in Congress, and such predictions, however well-informed, may well turn out to be wrong.

THE PARAMETERS OF CONGRESSIONAL POWER

The power of Congress as a policy-making body is, of course, the resultant of the whole context of the constitutional and political forces within which it operates, and the internal structure of power and organization of Congress reflects this context.

We have seen that the Constitution of the United States gives to each of the two Houses of Congress a high degree of legal autonomy, both in relation to each other and to the President. The President has no power to dissolve Congress, nor does he have any direct legislative authority. He can send messages to Congress requesting action, and he can veto Congressional acts of which he disapproves. The two Houses of Congress have equal power under the Constitution, except that the Senate is given the function of ratifying treaties on behalf of the United States, and of confirming the appointments to senior Federal executive and judicial posts. The Constitution also provides that all bills for raising revenue must *originate* in the House of Representatives, but the Senate retains the right to amend or reject such proposals. Just as important for congressional autonomy, however, is the fact that the decentralized party system provides no basis for the effective disciplining of Senators or Congressmen. No single man, or body of men, at the national level, can endanger the political career of a legislator simply because he has refused to follow their leadership. From time to time Congressmen are 'disciplined' by their Congressional party. Representative John B. Williams, a Democrat from Mississippi, supported the Republican candidate for the Presidency in 1964, and as a consequence the caucus of the Democratic Party in the House stripped him of his seniority in the Party. But no one in Congress or in the Administration could prevent, or even consider attempting to prevent, his re-election to Congress in 1966. The method of selecting candidates, in particular the system of primary elections, places the effective power of discipline in the hands of the local party, or of the Congressman's constituents, and not in the hands of national leaders. The diversity of the local political systems that we have surveyed, and the truly *local* basis of power in those systems, is the fundamental guarantee of congressional autonomy.

The most important consequences of this constitutional and political context are, first, that there is no single united source of leadership in Congress comparable to that exercised by the government in a parliamentary system; second, that Congress has organized itself to allow full play to the sectional and local interests which dominate the fates of its members, and to the group pressures which can fill the vacuum left by the absence of strongly party-oriented programmes; and third, that the changing patterns of voting in Congress on the issues which come before it are determined by a very complex interaction between local, sectional, and pluralistic influences, by the individual characters of Congressmen, and by the influence of the President and the Administration. Thus the individual Senator or Congressman stands at the centre of a great web of relationships, constitutional and political. Some of these relationships greatly strengthen his ability to exercise his judgement independently of the overriding authority of any person or group, but of course the exercise of this judgement is a matter of the highest political sensitivity. He can exercise his judgement only in a political context, which has a number of dimensions. If he is a member of the same party as the President he will feel the pull of allegiance to the national leader of his party; he will also have a loyalty to the congressional leadership of his party in House or Senate. The extent of the loyalty owed to these two types of party leader will depend upon a number of factors, and they will not always coincide. He will be particularly concerned with his perception of his constituents' attitudes, and also with the views of interest groups who may put those views to him with varying degrees of importunity. He will be concerned also with the positions adopted by other members of Congress with whom he has some affinity : the other members of the committees upon which he sits, the other members of the State delegation of which he forms a part, or the views of other members whom he respects as authorities upon their particular subjects.

This is the context within which a Senator or Representative operates, and his exact reaction to a particular legislative proposal will depend upon the relative importance of these differing factors in the light of his own personal circumstances. Often the cues which he receives from party leaders, constituency, or pressure group will conflict, and he must make up his mind which to respond to. His decision may depend upon how near he is to re-election, the relative strengths of the reactions from these differing sources, or his perception of the importance of a particular issue. Thus potentially the study of congressional behaviour is the description of how 535 men and women, each in a slightly different political context, will react to particular situations. Fortunately for us, however, the patterns of congressional behaviour are not random or haphazard, and we can discover the political and institutional structures which give a relative stability to the way in which the legislature goes about its business. We shall look at the influence of parties, and at the other determinants of congressional voting behaviour, then at the organizational structure of power in Congress, and finally at some concrete examples of the way in which the complex decisions on modern legislation are taken. First of all, however, let us take as an example the 1966 session of Congress, in order to gauge the overall pattern of its activity.

A PROFILE OF A CONGRESSIONAL SESSION

Each Senator or Member of the House of Representatives is free to introduce as many bills or resolutions as he wishes into Congress, and in 1966 this resulted in the introduction of 9,684 pieces of legislation.* Of this total 'input' 461 Acts became law, President Johnson having used his veto power seven times. Only half these Acts had been requested by the President, although nearly all the major legislation that was passed originated with the Administration or had its support. During the year President Johnson requested passage of 371 pieces of legislation of which fifty-five per cent was enacted by Congress. Nearly twenty per cent of his requests for legislation were specifically rejected by Congress, while the rest of his programme was stalled somewhere in the legislative machine when the session ended. This was a less satisfactory record than that of 1965 when nearly seventy per cent of the President's programme was enacted, but it was a great deal better than the low point of the session of 1963 when only twenty-seven per cent of the proposals submitted by President Kennedy were given force of law. Of course

*The statistical details which follow are drawn from the *Congressional Quarterly Almanac*, Vol. XXII, 1966, Washington D.C., 1967.

these figures give only a crude idea of the performance of Congress, for they treat trivial bills and great pieces of legislation as if they were of equal weight. Nevertheless the picture is a reasonably accurate one, for although Congress passed some 113 major pieces of legislation asked for by the Administration in 1966, it failed to pass nineteen important measures that had been requested, including a Civil Rights Bill. Furthermore, when Congress did act positively on a Presidential proposal it did not always give the President just what he wanted, for many of the bills that were passed were substantially amended during the process.

Many of the votes which are taken in Congress are not recorded, but on many important issues recorded roll call votes are held, and a study of these votes gives us an outline of the behaviour of the members of Congress. In particular they give us an insight into the extent to which the influence of the President affected voting patterns. There was a total of 428 roll call votes in 1966, and the President stated his position on the issues involved in 228 of the roll calls. Some Senators and Representatives had a record of strong support for the President's position. At the top of the list was the Democratic Senator Monroney of Oklahoma, who voted the way favoured by the President on seventy-eight per cent of the roll calls, but the Republican Senator Javits of New York was not far behind in the support of the President's position; he voted the President's way seventy-five per cent of the time. The Leader of the Democratic majority in the Senate, Senator Mansfield, was recorded in support of the President on sixty-seven per cent of the roll calls, and was in open opposition on fifteen per cent of them. The average degree of support for the President from the individual members of his own party in the Senate was only fifty-seven per cent. Democrats in the House were rather more consistent in his support, coming out on his side, on average, sixty-three per cent of the time. Fourteen Democratic Representatives were recorded in favour of the President's position on over ninety per cent of the votes, but almost as many of their party colleagues *opposed* the President's position on more than fifty per cent of the recorded votes. The Democratic Majority Leader in the House, Representative Carl Albert, supported the President on sixty per cent of the votes and expressed open opposition on only two per cent of them.

PARTY UNITY IN CONGRESS

How internally united were the legislative parties in 1966? When looking at the cohesion of the American parties in Congress it is necessary to be very clear about the measuring rod we are applying. We must not apply the same standards of party unity which are usual in the more ideological politics of Europe. Usually when studying party cohesion, students of American politics define a 'party vote' as one in which a *majority of one party is opposed by a majority of the other party*. Thus let us assume a hypothetical legislature with 100 members, in which party A has sixty seats and party B has forty seats. At the extreme a 'party vote' would include one in which the House divided on a vote fifty-fifty, made up in the following way :

	Ayes	Noes
Party A	31	29
Party B	19	21
	—	—
	50	50

This falls within the definition because a majority of party A voted 'Aye' and a majority of party B voted 'No'. Nevertheless it is rather startling as an example of a party vote, for both parties are equally split almost right down the middle. But fiction is rarely stranger than fact. In August 1966 a roll call vote in the United States Senate was held on an amendment to a defence appropriation bill. The amendment was supported by President Johnson, and it was lost because the vote was tied. The vote was forty-three for the amendment and forty-three against. The supporters of the amendment were twenty-eight Democrats and fifteen Republicans; the opposition to the amendment came from twenty-seven Democrats and sixteen Republicans. This was, therefore, one 'party vote' in the 1966 session of the U.S. Senate. Of course, on many other votes the parties were much more united internally and much more clearly divided from each other. However, taking this definition of party votes, the average Democrat voted with the majority of his party against a majority of Republicans only sixty-one per cent of the time. The Republicans were rather more united: the average Republican voted with a majority of his party against a majority of Democrats on sixty-seven per cent of the roll calls. Some members of the House and the Senate were more often in *opposition* to a majority of their party than in agreement with it. In the House, four Southern Democrats disagreed with a majority of their own party on over eighty per cent of the recorded votes! The degree of dissent among Republicans was not so great, but even so three Republican Representatives opposed the majority of their own party on over fifty per cent of the roll calls.

THE 'CONSERVATIVE COALITION' IN 1966

The greatest source of disunity within the Democratic party is, of course, the sectional split between Northern and Southern Democrats. Altough the major divisive element between these two groups is the civil rights issue, their differences are by no means confined to this question. The split between these two factions is to be found in votes on foreign policy, social welfare, labour legislation, and legislation on urban affairs. On no fewer than 124 of the 428 roll calls a majority of the Southern Democats voted against a majority of the Northern Democrats. This deep division within the Democratic party gives rise to the so-called 'conservative coalition' which has been of such great importance in Congress since the days of the New Deal. The coalition consists of a combination of a majority of Southern Democrats allied with a majority of the Republicans. This coalition was able for many years to check legislation, particularly on civil rights, which was proposed by the President, and supported by Northern Democrats together with some Republicans.

For several years the power of the coalition has been on the decline, and some observers have prematurely announced its demise. The realization of the urgent need for civil rights legislation led the Republicans to repudiate the coalition for a time and to cooperate with the Administration in obtaining the passage of important measures in that field. On this issue there was for a while, therefore, a different coalition, one between the Northern Democrats and the Republicans, to defeat the Southern Democrats. This coalition produced some of the most sectional votes in Congress in recent history. The vote on the Civil Rights Act of 1964 was a good example of legislation which could be passed only with strong support from the Republicans. The bill was passed in the House by a majority of 290 votes for, with 130 against. The majority was composed of 152 Democrats and 138 Republicans and the vote against the bill was made up of ninety-six Democrats and thirty-four Republicans. The sectional nature of the vote was quite striking. Of the Northern Democrats 141 supported the bill and only four opposed it, but ninety-two Southern Democrats came out against the bill and eleven supported it. In some States of the deep South, like Alabama, Georgia, Louisiana and Mississippi, where the entire State delegation to Congress was composed of Democrats, they all voted solidly against. In a few Southern States which have a sprinkling of Republican Representatives, like Virginia and North Carolina, the Republicans voted solidly with their Democratic colleagues against the legislation. At the other extreme, in Pennsylvania every one of the State's twenty-six Representatives, twelve Democrats and fourteen Republicans, voted solidly for the legislation. The same thing happened in Illinois, Indiana, and Massachusetts and in a number of other States. In New York State twenty Democrats and twenty Republicans voted 'Aye' and only one Republican voted 'No'. In other State delegations the divisions were more complex, but the sectional pattern of the voting was very strong indeed.

In 1966, however, there was a resurgence of the power of the conservative coalition of Southern Democrats and Republicans. The coalition defeated the Administration's Civil Rights Bill, and a majority of Southern Democrats was allied with a majority of Republicans against a majority of Northern Democrats on twenty-five per cent of the roll calls in 1966. The coalition won nearly half the votes which it contested. How long it will continue to operate it is impossible to say. Many Republicans see it as a handicap to their attempt to become established in the

South, but until the party system in the South is transformed, the coalition is likely to continue in one form or another.

INFLUENCES ON CONGRESSIONAL VOTING BEHAVIOUR

It is very clear from the evidence that issues that come up for decision by Congress are not simply decided on party lines. Each vote is the result of the complex of pressures acting on Congress, and the patterns of voting differ from issue to issue. Coalitions within Congress form and re-form to decide particular questions of policy. Party allegiance is an important, but by no means determining factor, in the way in which these patterns form. The effect of party loyalty is at its greatest on procedural or organizational votes: for example, the election of the Speaker, or the control over committee assignments. On substantive issues of policy, however, the alignments in Congress depend upon the issue under consideration, and the importance of party membership as an influence upon voting behaviour will depend upon the nature of these issues. What then is the significance of party on the way in which Senators and Representatives vote?

It is impossible to give an answer to this question in a straightforward way which would suggest a simple causal relationship between party membership and voting. It has been shown that there is a greater statistical correlation between party and congressional voting patterns than between the latter and any other single factor. Yet we have shown above that Senators and Congressmen habitually vote against the majority of their party without any adverse effects, either from the leadership of their party or from their constituents. Why then should party allegiance affect voting at all? There are a number of reasons. First of all, particularly for Members of the House, there is an important relationship between constituency attitudes and party image. Representatives do not have the publicity exposure of Senators. They must rely to a large extent upon the image which the electorate has of their party. Often a particular Congressman can rise above this and make a personal impression on his electorate, but he is bound to be concerned with the party attitudes which many of his constituents have. This image will vary to some extent from one part of the country to another, but the behaviour and policies of the President will be an important component of that image. When there is no strong constituency opposition to the President's policy, therefore, the member of Congress will tend to go along with his party leader. If, however, constituency attitudes are clearly opposed to the President's policy, then the member of Congress will put constituency loyalty first and party loyalty last. On very many issues that come to a vote in Congress, a member's constituents will be ignorant or apathetic, and in such circumstances he is free to listen to the urgings of pressure groups, or to vote the way the Administration or congressional leaders wish him to. The President has inducements to offer – patronage, or support for Federal expenditures in his district – and congressional leaders can provide publicity, good committee assignments, help at election time, and special facilities on Capitol Hill. Thus there will be a natural tendency for the Congressman to go along with his party, unless there is some strong reason to the contrary.

Groups of Congressmen of the same party who come from similar constituencies will naturally tend to react in the same way to the issues that confront them. The most important result of this is the way in which intra-party blocs form on overlapping sectional and ideological lines in Congress: thus, in the Democratic party we find the Southern bloc and the liberals, whilst in the Republican party there is also a liberal wing, and divisions between the representatives of different regions, particularly on foreign policy. Detailed analysis of congressional voting has shown a high degree of stability of the blocs in the Democratic party, and a much greater fluidity in the voting patterns in the Republican party.

On many issues, however, the Administration will not even state a position, or try to influence the vote. The Administration cannot dictate to Congress, and if it tried to use its persuasive powers all the time they would soon become ineffectual. Thus it is rather misleading even to think in terms of 'party discipline' in Congress. When a President badly wants a measure to be passed he will of course employ every weapon at his command. He may appeal to constituents over the head of Congressmen, he may promise, threaten or cajole. But he does not, and could not, conduct a continuous and consistent effort to direct congressional voting behaviour on every issue. Equally, congressional leaders must attempt to persuade rather than wave a big stick. Thus the statistical correlation between party and voting does not mean that Senators and Representatives are *forced* to vote the party line. It usually means that it is their natural inclination to do so. But when other factors enter into the picture then party loyalty may soon be forgotten.

The most important factor which can disrupt party voting is the Congressman's perception of the attitudes of his constituents. Congressmen are highly responsive to what they believe their constituents desire. They go to great lengths to test opinion in their constituency, by taking public opinion polls on issues, by extensive personal contacts, and by paying close attention to the huge deliveries of mail every Congressman receives. Undoubtedly when national party policy conflicts with constituency opinion, as they perceive it, they will choose the latter. This is particularly clear in the field of civil rights where Congressmen are very sensitive to constituency opinion. On other issues 'constituency opinion' may be irrelevant because largely non-existent.

There is a third component, however, and that is the influence of pressure groups. The power of pressure groups to influence congressional voting is easy to explain in two types of case. First, when there is no particular constituency interest involved, and when the Administration takes up no position on an issue, then a Congressman must look somewhere for the information and the 'cues' which will determine his vote, and these the pressure groups can provide. Second, when the appeals of a pressure group *reinforce* constituency interest, the Senator or Congressman will be completely deaf to appeals to party loyalty or to his duty to the Administration. The more difficult case to explain is what happens when the constituency interest is neutral and there is a sharp conflict between the party leadership and powerful pressure groups. Very often in such battles the Congressman seems bemused by the conflicting demands being made upon him. In such circumstances he may look to other groups in

Congress with whom he has shared interests – the other members of the congressional delegation from his home State, the members of the committees on which he serves, or other individuals in Congress whose opinion he respects because of their expertise or experience.

Finally, the importance of personality must not be overlooked. It is true that on the vast majority of the issues which come before Congress the attitudes of its members are 'determined' by Administration pressure, or by constituency or group attitudes, but there are always 'mavericks' whose behaviour is unpredictable, and in many cases where the considerations of party, constituency and group pressures are nicely balanced, the Congressman's or Senator's personal inclinations may be decisive in determining the way he casts his vote.

This then is the overall picture of congressional voting behaviour. It suggests a rather anarchic situation, but this is only a half-truth. Congress is in fact a highly organized, highly structured body. Indeed, if it were not, then anarchy would certainly reign. It is the fluidity of the voting patterns and the slackness of party ties that makes the organizational structure of Congress so important, and which gives to the committee system in particular its vitally important role.

THE STRUCTURE OF CONGRESS

The task which Congress has to perform imposes upon it the necessity of a highly organized procedure for dealing with legislation. Priorities have to be determined between conflicting claimants for limited Congressional time; procedures have to be devised to enable legislation to be dealt with in an orderly manner and the requirements of adequate representation of the interests involved have to be met. In a parliamentary system it is usually the government which undertakes the task of determining the legislative programme for the session and ensuring that it is seen through the complex legislative procedures. But there is no government in Congress. The constitutional separation of powers, as it has been interpreted since the early days of the Republic, prevents the President or his advisers from participating in the

formal processes of legislation other than by transmitting messages to Congress. They cannot vote, or even speak in debates,
and they are not allowed to have seats on the floor of the House.
Of course the formal relationships between Congress and Administration are supplemented by a wide range of informal contacts, but it remains true that the leadership which a President
must attempt to exercise over the operations of Congress must
be conducted from outside that body.

This lack of a directive 'government' inside the legislature has
meant that Congress has evolved its own leadership. The organization of Congress, the control over its procedures, and the
legislative programme, are all decided upon within Congress.
The division between the presidential party and the congressional party is, therefore, highly institutionalized, and although
the two sets of leaders usually work tolerably well together, they
retain their distinct points of view, and occasionally come into
sharp conflict. Furthermore, the decentralized character of
American politics is fully reflected in the organization of Congress. Congressional leadership is decentralized, some might say
fragmented, with groups of leaders drawing their strength from
differing sources. The legislative procedures, especially the role
of standing committees in the passage of legislation, give full
opportunities for the local, sectional and pluralistic forces in
American politics to have their say.

The extent of the decentralization of power in Congress is
epitomized by the very existence of the United States Senate.
Here is a legislative Chamber which is at first sight an ana-
chronism. It is composed of two representatives of each State of
the Union regardless of population. It is a second or 'upper'
chamber in a century which has seen the sharp decline or virtual
disappearance of Second Chambers. Yet the Senate is probably
the more powerful, and certainly the more prestigious, of the
two chambers of the American legislature. Its power relative to
that of the House of Representatives has increased rather than
diminished. Since it has fewer members than the House, the
individual Senator has a prestige and position which very few
members of the 'popular' chamber can hope to attain. Senators
have terms of office three times as long as members of the House;

the Senate's procedures are less restrictive of individual members; it has special functions in relation to foreign affairs and nominations; and it has equal legislative powers with the other chamber. Thus not only is political leadership in the United States divided between President and Congress, it is also divided within Congress between Senate and House, and the leaders of the two Houses will not always see eye to eye. Furthermore, *within* each House of Congress the leadership is decentralized and divided.

CONGRESSIONAL LEADERSHIP

The leadership in each House of Congress is divided into two distinct but overlapping groups. The first group consists of party leaders – the Speaker in the House of Representatives, the Majority and Minority Leaders in both houses, the Majority and Minority Whips, the chairmen of the party caucus or conference, and of party committees. The party caucus – or conference – consisting of all the members of the party in the House or Senate, elects these party leaders. There was a time, notably during the first Administration of President Woodrow Wilson (1913–16), when the party caucus, by a two thirds vote of its membership, could bind the party to support policy decisions and to vote accordingly in the legislature. Today, however, the more fragmented nature of the parties rules out any attempt on the part of the caucus to determine policy issues, for to do this would be more likely to provoke disintegration than to promote unity. It is on organizational questions that party allegiance plays a vital role. Congress must be organized, party leaders elected and committees constituted, and the parties show the highest degree of cohesion on these questions of the distribution of congressional offices.

However, the power of the party caucus has increased in recent years, particularly in the Democratic party in the House of Representatives. Until recently the second group of congressional leaders, the chairmen of the Standing Committees, were effectively chosen under the 'Seniority System'. These committee chairmen play an extremely important role in the legislative process, as we shall shortly see, and until 1971 a Senator or Representative became chairman by virtue of being the member of the majority party with the longest record of *continuous* service on that committee. The role of the party caucus was simply to rubber-stamp the outcome of this process of natural selection. Since 1971, however, there has been something of a revolution in this area of the American political system. In the House of Representatives both parties have now changed their rules to ensure that the majority of the party caucus can exercise effective control over appointments to committee chairmanships, disregarding the claims of seniority. Indeed, in January 1975 the chairmen of three important House committees were deposed by the Democratic caucus and replaced by more 'junior' Congressmen. In the Senate also both parties have taken steps to limit the operation of the seniority system, although so far with little practical effect. However, the erosion of the seniority system may eventually have far-reaching consequences for congressional politics.

THE SPEAKER

The role of the Speaker in the House of Representatives is very different from that of the Speaker in the British House of Commons. True the American Speaker has the responsibility, as presiding officer, of regulating the procedures of the House in a manner which will be fair to both sides, but at the same time he is also the foremost leader of his party in the lower chamber, actively and continuously furthering its interests. His power to interpret the rules of the House, and his control over its procedures, gives him considerable influence over its members. He has a discretionary power to recognize those who wish to speak from the floor, and in doubtful cases he can determine to which committee proposed legislation shall be sent. As the leader of his party in the House he has access to the President. The size of the House of Representatives and the volume of work it has to get through turns these into formidable powers in the hands of a skilful Speaker. The Speaker usually sees his function as the most devoted supporter of the President's programme in the House. This does not mean that he accepts the President's

policies uncritically, rather he is the main instrument for effect-
ing compromises between the President and his party in the
House, when they can be obtained. He can tell the President
what is possible and what is not. At the extreme a Speaker who
fundamentally disagreed with the President might resign, but
usually the President will respect and accept the Speaker's views
about policy in the House, because the latter is himself a man of
power to be reckoned with.

THE MAJORITY AND MINORITY FLOOR LEADERS

The Vice-President of the United States is the presiding officer
of the Senate, so that there is no direct equivalent of the Speaker
in the upper chamber. The senior party leaders in the Senate
are the Majority and Minority Floor Leaders. The Majority
Leader is the liaison between the President and his party in the
Senate, and upon him lies the responsibility of doing his best for
the President's programme. The position of the Democratic
Majority Leader is strengthened by the fact that he is, *ex officio,*
the chairman of three important party committees. There is a
Majority Leader also in the House, but he is simply the lieutenant
of the Speaker. The Minority Leaders in both Houses are also
important in the legislative process, because in the conditions of
the divided parties of today the Administration must often
depend upon their co-operation to obtain the passage of important legislation, against the opposition of its own nominal supporters. The leaders on both sides tend to be drawn from the
more moderate, middle-of-the-road members of the legislature,
for essentially their function is to act as brokers between the
various wings of the parties, and to elicit the greatest possible
degree of agreement.

THE MAJORITY AND MINORITY WHIPS

Like the Speaker, the Whips in the House and Senate perform
a role very different from their namesakes in the House of Commons. Like the British Whips they are two-way channels of
communication, informing the leadership of the views and vot-

ing intentions of members of the party, and passing down information on the position of the leadership on legislative issues. In the House there is a system of assistant Whips, organized on a regional basis; in 1966 there were eighteen assistant Whips on the Democratic side and sixteen on the Republican side. The Whips also have the task of trying to get members of the party on to the floor to take part in voting, but they cannot exercise any disciplinary authority or hope to pressure members of Congress into following the wishes of the leadership, if those members are determined to oppose them. Indeed, the assistant Whips themselves often deviate considerably from the position of the Floor Leaders. In 1966 the Democratic Floor Leader in the House voted against the President's stated position on only two per cent of the roll call votes that were held, but assistant Whips Thomas N. Downing, from Virginia, and John J. Flynt, Jr, from Georgia, opposed the President on forty per cent and twenty-five per cent of the roll call votes respectively.

PARTY COMMITTEES

There are a number of party committees in each House of Congress – campaign committees, policy committees, and committees on committees. The last-named are the most important, for it is they who assign members of the party to the Standing Committees of Congress. The Standing Committees are of varying degrees of importance and, therefore, of varying degrees of desirability. Members hope for assignment to the plum committee positions in order to impress their constituents, and also in order to be able to influence the most important decisions in the legislature. In the Senate this function is performed by the Democratic Steering Committee and by the Republican Committee on Committees; in the House by the Democratic Steering and Policy Committee and by the House Republican Committee on Committees. The working of these committees varies according to political conditions. Thus House committee assignments used to be made by the Democratic members of the House Ways and Means Committee who were accused of favouring conservative and Southern Representatives. When Lyndon Johnson was

Senate Majority Leader he used his position to dominate the Steering Committee in order to secure compliance with his policies in the Senate.

Thus in addition to the caucus (Democrats) or the conference (Republicans) there are party policy committees in each House, but their leadership role on policy matters is severely limited. They are able to make strong pronouncements on policy only on the rare occasions when there is virtual unanimity in the party. Their major function is to consult with the party leadership on problems of scheduling the legislative programme.

There is, therefore, a sizeable group of men in the two Houses who exercise some degree of leadership. The Speaker in the House and the Majority Leader in the Senate are by far the most important of these, but neither of them is anything like as powerful as a party leader in a strongly disciplined legislative party. They must work mostly through persuasion and with the relatively few sanctions available to them. They must attempt to steer the legislative programme through Congress even though the process of legislation is only partially under their control. They must work with the standing committees which dominate the legislative process, and they must also cope with two extra difficulties – the power of the Rules Committee in the House, and the operation of the filibuster in the Senate.

THE HOUSE RULES COMMITTEE

In order to understand the importance of the Rules Committee in the House it is first necessary to outline briefly the process by which legislation goes through Congress. Bills are introduced by Senators and Congressmen and after a formal first reading they are sent to the standing committees for consideration. We shall look at the operation of the standing committees shortly, but the important point here is that a large number of standing committees are working simultaneously on many pieces of legislation, and when they have dealt with them they are reported to the House or Senate for debate on the floor, preliminary to their passage or rejection. Thus there arises the question of which of the many bills which are reported by standing committees should be taken first. Given the limited time available in a session of Congress the determination of priorities is all-important, for bills which are not given time on the floor will die with the end of the session.

It is here that the Rules Committee of the House of Representatives exercises its authority. Bills must be given a 'rule' by the Rules Committee before being considered on the floor of the House. The rule will allocate a certain length of time to the bill, and may lay down conditions for the consideration of amendments. Thus the Rules Committee is the funnel through which all legislation must pass, and it may attempt to delay consideration of a particular measure or to block its passage altogether by refusing to grant a rule.

The vital function of establishing the priorities of the legislative programme is not in the hands of the Speaker or the elective leadership of the House; it is the hands of the Rules Committee, which enjoys a status peculiar to itself. The Rules Committee is not a party committee, but one of the standing committees of the House. It is composed of both majority and minority party members, the former numbering twice the latter. As a standing committee, its chairmanship is allocated under the seniority rule, so that the man who holds this key position is not an elected leader of the party and may well be out of sympathy with the elected leadership. Yet the committee and its chairman play an essential part in the processes by which the President's legislative programme is dealt with by the House.

Thus there is a built-in tendency towards conflict between the elective leadership and the chairman of the Rules Committee. In the years following the Second World War this potential for conflict was fully realized. Because of the operation of the seniority rule, and because the method of making committee assignments tended to favour conservatives, the Rules Committee became dominated by the conservative coalition in Congress. The chairman of the Rules Committee, Judge Howard W. Smith of Virginia, became, in effect, the leader of the conservative coalition in the House, and his key position on the Rules Committee gave him a power out of all proportion to the votes which the Southern Democrats could muster in the House itself. When

President Kennedy was elected in 1960 the Rules Committee was considered to be the major obstacle to the passage of the legislation which he intended to propose to Congress, and a change in the composition of the Committee seemed an essential prerequisite for the passage of his programme. Speaker Sam Rayburn therefore conducted an operation in the House to expand the Committee from twelve to fifteen members, making possible the appointment of some liberal Democrats.

However, although the power of the conservative coalition on the Committee was moderated, the Rules Committee still failed to grant rules for twenty pieces of legislation in the years 1961–3, and in 1965 a further diminution in its power was decreed by the House. Previously the only way around the power of the Rules Committee to block legislation had been the procedure of 'discharging' the Committee from further consideration of a bill. But a discharge petition requires the signatures of a majority of the total membership of the House, so that it was very difficult to operate the procedure. In 1965, however, 'the twenty-one-day rule' was introduced, which gave to the Speaker the power to call up a bill for consideration on the floor if the Rules Committee had failed to grant a rule after twenty-one days, and then by the vote of a majority of those present the House could adopt its own rule for the discussion of the bill. Thus the Rules Committee was brought more closely under the direction of the elective leadership of the House. The twenty-one-day rule was used to discharge the Rules Committee six times in 1965 and twice in 1966. Perhaps more important was the fact that the very existence of the new procedure probably induced the Committee to grant rules in a number of other cases. Even so the failure of the Rules Committee to act killed seventeen bills in 1966, some of which had been requested by the President and the Administration, and in 1967 conservatives were able to gain the repeal of the twenty-one-day rule.

THE FILIBUSTER IN THE SENATE

The problem of determining priorities for legislation, upon which the power of the House Rules Committee is based, gives little difficulty in the Senate. In that more relaxed chamber the Majority Leader, in consultation with a *party* committee, the Policy Committee, and with the co-operation of the Minority Leader, arranges the legislative programme The strict control which is exercised over debates in the House, however, does not exist in the Senate, so that the increased power of the leadership to schedule legislation is offset by its almost complete inability to control the actual length or relevance of debates on the floor of the Senate. The privilege of unlimited debate has traditionally been the pride of the Senate, conferring upon the individual Senator the power to dramatize the importance of an issue by staging a long performance on the floor of the Senate, during which time all other business is held up. In recent years two such efforts attracted public attention. In 1953 Senator Wayne Morse of Oregon held the floor without a break for twenty-two hours twenty-six minutes, and in 1959 Senator Strom Thurmond of South Carolina spoke for twenty-four hours and eighteen minutes against the passage of the Civil Rights Bill.

In defence of unlimited debate it is argued that in a heterogeneous country like the United States, which is, in a sense, 'composed' of minorities, no group should be forced against its will to accept legislation which it considers destructive of its major interests. No individual Senator can hope to block legislation through the use of this privilege, but a relatively small group of ten or a dozen Senators who are determined to prevent the passage of a bill can hold the floor in turn indefinitely, and so force the leadership of the Senate to abandon a measure. This is the filibuster, and it is a technique which was successful in preventing the passage of civil rights legislation for many years; for even the threat of a filibuster is enough to deter the leadership from introducing a bill on to the floor of the Senate if it is going to disrupt the work of the whole session. Although the main beneficiaries of the procedure have been the Southerners, who were prepared to fight civil rights measures in this way, many other Senators are loath to see limits put on debate, because in the future it *might* be *their* minority interests which would benefit from this type of defensive action.

Until 1917 there was no means of bringing debate to a close in the Senate so long as a single Senator wished to continue speaking, but as a result of the filibuster which was conducted by a handful of Senators against a proposal to arm American merchant ships, a closure rule was introduced. The present rule, adopted in 1975, provides for closure of a debate if three fifths of the entire Senate vote for it. Before 1975 a vote of two thirds of the Senators present and voting was required to end debate, so that just over one third of the Senate could prevent the passage of a bill if they were determined enough. Senators are reluctant to vote for closure, and filibusters have been difficult to prevent. Between 1917 and 1975 closure motions were introduced 104 times, but only 24 filibusters were ended in this way. The new rule makes it easier to end debate, but still gives a determined minority a good deal of power.

THE CONGRESSIONAL COMMITTEE SYSTEM

The most effective work in Congress is done away from the floor of the House or Senate in the Standing Committees. It is difficult to exaggerate the importance of these committees, for they are the sieve through which legislation is poured, and what comes through, and how it comes through, is largely in their hands. The importance of Standing Committees in the legislative process is well illustrated by the significant difference in the positioning of the committee-stage in Congress compared with the committee stage in the British House of Commons. In the latter body the formal first reading of a bill is followed by a full-scale second-reading debate. The vote at the end of the second-reading debate signifies that the House has accepted the principles of the bill, and the function of the committee, to which the bill is then sent, is to make an effective and unambiguous piece of legislation within those principles. Standing committees of the House of Commons have no power to question the principles of the legislation or to propose major amendments to it. In the United States Congress, however, the committee stage follows immediately after the formal introduction of the bill, before the chamber as a whole has an opportunity of considering it. Thus the committee is not in any way inhibited in its approach to the bill. It can propose amendments which alter the whole character of the proposal, or it can even strike out everything after the enacting clause and substitute a completely new bill. It can report a measure to the House or Senate with or without amendments, or it can simply pigeon-hole it by failing to take any action on it. The latter fate is that of most bills, for far more legislation is introduced by Senators and Congressmen than could possibly be enacted. Indeed some legislation is undoubtedly introduced by Congressmen as a gesture of good will to interested groups, safe in the knowledge that the committee will never let it go any further. But similar treatment can also be accorded to important legislative proposals originating in the Administration if the committee does not wish to report them out. A committee can be discharged from further consideration of a bill if it refuses to act on it, but as we have seen, the discharge procedure is a difficult one to operate.

The Standing Committees of Congress are specialist committees to which legislation concerning their particular field must be sent. The most important of the eighteen Senate committees are Budget, Foreign Relations, Appropriations, Armed Services, Judiciary, Agriculture and Forestry, and Interstate and Foreign Commerce. There are twenty-two House committees, the most important ones including Rules, Budget, Appropriations, Ways and Means, Judiciary, Banking Currency and Housing, Agriculture, Interstate and Foreign Commerce, and Public Works and Transportation. There are also a number of joint committees of both houses that coordinate the supervision of administrative agencies or make recommendations to Congress on specific subjects. The most important Joint Committee, and the only one which has the power to report out legislation, is the Joint Committee on Atomic Energy. Many of the committees are divided into a number of sub-committees, each with its own responsibility for a specialized area of the committee's field of interest. Some of the larger committees have a considerable range of specialized sub-committees – twelve sub-committees of the House Appropriations Committee, fifteen sub-committees of the Senate Judiciary Committee. The committees and their subdivisions hold hearings at which members of the public, representatives of interested groups, or members of the Administration can give evidence in support of, or in opposition to, proposed legislation. The witnesses may be cross-examined by members of the committee, and for members of the Administration this can be quite an ordeal, far more searching and detailed than the questions asked at question-time in a parliamentary system. Witnesses may prepare complex, detailed briefs to submit to the committee, and these together with a transcript of the proceedings are made public.

Until 1973 the public were excluded from the 'executive sessions' of committees in which most of the real work was done, and in which a bill could be changed out of all recognition. In 1973 the House adopted a rule that all committee sessions should be open unless a majority on the committee voted for a closed session. Senate committees may make their own rules about open sessions. As a result, in 1974 most House committee sessions were open to the public.

The committees can become extremely expert in their field of interest, as members of Congress may serve continuously on a committee for many years. They are provided with a specialist staff which, although it cannot compete with the resources of the departments of the Administration with which the Committee must deal, can brief the members on the subjects to which it must give consideration. This expertise, and the fact of working together over long periods, tends to build up a corporate spirit on a committee which may transcend party loyalties. The committees are the principal arena in which compromise takes place, and by the time the members of a committee have hammered out a compromise they will be reluctant to see it upset either by the leadership of their own party or by amendments from the floor. Some committees, notably the Senate Foreign Relations Committee, have managed to develop considerable internal unity, regardless of party. The activities of the committees make it possible for a large proportion of the business conducted on the floor of the House or Senate to be dealt with by 'bi-partisan majorities' – that is, votes in which a majority of each of the two parties joins to decide an issue. In 1966 fifty-four per cent of the roll call votes were settled by bi-partisan majorities. Conversely, if a committee is opposed to the passage of a bill it is very unlikely to be acceptable to the chamber as a whole. Thus, although Standing Committees are composed of members of both parties in proportion to party strength in the house, the practical result of their operations is to provide another focus of loyalty which cuts across party lines.

The Chairman of a Standing Committee has considerable influence over the fate of legislation. Over the years he will have built up a network of influence and will know how the system works. He has control over the calling of the committee and over its agenda. Until recently, as explained above, committee chairmen were chosen on the basis of the seniority system, which meant that they were almost inevitably from safe seats, and, when the Democrats were in control, a disproportionately high number came from the Southern States. In 1966 the Chairmen of more than half of the Senate Committees came from former Confederacy States, whilst six came from Western States and one from West Virginia. There were no committee chairmen from New England or New York, none from great Eastern States like Pennsylvania, or from industrial States like Michigan or Illinois. In the House eleven of the twenty chairmen were from the South. Inevitably, the Southern committee chairman, who has been in Congress representing a safe constituency for many years, tends to be somewhat out of touch with, and unresponsive to, the 'public opinion' of the great cities of the North. Yet it is these cities which are so significant in the election of the President, and where so many of the pressing problems of America today are to be found. However, since 1970 there has been a decline in the hold of the South over Senate committee chairmanships. At the beginning of the 1975 session only five Southerners chaired committees, and in the House, partly as a result of the reformed procedures for the selection of chairmen, the Southerners had fewer than half the committee chairmanships.

The influence of the committee chairman is by no means finished when his committee has reported out a bill. The committee appoints a floor manager for each bill, often the chairman himself, and his role is to see the bill through to the final vote. In the House of Representatives the Rules Committee will have allotted a certain amount of time for the bill, which will be divided equally between its supporters and its opponents, and the floor manager and a senior member of the committee in opposition to the bill will allocate this time among those who wish to speak. Usually the members of the committee will dominate debate on the floor and will greatly influence the extent to which the measure is amended.

CONFERENCE COMMITTEES

The two Houses of Congress consider legislation independently of each other, so that a bill passed by one House may fail to pass the other. Usually on important matters identical bills are introduced into both Houses, but by the time they have been through the legislative process it is unlikely that they will still be identical, and it will be necessary to iron out the differences between the Senate and House versions of the legislation. Sometimes these differences may be reconciled by the supporters of the legislation securing similar amendments in both Houses, but if important differences persist then a Conference Committee must be set up, with members from both Houses, to hammer out a compromise. This is a rather contradictory consequence of the autonomy of the two Houses of Congress, for after each of them has spent a great deal of time and effort working on a bill, they must turn the final decisions over to a small number of their members, working in secret, to produce a draft which may differ considerably from the version so recently enacted by them. It is true that the Conference Committee simply submits a report to both Houses which must be accepted by them if the legislation is to pass, but the power of the committee lies in the fact that each House must accept or reject its report outright. Any attempt to amend the bill as reported by the Conference Committee would necessitate another conference, and the agreed compromise upon which the conference report was based might be shattered.

Thus Conference Committees have considerable power, and appointment of the managers, as they are called, to represent each House, on an important piece of legislation is crucial in determining the sort of compromise which will be reached. Formally the power of appointing managers lies with the Speaker and the President of the Senate, but they usually follow the wishes of the chairmen of the Committees concerned with the bill. The members of Conference Committees tend to be the more senior members of either House, and the influence of the two Standing Committee chairmen in the proceedings of the Conference Committee is bound to be considerable. There is thus a danger that when the more senior members of the committee have been forced on the floor of the House to accept amendments of which they disapproved, the offending amendments may be quietly dropped in conference, on the grounds that it was necessary to do so in order to get agreement with the managers from the other House. Even at this late stage in the legislative process, the President, congressional leaders, or interest groups, and in particular the administrative agencies concerned with the legislation, may try to influence the outcome of the negotiations in the Conference Committee.

THE PRESIDENTIAL VETO POWER

Once legislation has passed both Houses in an identical form it is sent to the President for his signature. He can veto the bill by returning it to Congress, with a message giving his reasons for refusing to sign. If, however, he fails to do so within ten days whilst Congress is in session, the bill becomes law without his signature. The President also has a 'pocket veto'; if after Congress has adjourned the President fails to sign a bill within ten days, excluding Sundays, then it lapses. This is quite a significant power in practice, because many bills are passed in a hurry at the end of the session, and the President can use his pocket veto without having to give his reasons, and without fear that his veto will be overridden. The veto power is an important weapon in the presidential armoury, for the threat of the use of the veto can be used to gain amendments to legislation. However, it is also a somewhat clumsy weapon. The President can only accept or reject a measure in toto, for he has no power to veto particular items in a bill. Congress sometimes uses this fact to add 'riders' to bills they know the President will not veto, including in a measure clauses unrelated to the main subject-matter of the bill, because they know that the President would use his veto against them if he could.

Presidential vetoes can be overridden if both Houses of Congress pass the bill again by a two-thirds majority of each House. Only a small proportion of presidential vetoes are overridden, because the President can usually expect to muster over one third of the votes in each House of Congress. However, it is possible for important legislation to be passed in this way over the strong opposition of the President. In 1947 President Truman used his veto against the passage of the Taft-Hartley Act, which he described as unworkable and unfair to organized labour, but his veto was overridden by Congress.

This, then, is the complex legislative procedure of Congress. It can be seen that it allows a great deal of freedom to individuals and groups in Congress to affect the outcome of the legislative process. True, most important legislation originates with the Administration, although not all of it. But Congress retains the power to refuse to pass legislation or to amend it significantly during passage. Sustained pressure by the Administration over a number of sessions of Congress will usually eventually build up enough support to pass measures that a President is committed to, but in the process he may have to accept considerable modifications to his proposals. Furthermore, the timing of legislative policy is often as important as its content, and this is more in the control of Congress than of the President. Before going on to look at other aspects of the work of Congress let us look at the way in which one piece of proposed legislation, the Civil Rights Bill of 1966, was dealt with in Congress. In some ways it is not exactly a 'typical' legislative history, but then few things that happen in Congress can be classified in that way.

THE POLITICS OF DEADLOCK –
THE CIVIL RIGHTS BILL OF 1966

In 1954 in a historic decision the Supreme Court of the United States declared that the segregation of white and coloured children in separate schools was unconstitutional. This was an act which broke the log-jam of government action on civil rights which had existed for nearly a century. The mounting tide of Negro resentment against discrimination, and the realization of the internal and external consequences of the racial situation in America, led Congress to pass a series of civil rights measures culminating in the Voting Rights Act of 1965. The major concern of this legislation was to guarantee to the Negro community its political rights, particularly the right to vote. The legislation had relatively little impact upon the Northern States, and it did little to deal with the major social problems of the Negro, in particular in relation to the existence of Negro ghettos in Northern cities. As the 1960s progressed the militancy of the Negro community increased, and each summer riots broke out in many Northern cities with large Negro populations.

By 1966 a rather complex political situation had developed in Congress. The coalition of Northern Democrats and Republicans which had obtained the passage of previous civil rights measures was no longer so secure, and when President Johnson announced new proposals for the civil rights programme in his State of the Union Message in January, the Republican leadership was immediately hostile. The programme included for the first time an attempt to deal with the problem of discrimination in the sale and rent of housing. This, the so-called 'open housing' provision, would have an immediate impact upon urban and suburban areas in the North. Other provisions of the Administration's proposal, relating to the selection of juries, giving power to the Attorney-General to initiate actions in the courts to desegregate schools and public accommodations, and concerning the protection of people engaged in civil rights work, were not so controversial, but the open housing provision immediately raised a storm of controversy.

At the end of April and the beginning of May identical bills were introduced, into the House of Representatives by Representative Emmanuel Celler of New York (HR 14765) and into the Senate by Senator Philip A. Hart of Michigan (S 3296). Representative Celler was chairman of the House Judiciary Committee and also chairman of sub-committee No. 5 of that Committee.

Almost immediately sub-committee No. 5 began public hearings on the legislation, extending over three weeks. The Attorney-General of the United States, Nicholas Katzenbach, explained and argued the bill at length before the sub-committee. Other members of the Administration gave evidence in support of the bill, as did representatives of the National Association for the Advancement of Coloured People, a Negro representative of a group of religious associations, the Catholic Welfare Conference, the National Council of Churches, and the Synagogue Council of America, representatives of the Civil Liberties Union, the National Urban League, the Americans for Democratic Action, and a large housing construction firm. Arguments against the bill were presented by the National Association of Real Estate Boards, the Liberty Lobby, and the Texas Real Estate Association.

In June the sub-committee reported to its parent committee. It proposed some amendments to the bill, and it recommended in general that the bill should be passed, but it reported the open housing provision without any recommendation. The open housing provision met strong opposition in the Judiciary Committee and at this point a battle developed over the extent to which it would be necessary to modify the proposal if it was to get the approval of the House of Representatives. The discussions centred round the Democratic chairman of the Committee, the Attorney-General and the Department of Justice, a Republican member of the Committee, Charles McC. Mathias Jr, of Maryland, and the Leadership Conference on Civil Rights, a composite organization representing a number of groups concerned with civil rights issues. As a result the Committee accepted two amendments to the bill, one exempting owner-occupiers of dwellings with up to four families, and the other, which was opposed by the Administration, which provided for the setting-up of a Federal agency to enforce the legislation. With these amendments the Committee reported the bill to the House at the end of June, with strong dissenting opinions from Southern Democrats.

By the 25 July the House Rules Committee had failed to grant a rule to bring the measure to the floor of the House, and Representative Celler, acting under the twenty-one day rule, introduced a resolution to by-pass the Rules Committee and so to bring the bill to a vote. His resolution was approved by 200 votes to 180, the majority including twenty Republicans. There followed twelve days of debate on HR 14765, and a number of amendments were made; finally on 9 August the House passed the bill and sent it to the Senate. The final vote was 259 for and 157 against. The majority was composed of 169 Northern Democrats, fourteen Southern Democrats, and seventy-six Republicans, whilst the opponents were seventeen Northern Democrats, seventy-eight Southern Democrats, and sixty-two Republicans. The Democratic Majority Whip, Hale Boggs of Louisiana, voted against the passage of the bill. Throughout the time that the House was considering the Civil Rights Bill there were strong lobbying actions going on. The Leadership Conference on Civil Rights set up a headquarters on Capitol Hill, and the National Association of Real Estate Boards conducted a campaign to defeat the bill.

During the months that the House had been considering the Civil Rights Bill the identical measure, S 3296, had been languishing in the Senate. The Sub-Committee on Constitutional Rights of the Senate Judiciary Committee had held hearings on it, but the chairman of the sub-committee, Democratic Senator Sam J. Ervin of North Carolina, had openly attacked the bill. He had circulated a questionnaire on parts of the bill to the chief judges of all Federal District Courts and their clerks, and their replies, he announced, amounted to a 'striking indictment' of the bill's provisions. Nevertheless the sub-committee reported the bill to the Senate Judiciary Committee on 1 August, but the parent committee took no action. The supporters of the Civil Rights Bill feared that the Chairman of the Committee, Senator James O. Eastland of Mississippi, would pigeonhole the measure, and time was getting short because of the almost certain threat of a filibuster on the floor of the Senate. Senator Mansfield, the Democratic Majority Leader, therefore adopted a rather unusual procedure. Instead of waiting for the Senate bill to emerge from the Committee, he attempted to bring the bill which had passed the House directly to the floor of the Senate, so by-passing the

Judiciary Committee. To do so it was necessary for the Senate to agree by a majority vote to consider the House bill.

On 7 September Senator Hart introduced a motion that the Senate give consideration to HR 14765, and debate upon this motion continued, with interruption to deal with other business, until 19 September. During this whole period it was the motion to consider the bill, rather than the bill itself, which was before the Senate, but it was clear that the Southern Senators would not even allow this motion to come to a vote. The only way to break the filibuster was to pass a closure motion limiting debate on the bill, but to obtain the necessary two-thirds majority to pass a closure motion the active support of the Republican Minority Leader, Senator Dirksen, would be required. The Minority Leader had, however, already expressed his opposition to the open housing provision.

Senator Mansfield moved two closure motions to try to bring an end to the debate, one on 14 September, the second on the nineteenth. On both occasions he failed to get the necessary two-thirds majority. On the first occasion the vote was fifty-four for closing the debate and forty-two against. The Senators voting against closure were four Northern Democrats, seventeen Southern Democrats and twenty-one Republicans. Only twelve Republicans joined the Northern Democrats and a handful of Southerners to try to bring the debate to an end. Thus the old coalition of Republicans and Southern Democrats had re-emerged, for a time at least, to prevent the passage of civil rights legislation.

CONGRESSIONAL CONTROL OF FINANCE

Ultimately, in all government activities, finance is the controlling factor. Laws must be enforced, policies must be implemented, and they always cost money. The raising and spending of money provides the ultimate control by Congress over the Administration, and it provides also an area of American government which exemplifies the paradoxical relationship between President and Congress in the mid twentieth century. The broad outlines of the annual budget are fixed by circumstances and previously adopted policies, and are, therefore, outside the control both of President and Congress; but at the margin, and it is a 'margin' involving thousands of millions of dollars, there is a game of tug-of-war between the two branches of the government that illustrates both their weaknesses and their strengths. The initiative in financial matters must come from the Administration, and the attempt to use the financial operations of government as an instrument of overall economic policy must also largely be that of the President and his advisers. Nevertheless, this is an area of government over which Congress has been most tenacious in its bid to retain the ultimate control, rejecting all proposals which would loose its hold on the purse-strings. Furthermore, it is in the field of financial planning that the Administration has, over the years, made its biggest bid to achieve internal coordination, even if not wholly successfully; yet it is in the financial sphere that the *decentralized* character of congressional power is most apparent.

Estimates of expenditure required for the forthcoming year are prepared by the departments and agencies, and sent to the Office of Management and Budget to be coordinated. The budget is submitted to Congress in January and immediately the effect of the decentralized power structure of Congress comes into operation. The process of providing funds for government is dominated by the built-in tensions of the legislative process, for appropriation bills must go through much the same procedures as ordinary legislation. The Congress is concerned to safeguard the expenditure of public money, but it is also responsive to constituency and interest pressures. Thus at one and the same time it may attempt to cut back some Administration requests and to appropriate more than the Administration wishes in other directions; the House and the Senate may differ quite considerably on the amount to be appropriated for different purposes, and these differences have to be reconciled in Conference Committees; the legislative committees of Congress, each with their pet programmes, may come into conflict with the Appropriations Committees which have the primary responsibility for ensuring an economical use of public funds; and finally the Appropriations Committees are themselves divided up into a large number of sub-committees, each of which has become almost autonomous in its control over the particular appropriations for which it is responsible.

The House of Representatives has always claimed a pre-eminence in the financial field, and all money bills originate in the House, although in fact the Constitution insists on this point only in respect of bills for raising revenue. Furthermore, the House usually tends to take a more restrictive view of the needs of the government for funds. The 'normal' pattern is for the House to reduce the amount requested by the President by a substantial amount, for the Senate to propose an appropriation considerably in excess of that suggested by the House, although still lower than the presidential request, and then for the Conference Committee to approve finally an amount about half-way between the House and Senate figures. Of course the Administration is well aware of this general tendency, and no doubt it adjusts its requests to the expected behaviour of Congress – some observers rather cynically suggest that after all the effort expended by Congress the Administration usually gets just about the amount it had originally aimed at.

However, although this is the broad pattern of the financial operations of Congress it would be a mistake to think that the outcome of the battle over particular appropriations can always be forecast in this way. Sometimes Congress appropriates more money than the President has requested for a particular programme, either in an attempt to force a particular policy upon the Administration, or as a result of the desire to benefit constituents. One of the most consistent examples of the appropriation by Congress of more money than requested has been the way in which over a period of ten years or so Congress appropriated more for the maintenance and development of the manned bomber force than the President wished. This action reflected a dispute within the Administration between Air Force Generals who wished to prevent cuts in the bomber programme and the officials of the Defense Department who wished to rely to a greater extent upon missiles. At times this dispute has been painfully open. In 1956 General Curtis LeMay, Chief of the Strategic Air Command, was successful in getting Congress to

add $800 million to the defence appropriation for the production
of B-52 bombers against the opposition of President Eisenhower's Secretary for Defense Charles Wilson. In 1964 General
LeMay, then Air Force Chief of Staff, again persuaded Congress,
against the opposition of another President and another Secretary of Defense, to appropriate $52 million for research into a
'follow-up' bomber to replace the ageing B-52s.

Another area in which Congress tends to appropriate more
money than requested is in the field of so-called 'pork barrel'
legislation, where money is appropriated for public works expenditures which will bring work and business, and other benefits,
to the Congressman's home district. Particularly important in
this respect are the construction of dams and flood control
projects and irrigation schemes. Many of these are projects which
will be carried out by the U.S. Army Corps of Engineers, a
particularly powerful administrative agency, nominally under
the control of the army, which works closely with members of
Congress. In 1966 Congress appropriated money to start work on
sixty-three new water construction projects although only
twenty-nine had been included in the President's budget. In
other fields, however, the tendency has been for Congress consistently to cut down Presidential requests below that which
might be considered the normal removal of 'padding'. One of
the biggest annual battles is on the foreign-aid programme. In
1964 Congress cut the Presidential request for foreign-aid funds
by 33.8 per cent! In other years the foreign-aid programme has
fared better, but cuts of eighteen to twenty-eight per cent have
been common.

The House Ways and Means Committee and the Senate
Finance Committee share a similar responsibility for recommending tax measures, as do the Appropriations Committees for
recommending expenditures. These four committees tend to be
even more autonomous than the other Standing Committees
of Congress. In particular, the House committees have great
prestige and a reputation for considerable expertise. Their
recommendations are almost always accepted by the House without amendment, and tax bills are usually considered by the
House under a rule which even forbids consideration of amend-

ments unless they have been accepted by the committee. It is also relatively rare for the Appropriations Committee of the House to make amendments to the reports of its numerous sub-committees, which deal with the appropriation bills for various departments and agencies. Thus although the chairmen of these committees attempt to coordinate activities within their own spheres of responsibility there is no one body in Congress which is in a position to take an overall view of financial affairs. Attempts have been made, without success, to get these four committees to work more closely together, or to introduce procedures which would give greater continuity to the appropriations process over a number of years. However, Congress has successfully resisted any attempt to diminish its annual control over the raising of revenue and the authorization of expenditure.

As a result of President Richard Nixon's attempts to circumvent congressional control of finance the Congressional Budget and Impoundment Control Act was passed in 1974, which established a congressional budget system to attempt to give to that body an effective control over the national budget, and to over-ride attempts by the President to impound funds voted by Congress.

OTHER CONTROL FUNCTIONS

Congress conducts many investigations of the activities of the Federal Government in an attempt to keep control of this vast machine. Each year the Appropriations Committees and sub-committees investigate departmental operations, and Standing Committees conduct enquiries relevant to their sphere of legislative responsibility. The most notorious committee investigations were those of the House Un-American Activities Committee (since abolished), and the investigatory subcommittee of the Senate Government Operations Committee, chaired in the early 1950s by Senator Joseph McCarthy. Senate committees and some House committees have the power to subpoena witnesses and documents, and if a witness refuses to answer questions put to him he may find himself in jail, convicted of contempt of Congress.

The House Un-American Activities Committee was the main source of citations for contempt of Congress in recent years, many of them for failing to answer questions or produce documents about supposed Communist activities, though few of these contempt citations have actually resulted in convictions in the courts. In 1966 seven leaders of the Ku Klux Klan were cited for contempt for refusing to give the Committee records of the Klan's activities, and the Imperial Wizard of the Klan was convicted by a Federal Court and sentenced to a year's imprisonment.

At its worst the investigatory power of Congress can be used to harass individuals who offend against the political opinions of committee members, or to further the political ambitions of members of Congress. At its best it can be a valuable instrument for investigating the activities of the government in order to prevent abuses of power, both public and private. Recent investigations have been directed at the Ku Klux Klan, interstate criminal activities, racketeering in labour unions, the invasion of privacy through the use of electronic devices and lie-detectors, and the allocation of government defence contracts.

The Senate has special power under the Constitution to confirm the appointments to office of executive and judicial officers, including members of the Cabinet and Federal judges, which are made by the President. Thousands of nominations are made each year, and most of them are quickly confirmed. Very few nominations are actually rejected, although a small proportion are withdrawn by the President when opposition is manifested in the Senate. Occasionally, a nomination can lead to a protracted battle, with a public investigation of the nominee by a Senate Committee and heated debates on the floor of the Senate about his record and qualifications. Sometimes objections are made to the nominee because of the policies he is expected to pursue, and sometimes on personal grounds. The President usually avoids serious difficulty by consulting congressional leaders on appointments, and in one respect he must be quite meticulous in his consultation. The convention of 'senatorial courtesy' ensures that the President will clear every nomination with the Senator of the President's party from the State from which the nominee comes. If he fails to do so the Senator concerned may state on the floor of the Senate chamber that the nominee is 'personally obnoxious' to him, and the Senate will normally reject the nomination. An exceptional case of the refusal to confirm the nomination of a member of the Cabinet was the rejection of Lewis L. Strauss as Secretary of Commerce in 1959. He was nominated by President Eisenhower at a time when there was a Democratic majority in the Senate; Strauss had formerly been the Chairman of the Atomic Energy Commission, and the fight against his nomination was led by Senator Clinton P. Anderson, Chairman of the Joint Atomic Energy Committee. The battle lasted nearly six months, with the President throwing all his weight behind the attempts to secure confirmation of the nomination. Democratic Senators opposed Strauss because of his 'conservative' attitudes, because of some of his decisions as A.E.C. Chairman, and because of his role in the J. Robert Oppenheimer case in 1954. The final vote in the Senate was forty-nine against confirmation and forty-six in favour. Two Republican Senators voted against their President's nomination. If they had voted the other way the nomination of Strauss would have been confirmed.

Another field in which the Senate is given special powers is that of foreign policy. The Constitution requires that treaties made on behalf of the United States shall be subject to ratification by two thirds of the Senators present and voting. Perhaps the most shattering exercise of the power of the Senate was the rejection in 1919 of the Treaty of Versailles, which had been largely moulded by President Woodrow Wilson. By so doing the Senate prevented the United States from becoming a member of the League of Nations. The power of the Senate in this field has declined, however, owing to the practice of concluding 'executive agreements' between the President and foreign governments, agreements which do not require senatorial confirmation.

Traditionally the conduct of war was an area which Congress left almost exclusively to the President. The Constitution gives Congress the power to declare war, but in practice this was far overshadowed by the President's role as Commander-in-Chief and his consequent ability to order troops into action in any part of the world. However, in 1973 the public revulsion at the continuance of the war in South-East Asia drove Congress to reassert

itself in this field. The Resolution on the War in Cambodia prohibited the use of public funds 'to finance combat activities ...
over or from off the Shores of North Vietnam, South Vietnam,
Laos or Cambodia'. This was followed by the War Powers Resolution of 1973 which forbad the President to commit troops to
hostilities, except after a declaration of war, or under specific
statutory authorization from Congress, or in a national emergency created by an attack on the United States or its possessions.
Even in case of a national emergency the President is required to
consult with Congress 'in every possible instance'. The practic-
ability of this assertion of the power of the legislature has already
been put in question by President Ford's action in retaking the
merchant ship *Mayaguez* in May 1975.

CONGRESS AND POLICY-MAKING

The structure and operation of the Congress of the United States
closely reflects the decentralized and heterogeneous character of
the American political system. All the threads of class, pluralistic,
and sectional politics can be found in the operation of its committee system and in the changing patterns of voting as different
issues come up to be decided. The sectional element in the American political scene is exaggerated in Congress by the way in
which groups of Congressmen and Senators feel the necessity of
reacting to the views of a majority of their constituents, although
a sizeable minority in the region may disagree with their views,
or at least with the fervour with which they are expressed. The
representative system in Congress does not claim to produce a
proportional representation of opinion through the country, but
neither does it produce a stable, continuously coordinated government, which is usually represented as the great boon of the Anglo-
Saxon system of single-member, simple-majority electoral systems.
The tendency towards multi-party politics that we found earlier
is barely restrained by the needs of organizing Congress and by
the advantages of maintaining control of certain key congressional
positions. Thus policy-making is haphazard and discontinuous.
Congress approves programmes and then refuses to appropriate
money for them; it demands economy and then spends more

money than ever on projects which will benefit constituents. The nature of Congress, and its continuing though declining power, raises the whole question of ensuring governmental responsibility for policy: how can the citizen affix responsibility for governmental policies, or the lack of them, if he is faced with a continually changing kaleidoscope of coalitions in Congress? And yet in a very real sense there is more genuinely responsible government in Congress than in most of the party-dominated legislatures of the world. For we have seen that there is nothing which ultimately is of more importance to a member of Congress than the views of a majority of his constituents.

The efforts which Congress has made in the period since 1973, to increase its control over the executive branch in the spheres of financial and foreign policy are likely to founder simply because of this fundamental characteristic of the legislature. It lacks the necessary coherence to provide such leadership. That leadership can only come, if it is to come at all, from the President.

The description of the American political system that we have developed to this point is one of enormous variety and diversity : a set of sectional, class, pluralistic and individualistic forces which can only with difficulty be compressed into a few broad categories. The institutional structures which we have examined have fully reflected and expressed this diversity : the federal system, the structure of pressure-groups, the political parties, the working of Congress – all of these give full rein to multifarious interests, each intent on furthering its economic aims, defending its social position, or gaining a hearing for its point of view. Each of these structures channels and articulates these demands, gradually contributing to the process of bargaining and compromise that decision-making requires. Yet the very nature of all these structures emphasizes their own pluralistic character, for pluralism is built into all of them as a dominant characteristic. It is only when we come to the Presidency of the United States itself that we reach a part of the political structure where a single will must be expressed, a single mind made up. This is not to say that all the enormous pressures of the pluralistic political system do not reach expression in the Presidency. They are indeed felt, and their impact is very considerable, as we shall see. But here at least there is the *possibility* of a unity, which exists nowhere else in the system, and consequently the possibility of the exercise of leadership. It is in the area of leadership that the American political system may be thought to be most defective, and it is the function of the President to try to remedy that defect. Given the nature of the American system, and of the political culture which sustains it, the task of the President is a superhuman one. He is therefore inevitably doomed to failure before he begins. This is the challenge of the Presidency, its fascination and its tragedy.

When the President is greeted at a public function on his arrival at an airfield or a military parade, the band strikes up the familiar tune 'Hail to the Chief'. The President is a chief in many senses – chief of state, party chief, commander-in-chief of the armed forces, chief administrator, and chief initiator of legislation. At the same time he embodies the power and authority of the nation. On this solitary individual, for four years or more, is placed the final responsibility for the external, and much of the internal, affairs of the United States. But just how powerful is a President? What are the tools at his disposal for the discharge of his political functions? What are the built-in limitations on the power of the President? These are the questions we shall look at in the present chapter.

Of course it is true to say that the nature of the Presidency at a particular moment depends considerably upon the incumbent of the office – great men make great Presidents. But although the personality of the President may make a considerable difference to the course of day-to-day policy-making there are very real institutional limitations on the President – things he may do and things he may not, as well as things that he cannot escape doing. In certain circumstances a President may set the country on a new course, achieving a new economic policy, setting off in a new direction in foreign affairs, initiating great social changes. But all the time he is subject to very real constitutional and political limitations. In recent years in Britain there has been much discussion of the extent to which the office of Prime Minister has been moving more and more towards a presidential form, and by implication the discussion is usually cast in terms of the extent to which the British Prime Minister is becoming more like the American President, and consequently becoming a more powerful and dominant political figure. But the comparison between these two great offices is in fact by no means as simple as this. The recognition of the increasing power of the Prime Minister *in relation to other members of his Cabinet* does seem to make him more like his American counterpart as head of the government, but in relation to other parts of the political system the comparison is much more complex. In order to assess Presidential power we must look at the Presidency from every angle, regarding internal affairs and external, considering his relationships to his Cabinet, his other advisers, to Congress, to the party system, to pressure groups and to the courts. For the working of the Presidency fluctuates between two poles – on the one hand an awesome exercise of power, power which is personal and seemingly unchecked, and on the other hand an impotent inability to gain acceptance for major policies which he considers essential to the well-being of the country, or even for relatively minor aims which he considers desirable. It is the ever-changing complex of inter-relationships between these two poles that constitutes Presidential politics, the ramifications of which we shall now explore.

THE POLITICAL FUNCTIONS OF THE PRESIDENT

The President has a number of *constitutional* powers which we shall look at shortly, but the way in which he exercises them is largely dictated by the context in which he operates, and by the functions which he performs in the political system. At the same time the provisions of the Constitution do constitute a very real framework for the exercise of Presidential power, for they provide the legal weapons which other political actors can use in their struggle with the President.

The President has four main political functions. First, like Congress, although necessarily in a very different way, he has to act as a broker between the contending interests which make demands upon the government. No President can afford to ignore the demands, some trivial, some gargantuan, that are evolved in the political system. He may be looking for his own re-election, or simply attempting to secure political support in matters of vital concern to his Administration's policies, but in either case he must play the political game. He is potentially the ultimate target, direct or indirect, of every individual or group which wishes to promote or defeat legislation, to obtain the exercise of a Presidential power, or to affect the operation of the Administration. In a multitude of matters of governmental concern the attempt to gain the ear of the President will not be worth the effort, and no attempt will be made. The decision to attract Presidential attention will not necessarily depend simply upon the intrinsic importance of the matter at issue, but also upon the politics of access to the President. Individuals or groups who potentially have support to offer the President, whether it be the likelihood of voting support in a Congressional battle, or simply the friendship of someone whom the President may trust, will be in a privileged position as far as access is concerned. Whether this results in actual Presidential support for the policy is quite another matter – but access in itself is a vitally important factor when a single man must cram so much into a working day. In many matters of vital concern to interest groups his intervention, or refusal to intervene, may be decisive, although Presidential support for a particular point of view is by no means a guarantee of success. Thus the Presidency is a pluralistic institution like the other parts of the system, although in a very different dimension.

The first political function of the President, then, is to reflect and react to pluralistic pressures, but his second function, paradoxically, tends to cut across and even contradict this line of action. His second political function is to attempt to interpret and pursue the national interest as he sees it. The idea of the national interest is fraught with difficulties for the student of politics. Indeed, those who see the political system in extreme pluralistic terms deny that the concept can have any meaning. Objectively, it is true, there may not be any policy, or set of policies, which can be unequivocally designated as being in the interest of the whole nation, except perhaps when one can isolate a situation which would lead to its complete destruction. Nearly every policy will help or harm different groups in varying degrees. The decisions of governments inevitably strike some sort of balance between the advantages and disadvantages which they anticipate will result from alternative policies, so that the 'national interest' can almost always be resolved into sets of conflicting sectional interests. Nevertheless, whatever the *objective* realities of the national interest may be, the man who holds the office of President must do more than simply attempt to strike compromises between contending interests. He must identify policy goals *which seem to him* to provide the best long-run prospects, economic, social, and strategic, for the over-whelming majority of the American people, and attempt to attain these goals. For the pluralistic jumble of interests that faces him will not necessarily and automatically cancel out into some rational and successful pattern. The implicit assumption that it will do so lies behind much of the extreme adherence to the philosophy of pluralism, and represents a considerable danger in assessing the operation of modern political systems. It leaves no room for leadership, seeing the role of government merely as that of an umpire between contending interests. But a full explanation of, and understanding of, the Presidency requires more than simply seeing the office as a neutral machine for registering public opinion. Presidents can, and must, be leaders, even if that leadership proves to be a merely negative force. They stand at a fulcrum of the American political system, using levers which can, in many circumstances, although not all, turn the tide of events in one direction or another. There is no escaping this responsibility, even though in attempting to carry it out a President will often succumb to sectional pressures or to political expediency.

The third function is closely related to the first two. The President must try to act as the focal point of loyalty for this diverse American society, at one and the same time giving to each distinct group the sense that its interests are being defended against internal attacks and attempting also to give at least a minimal sense of unity to the whole country, particularly in relation to the rest of the world. No other single individual can ever lay claim to represent the whole American people. As Head of State as well as Head of the Administration, he must be seen abroad, and to some extent at home as well, as in some sense embodying the power and authority of the whole of the United States. It is this which in large degree has led the Presidency increasingly to take on a charismatic quality, giving to the President an almost mystical aura, sometimes seeming to endow him with the awesome quality of a monarch, but combined with the real hard-headed power of a skilled politician. Yet here again, the built-in complexity of the system produces another paradox. The President speaks for the nation, but he speaks also as a party

leader, and, as he must pursue controversial policies, he sometimes speaks simply as a leader of a faction. The line between the
national leader giving voice to the aspirations and demands of
the whole people, and the party or factional leader pursuing
policies which many of his countrymen bitterly oppose, is indeed a difficult one to maintain. It is usually easier for a President to pursue these potentially conflicting roles when his
foreign policies remain essentially non-controversial. When
foreign policy becomes a matter of bitter internal dissension, as
in the case of the Vietnam war, then the President's task becomes
a formidable one indeed.

The fourth, and perhaps the essential political function of the
President is to be 'coordinator-in-chief', indeed almost the only
coordinator, of the innumerable semi-autonomous parts of the
governmental machine, both legislative and executive alike.
The extraordinarily fragmented nature of the American governmental structure should by now be apparent to the reader, but
in addition there must be added two further dimensions which
will be looked at in more detail in later chapters – the loosely
integrated character of the American administrative machine,
and the powers of the courts to affect the outcome of political
situations. The President must, by an extreme act of will, attempt
to impose his point of view upon this vast and complex body of
people. In the last analysis the standing of a President depends
upon the success with which he performs this function. To
evolve and initiate policies is of little use if the acquiescence of
Congress, and of State and local governments, is not obtained:
and the passage of legislation, or the exercise of Presidential
authority, will be of little real value if the President's intentions
are frustrated by members of his own Administration. The President is by no means lacking in weapons with which to tackle the
problem of coordination, in its widest sense, and most of the
reforms which have been made in the Presidency in the past
thirty years have been directed at improving the President's performance in this area. However, in performing this function the
President faces two most formidable obstacles.

In the first place he reaps the benefits, and also the considerable
disadvantages, of the loosely organized party system, with its

consequent lack of party discipline. The advantage is that the President can hope to attract support for some of his policies from the members of both parties in Congress, but by the same token he cannot depend upon his own party to give him unequivocal support for his legislative proposals. Furthermore, the effects of this lack of party cohesion go beyond the sphere of the relations of the President with Congress. They reach into his own Administration. The President is not able to assume that party allegiance will assure ready compliance with his policies among the senior members of his Administration, even when they are members of his own party, which is not always the case. He may meet almost as much opposition, of a rather different kind, it is true, from within his Administration as from outside it.

Second, the President faces a formidable array of constitutional limitations upon his ability to obtain coordinated governmental action. Much of the politics of the Presidency consists of the efforts of the President to overcome these barriers to the smooth exercise of power. Let us look at the constitutional position of the President.

THE POWERS OF THE PRESIDENT

As in other respects, the Constitution's grant of power to the President is in very general terms, the main provision being 'The Executive Power shall be vested in a President of the United States of America'. The content and meaning of this bald statement has been filled in since 1789 by the accumulation of practice, and by the decisions of the Supreme Court. The Constitution did, however, expand a little on the role of the Chief Executive. He was also to be Commander-in-Chief of the army and navy of the United States, and of the militia of the Several States when called into the service of the United States. He could require the opinion, in writing, of the principal officer of each of the Executive Departments, and was also given power to grant reprieves and pardons for offences against the United States except in cases of impeachment. The other important powers granted to him were the power to make treaties, subject to their ratification by a two-thirds majority vote in the Senate, and to nominate ambassadors, other public ministers and consuls, judges of the Supreme Court, and all other officers of the United States, subject to the confirmation of the Senate. However, Congress was given the power to allow the President acting alone to make appointments 'of such inferior officers as they think proper', and the vast majority of official appointments are today made in this way.

In accordance with the Founders' belief in the separation of powers the President was given no positive role in the legislative process other than the duty, from time to time, to give to the Congress information on the State of the Union, and to recommend to their consideration such measures as he considers necessary and expedient. He has also the power to convene both Houses of Congress in emergency session, and to adjourn them if they disagree with respect to the time of adjournment (the last eventuality has never yet arisen). He does not have the power to dissolve Congress and so lacks what is sometimes considered to be the ultimate disciplinary weapon in parliamentary systems of government. As a check to the legislature, however, he was given a veto power over legislation, subject to the ability of Congress to override his veto by a two-thirds majority vote in both Houses.

By this grant of power the Founding Fathers in 1787 certainly did not intend to establish an office of the power and importance that has become the hallmark of the twentieth-century Presidency. Many of them may have wanted 'a mere Executive', one who would faithfully carry into effect the orders of the legislature: others wanted a more powerful President who would be able to check the dangerous tendencies of a democratic legislature, but none could have foreseen that the President would become the initiator of policy that he has become, working with every weapon at his disposal, constitutional and political, to further those policies, and to lead the country in the direction that he considers desirable. Some modern Presidents, President Taft for example, have tended towards the 'weak' view of the President's function, but the transformation of the office by Theodore Roosevelt, Woodrow Wilson, and above all by Franklin D. Roosevelt, into a dynamic centre of policy-making is a reaction to the demands made upon governments in this century which they are unable to ignore.

The Constitution thus gives little direct authority to the President to control the affairs of the nation, and sets formidable obstacles in his way. In legislative and financial matters he is constitutionally almost entirely dependent upon Congress, and the Senate has a veto on appointments and treaties. The Supreme Court also stands as a potential check to the power of the President, with the ability to pronounce his actions unconstitutional, as it did in 1952 in the steel seizure case (see chapter 9 below). Thus if the President is to exercise the leadership in national affairs that modern conditions demand he must use his constitutional authority in the context of the *extra*-constitutional power that he draws from his position as a national and party leader, in order to play a role not foreseen in the Constitution.

PARTY CHIEF AND NATIONAL LEADER

The two sources of extra-constitutional power available to the President are the allegiance of the supporters of his own political party, in Congress and in the country as a whole, and 'public opinion'. These two sources of power sometimes complement each other and sometimes conflict. A skilful President may ring the changes of differing combinations of public and party support to attain his ends, sometimes depending upon the former to attain limited aims which do not enjoy wide popular support, and at others using public opinion to override contrary opinions in his own party. In essence Presidential politics consists in the attempt to walk this tight-rope, and it brings the Presidency to its lowest ebb when Presidential policies come up against strong opposition both in the country at large and in the President's own party. Equally, however, when a President enjoys wide popular support and is backed by a relatively united party his power is impressive indeed.

As in so many other respects, however, these two sources of power are by no means simple and straightforward, either in their composition or in their usefulness as weapons in the Presidential armoury. The President's position as a party leader is an equivocal one. In office he is necessarily the titular head of his party, at least until a successor is nominated at the national convention. As the party is the organizational structure through which candidates are nominated and election campaigns conducted, there is a constant tendency to emphasize party unity. This desire for unity in the party works both ways, however. It gives the President some sort of claim to party allegiance, but it also imposes on the President a considerable restraint, in that he must attempt to avoid making demands which will seriously divide his party. The claims of party loyalty on State and local political leaders is necessarily a limited one. They will often make considerable efforts to maintain a semblance of unity, perhaps with considerable embarrassment in the context of their local politics, but the claims of party loyalty alone cannot override really strong local pressures. A party leader who is also President of the United States has, however, more to offer to those whose support he requires than the satisfaction simply of being a good party man. In return he may offer support for projects which a legislator or party chieftain wishes to further. Presidential approval of legislative proposals or Presidential commitment to the expenditure of money on public works in a State or locality, are powerful incentives to be a good supporter of the head of the party. In spite of the drastic curtailment of the spoils system, in which appointments to government positions all the way down the civil service hierarchy were potential political inducements, the President still has some thousands of offices to fill, and they include many plum positions, highly desirable to the friends and supporters of local politicians, and sometimes to those politicians themselves. The appointment of ambassadors and judges provides an important but by no means inexhaustible source of Presidential bounty. This patronage is *not* channelled through those members of the President's party who consistently oppose his policies.

Another of the weapons the President may use in his role as party leader is the use of publicity. What the President does or says is automatically newsworthy, and the way in which he handles his appearances, the references he makes to his party colleagues, the people he invites to accompany him on platforms or at public events, all these seemingly innocent considerations can be the subject of the most intense political manoeuvring. Presidents, and Presidential aspirants, may also become involved in the dangerous sphere of local political disputes, throwing their weight behind one faction or another, and hoping to benefit one day from the gratitude of the successful contender, although they may equally reap the bitter enmity of the opposing and not necessarily defeated faction. The dangers, and the likely lack of success, of too deep an involvement in local politics is illustrated by the experience of Franklin Roosevelt in the elections of 1938, but a more subtle and continuing use of Presidential influence is an inescapable part of a successful President's armoury.

The President may hope, therefore, to call upon party support, however engendered, for his policies, but he cannot rely upon it. Often, in order to get Congress to accept his proposals, he must turn to a wider and more inclusive source of support, the American people. It is, of course, difficult to distinguish clearly these two roles of the President. Usually, in appealing for support to the people, the President is attempting to demonstrate to his party in Congress that they would be unwise to flout his leadership. At the same time the President may be appealing to members of the opposing party, or to political independents to support him on a national, non-partisan basis, for the good of the country as a whole, and on many issues he can hope to achieve such support both in Congress and in the country. In the twentieth century the President's use of 'public opinion' has become of considerable political importance. The prestige and prominence of his office, the fact that the President alone can claim to speak for the nation gives him also a special right to speak to the nation. With the development of the mass media of communication the President has tended to appeal for support more and more to his unique constituency, the nation, against the members of Congress who can be seen with some truth as an assembly of local politicians. Franklin Roosevelt first used the radio as an effective political weapon in his 'fireside chats' in the 1930s, in which he told the American people what he was attempting to do and asked for their support. The fireside chats have been replaced by Presidential appearances before the television cameras, and the Presidential press conference has become an institutionalized part of the machinery of government.

The direct dialogue between the President and the representatives of the press was first put on a regular basis by Woodrow Wilson, who established regular press conferences. Franklin Roosevelt further developed this medium of communication in which the President could give background information and explain his policies to reporters, on the clear understanding that he would be quoted directly only when he gave his permission. In this way the President hoped for an understanding of, and representation of, his policies which would go beyond his public announcements. The Presidential press conferences were then held in the intimacy of the President's office in the White House, but President Truman gave them a rather different character by transferring them to a much larger room where hundreds of correspondents from all over the country, and indeed all over the world, could attend. This proved to be the initial step in transforming the press conference into something quite different. In 1955 President Eisenhower allowed his press conferences to be filmed for television, and instead of a cosy, off-the-record discussion, the press conference became an unprecedented opportunity for a President to answer, before a national audience, the questions put to him by reporters. President Kennedy took this process one vital stage further. Whilst the Eisenhower conferences were filmed and edited before transmission, Kennedy instituted the 'live' press conference, in which he stood before the television cameras giving his views on a wide range of subjects direct to the American people without the intervention of time or editors. The impact of this method of communication is difficult to measure, but its significance for Presidential leadership must surely be enormous. The President is, of course, thoroughly briefed by his Press Secretary, by the State Department, and his other advisers upon likely questions and the answers to be given. He is in a position of considerable superiority over his questioners, who treat him with deference and do not attempt to cross-question him. It is in fact an invaluable forum for the President to *make* opinion, and a great deal of time and effort is devoted by modern Presidents and their assistants to these problems of public relations.

However, like his role as party leader, this endeavour to project himself as a national leader, in order to persuade his opponents in Congress at least not to oppose him too actively, has its limitations. To obtain public sympathy and understanding for his position is one thing, but to translate this into *active* support which will make a positive impact upon Senators and Congressmen is quite another. Furthermore the obverse of the President's power to persuade through the mass media is the revelation of his weaknesses or the inadequacies of his policies. A misjudged attempt to persuade may quickly have the reverse effect from that which was intended. The intelligent use of the media of communication must avoid saturating or boring the public with Presidential exhortations. A dramatic appeal by the President might generate considerable public support, but dramatic appeals six times a week are likely to have a very different result. Presidential leadership can be exercised in part, therefore, through the management, almost the manipulation, of public opinion, but the danger is that it can also make the President into the prisoner of public opinion, for if he makes his effort to persuade and fails, it is extremely unlikely that he will succeed in any other way.

THE INSTITUTIONS OF THE PRESIDENCY

Up to this point we have treated the *Presidency* as if it consisted simply of the President alone. The dominant position of this individual should not, however, blind us to the fact that the Presidency is an institution, and that the modern Presidency involves an extensive structure of offices and functions. It is to this aspect of the Presidency that we now turn, to look first at the role of the Cabinet, and then at the Executive Office of the President.

THE CABINET

The Founding Fathers' attachment to the principle of the separation of powers in 1787 ensured that they would reject the system of cabinet government that was then in an embryonic stage of its development in England. They saw the Cabinet as a means of the maintenance of a royal dominance over the legislature and they did not wish to put such a weapon into the hands of the President. Some of the Founders, however, wished to establish some form of Council to advise the President, and the first proposal which was submitted to the Convention, the Pinckney Plan, incorporated such a body. However, the Constitution as finally submitted for ratification to the States contained no reference to a council, cabinet, or other collective body to work with, or advise, the President. It simply stated that the President might 'require the opinion, in writing, of the principal officer in each of the executive departments, upon any subject relating to the duties of their respective offices'. Thus the Constitution left the President in a solitary pre-eminence in the executive branch of government.

However, from the very beginning of the Union George Washington took to consulting his heads of departments collectively as well as individually, and as early as 1793 the term *cabinet* was being applied to this group of advisers. Today the Cabinet consists of the heads of the eleven executive departments – the Secretary of State, the Secretary of the Treasury, the Secretary of Defense, the Attorney-General, the Secretary of the Interior, the Secretary of Agriculture, the Secretary of Commerce, the Secretary of Labor, the Secretary of Health, Education and Welfare, the Secretary of Housing and Urban Development, and the Secretary of Transportation. These men have the formal status of Cabinet rank, but others may be present, either sporadically or frequently. Usually the Director of the Bureau of the Budget has been present to advise the President, as have other Presidential aides. The heads of agencies without Cabinet rank may be asked to attend from time to time for the discussion of particular subjects, and at times during the Cabinet's history the head of an important agency not yet promoted to the status of a department has been in continuous attendance.

Until President Eisenhower's term of office the Cabinet worked on an extremely informal basis. There were no Cabinet agenda and no minutes. The business was conducted as the incumbent

President wished. Eisenhower formalized Cabinet meetings, holding them weekly, introducing agenda and minutes, and appointed one of his special Assistants to the President as Secretary to the Cabinet. President Kennedy, with a completely different approach to the organization of his Administration, abandoned frequent meetings of the Cabinet and abolished the Cabinet Secretariat. The Cabinet virtually ceased to have any collective function, giving way to *ad hoc* meetings with the President of those members concerned with a particular problem. What then is the nature and significance of the American Cabinet?

Presidents have used the Cabinet as an organ of consultation and advice, but it has never enjoyed the role of a collective decision-taking body that the British Cabinet has had at some periods of its existence. There are a number of reasons for this, quite apart from the silence of the Constitution on the subject. The whole atmosphere of the American political scene is opposed to the idea of the collective responsibility of a tightly knit, cohesive Cabinet along the lines which used to be the ideal of Cabinet government in Britain. The cohesiveness of British Cabinets rested upon two inter-related characteristics of the British system – parliamentary government and the English party structure. The former makes it imperative for the Cabinet to maintain a unified front in order to safeguard its majority in the House of Commons, without which it must resign. The latter, based upon closely disciplined, ideologically oriented party organizations, produces a relatively like-minded body of men at the head of a political party, whose approach to the problems of government will be quite similar. Although the foundations of this party system may be crumbling in Britain today, and the concept of collective responsibility has lost much of its earlier significance, the members of a British Cabinet still tend to be very close to each other in their political ideas and ideals, compared with the attitudes of the leaders of the opposition. Furthermore, they will be a group of men most of whom have shared the same long apprenticeship in the House of Commons, working their way up from the back benches, through junior and then more senior ministerial positions, until they reach the Cabinet. They will also have shared the years of political wilderness in opposition. This forges a bond which is not lightly broken. None of these considerations applies to the American Cabinet.

First, the American Cabinet is not formally 'responsible' to Congress. In a constitutional sense its responsibility is to the President alone, but in terms of practical politics the heads of the great departments must pay almost as much attention to what Congress wants as to the President. It is congressional legislation that empowers them to act, it is money granted by Congress that finances their activities, and it is the committees of Congress that keep vigilant watch on their performance. Thus the Cabinet member looks to the President who hired him, and could fire him, and to the Congress, particularly to the chairmen of those committees with whom he must deal, but he does not look much to his Cabinet colleagues, except perhaps as potential rivals for Presidential favours and congressional funds.

Second, the relationships between the President and the members of his Cabinet may be very close, and yet they are of a different quality from those of a Prime Minister and his colleagues. The President may appoint to the highest offices in his Administhation men who were unknown to him personally until a few days before their appointment. He may appoint members of the opposing party to the most important positions in his Administration. Although he must have some regard for the representative nature of his Cabinet, ensuring that the regions of the country are represented and that no section of the community feels itself to have been slighted, the President is virtually unfettered in terms of the actual individuals that he appoints. There is no 'shadow Cabinet' in the American political universe, and so no clear expectations to be satisfied, unless the President has given hostages to fortune during the electoral campaign. He tends to appoint 'experts' to his Cabinet posts, in the sense of finding men qualified to do the jobs he wants done, rather than looking for any other qualification. They may be businessmen, academics, former State Governors, Congressmen, judges, lawyers, engineers, or from any other walk of life, and after they have finished with his Administration they will probably return whence they came. Thus their loyalty, their first allegiance, is to the man who appointed them, and to him as an individual.

It is not, however, their only loyalty. As we have seen, they must look also to important figures in Congress, and they must also look to their 'clientele'. Each of the great departments, even the Department of State, has a 'clientele', the people they serve and regulate, and to whom they develop a sense of responsibility. Sometimes the identification with a section of the community can become so strong, in the case of the Departments of Agriculture, Commerce, and Labor for example, that their aim seems to be to promote a particular interest to the government, rather than to represent the government itself. This is yet another divisive characteristic, forcing the members of the Cabinet to seek individual and confidential contact with the President in order to gain his support. Thus there is an important distinction to be made between the Cabinet as a collective body and the individuals who compose it. It is often emphasized, quite rightly, that it is the President who has the final responsibility for decisions. Even if the Cabinet is unanimously opposed to a Presidential policy they cannot outvote him, nor veto it. It is true also that the President appoints the members of the Cabinet and can dismiss them. Yet to see the individual members of the Cabinet as the mere 'creatures' of the President is a mistake. They can and do disagree with him. If he is determined to overrule them he will do so, but they and he operate in a political context. Each department head has his sources of support distinct from the President, and each has many decisions to make, so that the most active and well-informed of Presidents cannot be aware of all of them, nor afford to try to exercise a continual personal surveillance over them. Individual Cabinet members can attain a political influence which may be of some embarrassment to the President, and a very few have even rivalled his authority in their own sphere.

Given the nature of the American Cabinet, it seems difficult to understand why it should have persisted at all as a collective entity, and yet, although it seems at times almost to have ceased to function in this way, there would appear to have been a continuous need for a body of this sort. Presidents need to indicate in some way that the Administration is working as a team, and to demonstrate collective support and approval for policies, particularly at times of crisis. A meeting of the Cabinet, with its members representing their differing clienteles, authenticates the process of consulting the pluralistic interests that go to make up the American polity, but it represents very little in terms of actual decision-making, for the decisions are taken elsewhere. Similarly the Cabinet fails to make any significant contribution to the solution of that problem of coordinating the activities of the governmental machines which is so critically important in modern 'big' government. To help the President to perform this function, therefore, a quite distinct set of institutions has been evolved.

THE EXECUTIVE OFFICE OF THE PRESIDENT

The President heads an Administration which, in 1966, totalled more than 2,750,000 Federal civil servants, as well as nearly three million members of the armed forces. In addition to the eleven executive departments there are over forty independent agencies of the Federal Government together with a plethora of Advisory Boards, Committees and Commissions. The President stands in a solitary position of overall responsibility for the acts of this enormous machine. He must direct and coordinate its activities and to do this he must have information about its operations, assessments of policy needs and a means of ensuring that his decisions, and those of the Congress, are carried out effectively and in the spirit in which they were intended. The problem of channelling information and advice upwards to the President and of transmitting commands down through the machinery of government, as well as the complex problems of liaison with the Congress, have inevitably increased in the twentieth century with the enormous expansion of the functions of the Federal Government. The size of the Presidential staffs gradually increased in a rather haphazard fashion until the New Deal programmes of

Franklin D. Roosevelt imposed an intolerable strain upon the existing machinery. In 1937 the President's Committee an Administrative Management emphasized the need to equip the President with an organization to enable him to control and coordinate the Administration effectively. As a result, Congress passed the Reorganization Act of 1939 and empowered President Roosevelt to establish the Executive Office of the President. This he did by Executive Order 8248, in September 1939. Clinton Rossiter has described this an an innovation which saved the Presidency from paralysis, and the Constitution from radical amendment. The Executive Office has become the heart of the Administration, providing the President with information and advice, attempting to foresee future trends in government and to forecast future problems for the government. It conducts the President's relations with the Congress, with the press and the general public, and supervises the implementation of his decisions.

THE WHITE HOUSE OFFICE

The nerve centre of the Executive Office, and indeed of the Presidency, is the President's personal staff, the White House Office. Altogether over five hundred people work in the White House Office, but the twenty or so men and women who work closest to the President are the Special Assistants to the President, an Administrative Assistant, the Press Secrtary, Special Consultants appointed by the President, the Special Counsel to the President, and his Armed Forces Aide. The White House Office also includes the President's Physician, a Personal Secretary and a Social Secretary. The exact nature and role of this group of people depends entirely on the President. He has a completely free hand in their selection. At one extreme they could be merely a set of errand-boys running messages or carrying out routine tasks, but in fact the Special Assistants to the President have become the most coherent group of men in the Administration, taking a major part in the process of innovation and policy-making. John F. Kennedy surrounded himself with a group of talented men from different areas of national life, whose role was described by one of them, Theodore Sorensen, in the following way.

Two dozen or more Kennedy assistants gave him two dozen or more sets of hands, eyes and ears, two dozen or more minds attuned to his own. They could talk with legislators, newsmen, experts, Cabinet members and politicians – serve on inter-departmental task forces – review papers and draft speeches, letters and other documents – spot problems before they were crises and possibilities before they were proposals – screen requests for legislation, Executive Orders, jobs, appointments with the President, patronage and Presidential speeches – and bear his messages, look out for his interests, carry out his orders and make certain his decisions were executed.

The allocation of work among these men is again a matter of Presidential taste. He may ask a Special Assistant to cover a particular field, foreign affairs, defence, or liaison with Congress, or simply use them as generalists or 'trouble-shooters'. The potential importance of these men who are closest to the President lies in the nature of the void that they fill in the system of government, a void which the Cabinet is quite unfitted to fill. With a powerful, dominant personality like that of Kennedy in the President's chair they may be influential but clearly subordinate, but what if the President is not so dominant, or is physically weak? Is there not a danger that a non-elective, non-representative, official or group of officials could wield excessive power? Some critics of the Eisenhower Administration levelled this charge against one member of the President's staff, Sherman Adams. President Eisenhower appointed Adams as 'Assistant to the President', a title which had been created under the Administration of his predecessor, President Truman. Adams was given a broad grant of power which led his critics to label him 'The Assistant President'. Access to the President was channelled through Adams, who saw his function as that of 'Shielding the President from problems that could be settled on the lower echelons', and assuring that work of 'secondary importance' should be kept off the President's desk. Although Adams strongly denied that this position represented in any way a usurpation of Presidential authority, it inevitably meant that it was *his* judgement that determined what was, and was not, of secondary importance.

The relationship of the White House Office to the Cabinet is, therefore, of critical importance. The Cabinet, which should contain the main administrative lieutenants of the President, has been consistently downgraded, and a new, potentially extremely powerful, apparatus has been created around the President. The evolution of this relationship during the ill-fated presidency of Mr Nixon is particularly instructive. On taking office in 1969 President Nixon, concerned with the problem of coordinating government policies in the field of urban affairs and economic policy, created two new important posts in the Administration and two new coordinating bodies. The post of Counsellor to the President was established in the White House Staff, with the prime responsibility of coordinating the development of domestic policies and programmes. The President appointed Dr Arthur Burns to this position, and gave him Cabinet rank, thus putting him at a level never formally held by a member of the White House Staff. The President also appointed to his staff an Assistant to the President for Urban Affairs, Dr D. P. Moynihan. There were created alongside the National Security Council two new Cabinet-level organizations, the Council for Urban Affairs and a Cabinet Committee on Economic Policy. In July 1970 President Nixon effected an even more fundamental change in the relationship between the Cabinet and the Executive Office. A Domestic Council was established in order to co-ordinate the activities of the departments and agencies operating in the domestic field. The Council consists of the President, the Vice-President, and the heads of the departments, with the exception of the Secretaries of State and Defense, but it included also the two members of the White House Staff with the title of Counsellor to the President, as well as other presidential aides and the Chairman of the Council of Economic Advisers. Most of the White House Staff working on domestic affairs were absorbed into the staff of the new Council, which was not intended to operate as a single entity, but to divide into a number of committees each dealing with a particular area of policy. The development had begun of a new kind of 'cabinet', constructed in part out of some members of the traditional Cabinet, and in part out of the White House Staff, who were now to assume formally responsibilities which they had exercised before, if at all, only informally.

At the beginning of his second term, President Nixon pressed on further with this line of development. In January 1973 he announced the establishment of a 'super-cabinet' in which the dividing lines between the Cabinet and the White House Office disappeared almost entirely. Although the 'super-cabinet' was never really to operate because of the vast upheaval of the Watergate affair it is worth some study since some similar structure may yet emerge again in response to the need for coordination at the top of the Federal Government.

Nixon established five Assistants to the President to work under him, 'to integrate and unify policies and operations throughout the executive branch of the Government, and to oversee all of the activities for which the President is responsible'. The five Assistants were H. R. Haldeman (White House Administration,) John D. Ehrlichman (Domestic Affairs), Henry Kissinger (Foreign Affairs), Roy L. Ash (Executive Management), and George P. Schulz (Economic Affairs). Schulz, to be appointed an Assistant to the President in the White House Office, was to retain his Cabinet post as Secretary of the Treasury. Three other Cabinet members, in the field of domestic policy, were to be given broad coordinating functions over their Cabinet colleagues and other divisions of the Administration. These three members of the Cabinet were also to become members of the White House Staff as Counsellors to the President and to become chairmen of the committees of the Domestic Council dealing with their area of policy. Furthermore, the three domestic coordinators were to report to the President through Assistant to the President John Ehrlichman.

How this system would have worked had it not disappeared in the Watergate holocaust it is impossible to say. It is significant, however, that it formed the White House Office and the Cabinet into a single hierarchy of control under the President, and so blurred the distinction between Cabinet members and presidential Assistants that it hardly seemed any longer a guide to the significance of an individual – what was important was his position in the hierarchy. Since taking office President Ford has returned to the pre-Nixon relationship between Cabinet and White House Office; naturally enough the changes which Nixon introduced so soon before his downfall have been associated with his abuse of the power of the presidency – nevertheless the essential problem of coordination at the centre of the American Administration remains.

THE NATIONAL SECURITY COUNCIL

The conduct of defence policy presents special problems for the American Administration. The President is Commander-in-chief, and as in other fields the final decisions are his, but the unity of command implicit in this constitutional principle must be translated into reality in an extremely large and diffuse government machine. The Cabinet, as we have seen, is of no use for this purpose, and as a result Congress created a special 'defence cabinet' in 1947, the National Security Council. The Council has the duty to 'consider policies on matters of common interest to the departments and agencies of the government concerned with the national security and to make recommendations to the President'. It is composed of the President, Vice-President, Secretary of State, Secretary of Defense and Director of the Office of Emergency Planning. Other officials, such as the Joint Chiefs of Staff, may be asked to attend its meetings. Under President Eisenhower the Council met frequently to discuss current problems of foreign policy, the staff prepared policy papers to keep the members of the Council abreast of new developments in matters such as weapon technology, and there was a complete sub-structure of inter-departmental committees. Under Presidents Kennedy and Johnson, however, the Council met less frequently, problems being dealt with much more by the President in collaboration with groups of advisers. Like the Cabinet itself, the National Security Council cannot make decisions for the President, but only provide him with the information and advice on which to base his decisions. Certainly it would seem that few major decisions at times of crisis have actually been made in the Council. Under the control of the National

Security Council, nominally at least, is the Central Intelligence
Agency. Its major function is to coordinate the intelligence
activities of the government and to evaluate the intelligence that
is received. However, in the wake of the Watergate scandal, dis-
closures about CIA activities led to investigations of its activities
by Vice-President Rockefeller, and by Congress. The extraordinary
revelations of its operations, culminating in bizarre, James Bond-
like plots to assassinate foreign heads of State raise profound
questions about the nature of the American governmental
machine. Whether CIA activities are characteristic of the secret
services of other States we cannot know – they do not allow their
legislatures to investigate secret activities in the way in which
Congress has done. The more important question, however, is
the extent to which these almost unbelievable plots were evolved
with or without the knowledge of responsible members of the
Administration. The fragmented nature of the American administrative machine will be stressed later in this book, and the problems to which it gives rise are well-known. However what is
merely 'uncoordinated action' in one part of the Government
machine can in another lead the whole world into disaster.

THE OFFICE OF MANAGEMENT AND BUDGET

The problem of financial control in the American system is a
difficult one indeed – Congress is jealous of its prerogatives, and
the departments of the Administration use all their guile to retain
the maximum possible financial autonomy. The instrument
which the President uses to maintain control over the financial
operations of the government is the Office of Management and
Budget. It is important to realize that the United States Treasury
Department is very different in function from the British Treasury or most other European Finance Ministries. The U.S. Treasury has never had the role of supervising in detail the
expenditures of government departments, or of relating government expenditures in general to government revenues. Before
1921, indeed, there was no national executive budget (a term
which is applied to proposed expenditures, not to proposed taxation). Each department prepared its estimates for submission to

Congress and the duty of the Secretary of the Treasury was simply to compile them into a single book of estimates. In 1921 the Budget and Accounting Act provided that the President should submit an annual budget of the United States to Congress, and it established the Bureau of the Budget to aid him. The Bureau was nominally established in the Treasury Department, but the Act provided that the Director of the Bureau should report directly to the President and be responsible to him. This rather anomalous position was ended in 1939 when the Bureau was transferred to the newly-created Executive Office.

The Act of 1921 gave to the Bureau the authority 'to assemble, correlate, revise, reduce, or increase the requests for appropriations of the several departments and establishments'. As a result of its strategic position in regard to finance, and the fact that its functions involved it in the activities of all the agencies of the Executive branch, the Bureau was the natural instrument for Presidential attempts to coordinate the activities of the Administration and to promote administrative efficiency. So in addition to its functions in relation to the preparation and administration of the budget, the Bureau was charged with the task of conducting research into better administrative management and advising the departments upon better administrative organization and accounting practices, of coordinating departmental advice on proposed legislation, and with the coordination and improvement of the government's statistical activities. In July 1970 the Bureau of the Budget was absorbed into the newly established Office of Management and Budget in the Executive Office of the President.

Potentially the Office of Management and Budget is the most powerful coordinating device available to the President. It has knowledge of, and extensive contracts with, every part of the administrative machine. Its power to revise estimates is ultimately the power over policy. The head of the Office has direct access to the President, and at the same time his major responsibility is to see that Presidential policy is carried through. However, the practical significance of the Office must be assessed within the political and administrative context in which it operates. It is unlikely ever to have the degree of control over executive departments that the British Treasury wields, simply because the American administrative machine is much more loosely knit. Furthermore, the power of its head ultimately depends upon the extent to which the President is prepared actively to back him up. If a President is determined to use the Office as an instrument of policy, rather than as a mere accounting device, and if he makes it clear to his subordinates that he will uphold the Office point of view, then control over the estimates can become a reality. But with the best will in the world a President inevitably faces the difficulty that he has only a part of his time to devote to these matters, and for its head it becomes a political problem of how far, and how often, he can appeal for direct Presidential support in conflicts with departments. Finally, of course, the Office has to take account of Congress, and of the influence wielded by Chairmen of committees over the bureaux and agencies of the government, and on their behalf. The head of the Office, and the President too, must live with the knowledge that Congress *might* reverse their decisions. They do not, therefore, have the same authority in the settlement of disputes within the Administration that a Chancellor of the Exchequer has in the British administrative machine, for the latter is virtually certain that Parliament will pass the estimates in the form that he decides.

THE COUNCIL OF ECONOMIC ADVISERS

The function of the Office of Management and Budget is to control and coordinate the activities of government through the supervision of departmental expenditures, but modern governments must concern themselves with economic policy in a wider context. They must attempt, at whatever level of sophistication, to control the general direction and pace of economic development, to control inflation, prevent slumps, and sustain economic growth. The broad acceptance of this philosophy by Congress in the immediate post-war period led to the passage of the Employment Act of 1946, which set up the Council of Economic Advisers. The function of the Council is to advise the President on future economic trends, to develop and recommend to him policies which will 'promote maximum employment, production and purchasing power', to conduct studies of the economy and to recommend legislation which will contribute to this aim. The Council, consisting of a Chairman and two other members, together with a large staff, has the task of preparing for the President an Annual Economic Report for presentation to the Congress, setting out the Administration's view of what is likely to happen during the year in the economic sphere, and making recommendations on economic policy. Even more perhaps than other parts of the Presidential entourage the Council must be seen essentially as an advisory body. It has been described as the 'economic conscience' of the Administration, serving as a counter-weight to the Treasury Department and the Office of Management and Budget with their more restricted, and more immediate responsibilities. Undoubtedly it has served as an invaluable educative influence on Presidents and their staffs, working for more flexible and foresighted economic policies. It has meant that the influence of skilled economists has been brought to bear right at the apex of the American administrative machine.

THE PROBLEM OF THE PRESIDENCY

In September 1974 Richard Nixon became the first President of the United States to resign from office. He did so after it became clear that he would be impeached if he did not resign, and after some of the most extraordinary events in the history of the United States had taken place, events which were revealed, in the most exhaustive detail, to the whole world by newspaper and congressional investigations. An attempt will be made to put this, the lowest point ever reached by the institution of the Presidency, into perspective in the final chapter of this book. Here we are concerned to explore the nature of Presidential power, its extent, its bases, and its limitations. Recent events have given a bizarre colouration to this picture, but the underlying nature of the problem of the Presidency remains the same.

The central problem of the Presidency is its solitary character. The Cabinet rarely acts in any collective sense, and the final burden of decision-taking, or of the extent to which he will abdicate

it to others, rests upon the shoulders of one man. The creation of
the Executive Office in 1939 initially eased this problem, but now
it can be seen to have created new and perhaps more fundamental
problems. What then is the nature of this power that the President wields?

PRESIDENTIAL POWER

There are two rather contradictory statements used to describe
Presidential power. On the one hand it is asserted that the President of the United States is the most powerful elected official in
the world; on the other hand it is argued that the power of the
President is, in effect, simply the power to persuade. As we have
seen his power certainly is hemmed in by constitutional boundaries, but it is a mistake to try to characterize the power of the
President in a single, well-turned epigram. The reality is much
more complex. We are now in a position to analyse the nature of
Presidential power, and to explore its boundaries. Of course, we
cannot say anything about the nature or extent of Presidential
power in any *particular* future situation, for so much must
depend upon the exact circumstances, or upon the nature of
public opinion at the time: what is unthinkable at one moment
may be practical politics the next. What we can do is to define
the parameters of Presidential power, the constants within
which it must develop and be exercised according to the political
context. We can in fact distinguish three sets of conditions of
this sort, which overlap and combine into differing qualities of
potential power. Given a certain level of public and party support, therefore, the potential power of the President will vary
according to the way in which these factors add up in a particular instance.

THE PARAMETERS OF POWER

The potential power of the President to act will vary in the
following ways:

1. (a) If the action involves persuading Congress to confer new statutory powers on the Administration

(b) If the action can be taken under an existing Congressional statute

(c) If the action can be brought within one of the directly granted constitutional powers of the President

2. (a) If the action depends entirely upon the immediate appropriation of money by the Congress

(b) If the action requires the appropriation of money by Congress in the relatively near future

(c) If the action requires no exenditure of money other than the normal running expenses of the Administration

3. (a) If the action lies in the field of domestic policy

(b) If it lies in the field of diplomacy

(c) If it involves the exercise of military power.

Thus *with a given level of popular support* one can generalize that the potential power of the President will be least if he must persuade Congress to grant him new powers before he can act, if the required action needs the appropriation of money, and if it is in the field of domestic policy; his potential power will be the greatest if he can act independently of Congressional approval, in an area requiring little or no immediate expenditure of money and in the field of his responsibilities as Commander-in-Chief. In between these extremes there will be a number of diffrent degrees of potential power according to the combination of factors involved.

The President and the Administration exercise enormous statutory powers granted by Congress over the years. In the mid twentieth century this authority extends into a wide variety of fields of activity, touching the lives of every citizen of the United States. Every statutory authority granted to the Administration is potentially a weapon of Presidential policy, for powers originally granted for one purpose can sometimes be turned to the support of other policies. Furthermore, the authority granted by Congress may be used to the hilt or drawn upon very little. The way in which the Administration uses its powers depends in the last resort on the President. Thus the power to help Negroes to exercise their rights as voters may be very actively pursued, or allowed to languish. It is the President who will instruct the Attorney-General to pursue one policy or another, or at least give the latter support either in his actions or his inaction. In almost every field of government activity there are such powers which can be implemented in differing ways. Furthermore, the modern Administration has a considerable reservoir of delegated power, the power to fill in the administrative details of legislation, and to legislate itself within the authority granted by Congress. The principle of delegated legislative power, which seems on its face to offend against the doctrine of the separation of powers, has long been accepted by the judiciary, provided that the grant of power is not so wide as to be invalid through vagueness or is incapable of being policed by the courts. However, there are, clearly, limits to these possibilities. The Administration is bound by the law and must justify its acts if challenged in the courts, so that where there is doubt, or where a quite new programme is to be initiated, the President and his colleagues must go to Congress and persuade them with whatever means they have at their disposal of the need for further legislation.

Even when explicit powers have been granted to the Administration, however, the President's position is not wholly secure. What has been given can be taken away, and the Congressional grant of power may have been explicitly hedged with all manner of conditions and limitations. The President's potential power is greatest, therefore, in those areas where he has the independent power to act, based directly upon the Constitution, although in practice these constitutional powers will usually have been filled out and augmented by Federal legislation. Most of these powers are to be found in the field of military affairs and diplomacy, but they also have internal aspects. The President can call the State militia, the National Guard, into Federal service and use them to maintain law and order, usually, but not always, at the invitation of the Governor of a State. The President can use Federal Marshals or, in an extreme case, Federal troops to enforce Federal law and the decisions of the courts. The intervention of President Eisenhower in Little Rock, Arkansas, in 1957, and of President Kennedy in Alabama in 1961 and in Mississippi the following year, are good examples. From time to time Presidents have claimed 'prerogative powers' to act without statutory authority where the safety of the nation is involved, usually, it is true, moving quickly to gain *ex post facto* Congressional approval of their actions.

All these, then, are ways in which the President's potential power is dependent upon the extent to which he has existing authority to act, and upon the basis of that authority. But this is not the only dimension. The problem of finance must be considered. An existing authority, statutory or constitutional, is of little significance if the money to implement it is not forthcoming. Some statutory powers can be exercised with little or no expenditure of money, whilst others require large appropriations by Congress before they can be implemented. Congress keeps quite distinct the two operations of *authorizing* a programme and *appropriating* money for it. It is by no means unknown for it to do the former and to baulk at the latter. Furthermore, Congress insists upon the annual appropriation of funds, although the authority to pursue a particular policy may have been on the statute book for many years, so that the Administration must continually justify its demands and persuade Congress to give it the money it needs. Thus the use of Federal troops or of the National Guard to maintain order is a very different *financial* proposition from running an anti-poverty programme, even though the latter has been fully approved by Congress. Similarly, the decision to implement the Voting Rights Act with greater vigour may initially involve only a redeployment of the resources of the Department of Justice, but in the long run it will depend upon congressional willingness to maintain a large force of attorneys and Federal Marshals.

The third dimension of presidential power is the arena in which action is contemplated. The general considerations set out above about the character of the sources of power, and the financial implications of policy decisions, apply to the fields of domestic and foreign policy alike, and also to the problems of the military sector. Thus the foreign aid programme is one where congressional control is felt very strongly, because of the need both for statutory authorization, and for the annual appropriation of large sums of money. But there are a number of considerations which tend to enhance the power of the President when he moves from strictly domestic concerns into the field of foreign affairs, and even more so when he is concerned as Commander-in-Chief of the armed forces rather than as chief diplomat. These considerations overlap our first category of the nature of the sources of power, for in the area of foreign relations the President has far more directly granted powers to conduct the diplomatic affairs of the nation. The major restriction upon him, apart from the financial question, is the requirement that treaties must be ratified by a two-thirds majority of the Senate, but since the refusal of the Senate to ratify the treaty of Versailles, Presidents have resorted much more to the use of 'executive agreements' with foreign countries which do not require ratification.

But the major difference between the diplomatic and domestic roles of the President is that he is strategically in a much more powerful position in foreign affairs *in relation to internal American political forces*. His role of national leader is here most potent, and his claim to represent the whole nation against sectional forces the most persuasive. As the President, and only the President, must make the final decisions in matters of foreign policy there is a natural tendency to allow him to know best in this field. It does not mean of course that his decisions will not be challenged and indeed hotly contested in some quarters; but there is almost the presupposition in the attitude of the general public that the President should be supported. This attitude is buttressed by patriotic sentiments, which can be extremely powerful in American politics, which suggest that the President should be supported when under attack from foreigners. Thus it is possible for the President to move with greater freedom in this area, partly because of his original rather than derived powers, partly because of the initial strength from which he starts. Furthermore, in the field of foreign affairs the institutional power of the Presidency carries most weight. In internal affairs the President must function much more as a broker between contending interests, and the machinery of Presidential decision-making is very closely bound up with the interest-group structure. There are interest groups in foreign affairs of course, some very important, but their significance is much less than in internal affairs. The information and advice which the President gets from his White House advisers, from Cabinet members and from officials, will therefore be of greater significance than in the domestic field.

Thus the overwhelming difference between external affairs and internal politics is the potential power of the President to commit the country to a course of action, which, once embarked upon, is extremely difficult to repudiate or reverse. The President's powers as Commander-in-Chief are the extreme example of this. By being able to order American troops to take up positions abroad, or even to commit them to hostilities, he can present the Congress, and the people, with a *fait accompli*, where they must choose between repudiating their President, and so perhaps endangering their own men, or supporting his actions. This still remains true in an emergency situation, notwithstanding the War Powers Resolution of 1973.

THE TWENTY-SECOND AMENDMENT

The growth of Presidential power in this century, and in particular in the period 1932–45, has called forth a large volume of criticism and demands that it should be curbed. There have been two major lines of attack, one unsuccessful, the Bricker Amendment, and the other a successful move, the Twenty-Second Amendment to the Constitution. The latter is aimed at the tenure of office of popular Presidents. The length of the President's tenure of office is a matter of great importance for his power and influence. An incumbent President is in a strong position (though not an impregnable one) to gain re-nomination and re-election. As we have seen, the ability of a President to secure agreement for his policies depends very much upon a number of factors involving the use of his position as party leader and national leader, as well as his constitutional and statutory powers. If it is known that the end of his period of office is in sight much of the President's armoury falls away from him. Soon someone else will be wielding his powers and dispensing his patronage. It is true that even late in his term of office the President's position is still awesome enough to give him considerable influence in his own party – witness the way in which President Johnson was apparently able to affect the decisions on the party platform at the Chicago Convention in 1968 – but his ability to secure congressional support for his policies inevitably declines as his term nears its end. The influence of an incumbent President will therefore be likely to be greater as long as there is a chance that he will run again for election.

Given the power and prestige of the incumbent in the White House there has been a persistent fear, throughout the history of the Union, that a strong President might try to make himself into a permanent President through continual re-election, and attain a position not far removed from that of a dictator. However unreal this likelihood might seem, it has been a continual fear which has increased in some quarters during the present century as a consequence of the growth of power of the President. The Founders of the Constitution decided against writing into that document a limitation upon the number of terms the President might serve, but President Washington, who of all Presidents might have hoped for life tenure of the office, declined to stand again when he had almost completed his second term, explicitly warning against the dangers of too long a period of office. This attitude hardened into a two-term tradition which remained unbroken until 1940, although Presidents who had been elected for two terms persistently hoped for a third term of office, None, however, was successful until President Franklin Roosevelt, a man of unrivalled popularity in a time of great tension, was nominated for a third term, and four years later for yet another. This remarkable achievement, together with the fears that Roosevelt's policies engendered, led, after the war, to demands for curbs on Presidential power. The Republican-dominated Eightieth Congress in 1947 proposed an Amendment to the Constitution limiting Presidents to two terms. It was ratified in 1951 and became the Twenty-Second Amendment. It is as yet difficult to assess the significance of the Amendment, as it has so far been a limitation in principle only on the re-nomination of President Eisenhower for a third term, and he had no wish to run. Potentially, however, it has the effect of diminishing the influence and authority in his second term of the most effective of Presidents, for it removes whatever doubt might have remained of the likelihood of his running for a third term. It may also have a potentially more drastic effect upon the term of office of a Vice-President who succeeds to the Presidency. A Vice-President who succeeds to the Presidency and serves more than two years of the unexpired term (presumably even if only a few hours more), cannot be elected to the office in his own right more than once. Almost as soon as he is elected the speculation will begin about his successor.

The other attempt to limit the President's power was first introduced into Congress in 1951 by Senator John Bricker of Ohio, who proposed to amend the Constitution in order to subject executive agreements made by the President to the same control by the Senate as treaties, and to ensure that treaties would not be enforceable except through Federal legislation, which would be subject to the same constitutional limitations as other legislation. The Bricker amendment was proposed to Congress in a number of forms, and a much less restrictive Amendment was proposed by Senator Walter George in 1954, but none of them was successful in gaining the necessary two-thirds majority in Congress.

*

The Presidency is then the centre of the American political system, an institution that concentrates great power in the hands of one man, but which subjects him also to the humiliations of utter defeat; it is a single point in a great sea of ever-moving, ever-changing political forces of the most varied character, which threaten to engulf and beat him down, but a point which provides him with the one central, stable focus of authority to enable him, for some time at least, to dominate, to lead, and to innovate.

Politics
and the
Administration

8

So far we have been concerned largely with the complex manoeuvres and manipulations related to the formulation of government policy through its various stages, from the electoral process to the point where President and Congress issue their authoritative decisions. All of this has been eminently 'political', but in this chapter we turn to an area in which the importance of political influences is just as great but not so obvious. *Administration* may suggest simply the putting into effect of decisions taken elsewhere, and some civil servants and reformers in the past have argued that politics and administration should be kept in quite distinct compartments. According to this view the civil service should simply be the neutral instrument of the democratically elected politicians, and it should not itself have a policy-determining role. There have been attempts in the United States to implement this view, in particular in the case of those agencies which have been given regulatory functions in the industrial and commercial field. The proponents of this view argue that the only function of the bureaucracy, once its goals have been set for it, is to pursue them with the maximum efficiency, free from the considerations of personal gain or political advantage which would cloud their judgement or affect their behaviour if they were involved in any way in political intrigues.

But this simple view of the nature of administration just will not do. The executive is deeply involved in politics at many levels. Much of the legislation which eventually is enacted into law is first formulated in the departments and agencies of the government, and pressure-groups and members of Congress are of course well aware of this and may attempt to influence Administration proposals at a very early stage. The exact way in which the constitutional and statutory powers of the government are exercised may make a very considerable difference to these policies in practice, because so much discretion is inevitably left to those who implement the law. The officials who form the Administration may well be overtly involved in politics both by attempting to influence Congress in matters relating to their agencies, particularly appropriations, and by being influenced by Congressmen in the way they carry out their administrative duties. Furthermore, the departments of the government may battle with each other where their interests, or the interests of their 'clients' conflict, and even within a single department such conflicts may arise and become very sharp indeed. Thus the idea that the administrative agencies of government can be isolated from political problems is a chimera, and in America there are a number of social and political factors which increase the extent to which the officials of the government may become involved in political issues.

Nevertheless the demand for efficiency in government is a continuing and powerful force for reform, and it must be admitted that, up to a point, the demand that administration should be 'taken out of politics' has improved the quality and the performance of the Federal bureaucracy. But how far should it be taken? If the administrative machine is too insulated from the political battle might it not become out of touch with the needs and aspirations of the people? In a democracy should not the civil service be representative of, and responsive to, all the differing interests and points of view that make up the society? And if the President is to get his policies effectively translated into actions is it not essential that those who actually direct this work should be fired with enthusiasm both for him and his policies? This tension between 'technical efficiency' and 'democracy' can be seen throughout the working of the American governmental machine, and the exact balance which has been struck is the subject of the present chapter.

THE STRUCTURE OF THE ADMINISTRATION

The major characteristics of the American political system, which we have seen working their way through every aspect of the structure, have their impact also upon the organization and operation of the executive branch of government. Indeed, rather than presenting a picture of a unified, hierarchical, highly co-ordinated administrative machine, the American Administration is decentralized, fragmented, some might say almost anarchic. The separation of powers as it has evolved in its American version, far from creating an administrative instrument subservient to the Presidential will, has in practice given to Congress the power, and the inclination, to 'interfere' in the day-to-day working of the Administration. The structure of the federal system, necessitating as it does that the Federal Administration must work with State and local officials across the continent, subjects the operation of the machinery of the Federal government to a great variety of pressures which are felt both by the bulk of civil servants, most of whom work outside Washington, and by those executives who have to cope with the Senators, Congressmen, Governors, and State and local politicians who flock to the capital to put their views to the President and his subordinates. In fact, the pluralism of American politics is amply reflected in the structure and practice of the Administration.

The administrative apparatus of the Federal Government is divided up into three broad categories – the Executive Departments and agencies, the independent agencies, and government corporations.

THE EXECUTIVE DEPARTMENTS

As we have seen, the President's Cabinet is composed largely of the heads of the Executive Departments, and these form the core of the Administration, the part most under his control. They have gradually increased in number as the functions of government have expanded – in 1789 the Federal Government was inaugurated with the Department of State, the Treasury Department and the Department of War. President Washington included the Attorney-General in his Cabinet, but the department which the latter leads today, the Department of Justice, was not created until 1870. In 1798 the Department of the Navy was added, and with the Department of War was the continuing focus of much inter-departmental service rivalry. The emergence of the Air Force in the twentieth century was not acknowledged with departmental status until 1947, when it was detached from the Army, but only two years later all three service departments were subordinated to the newly-created Department of Defense. The Secretary of Defense became a member of the Cabinet and although the service departments continue to be called such, and have Secretaries at their head, these officers are not in the Cabinet. The Postmaster-General became a member of the Cabinet in 1829, but the Post Office became a fully-fledged Executive Department only in 1872. In July 1971, however, the Post Office was turned into a government corporation and the Postmaster General no longer has cabinet rank. The other departments set up in the nineteenth century were Interior, in 1849, and Agriculture, in 1889. The twentieth century, however, has seen the addition of no fewer than five Executive Departments, in addition to the Defense Department, reflecting the great expansion of government functions. A Department of Commerce and Labor was created in 1903, and then divided into the Department of Commerce and the Department of Labor in 1913. The government activity resulting from the New Deal policies of President Roosevelt during the 1930s meant the creation of numerous agencies and commissions, some squarely within the executive branch, others with a greater degree of independence; but no new Executive Departments were created during this period. In 1953, however, many of the agencies which had been created to administer social security and welfare programmes were amalgamated into a new department, the Department of Health, Education and Welfare. Other urgent problems facing the Federal Government were acknowledged by the creation of the Department of Housing and Urban Development in 1965, and in 1966 Congress authorized the setting up of the Department of Transportation.

The attainment of full Departmental status with a seat in the Cabinet represents for most of the Departments the culmination of a long process of the creation and amalgamation of lesser agencies and bureaux, sometimes as part of other Departments, sometimes as independent executive agencies directly responsible to the President. Some have gone through a complex process of development; for example, a Bureau of Labor was created in 1884 as part of the Department of the Interior. It later became an independent agency, but not of Department status, only to lose its independence as part of the Department of Commerce and Labor, and finally to re-emerge in 1913 as a fully-fledged Department of Labor. At any one time, therefore, a number of very important agencies may operate outside the structure of the Departments, headed by an Administrator or Director who is responsible to the President and not to a Cabinet officer. Some of these agencies may be very large and important, for example the Veterans Administration, or the National Aeronautics and Space Administration. From time to time the amalgamation of agencies into a Department tends to simplify the general structure of the Administration, but there are always a number of such independent agencies, and there is a continual pressure to create new ones to solve *ad hoc* problems as they arise.

In form the Departments follow a hierarchical pattern, with the Secretary at the head, supported by an Under Secretary or Deputy Secretary. The major administrative sections of the Department are headed by Assistant Secretaries, and below these are the operative units of the Department, the bureaux or offices, headed by a Director or a Chief. This level of bureau chief is a critical one in the Administration. Many of them are career officials, whilst above this level nearly all are political appointments. Yet the bureau chiefs become the focus of political pressure by Congressmen or lobbyists because it is at this level that the vital operative decisions are taken. Indeed, the apparently straightforward chain of command from the President downwards is highly misleading. The President can, in most cases, obtain compliance from his subordinates in the Departments provided that he has the time, the energy, and the information to exercise such control. But clearly he cannot be everywhere at once, and the nature of the Cabinet hardly makes it an effective coordinating body. Indeed some Presidents have encouraged conflict within the Administration as a means of ensuring their own pre-eminence, or to help work out within the administrative structure the different political problems with which it must contend. But conflict is by no means confined to relationships *between* Departments. The apparently monolithic structure of the Department is deceptive. Many bureaux are relatively independent of higher control, both formally and in practice. Two outstanding instances are the Federal Bureau of Investigation in the Department of Justice and the U.S. Corps of Engineers in the Department of the Army.

Congress has contributed to the fragmentation of power in the Administration by reinforcing the powers and independence of bureaux. It has given specific authority by statute to bureau chiefs to exercise powers independently of the control of President or Secretary; it has written detailed administrative procedures into law which may make the practice of a bureau quite different from the rest of the Department; and it has 'interfered' in the working of Departments by appropriating money in such detail that the head of the Department has little discretion over the way in which his Department uses its funds. The committees of Congress, or at least their chairmen, tend to develop direct relationships with the bureau chiefs, and the latter may use the political leverage given by the support of influential Congressmen and Senators against the authority of their superiors in the Administration. Thus the political problems involved in the implementation of policy may well prevent the exercise of effective control by the President or his immediate subordinates over the detailed operation of their own administrative machine. The fragmentive effect of politics on the Administration has considerable impact upon the Departments, at its core, where Presidential control is theoretically at its greatest, but the diffusion of authority and power goes much further than this, for in a number of vitally important fields of government action Congress has deliberately decreased the power of the President by setting up agencies which are very much more free of direct supervision, the Independent Regulatory Commissions.

THE INDEPENDENT REGULATORY COMMISSIONS

The Regulatory Commissions have been described as a 'headless fourth branch' of the United States government. These powerful and important bodies are *in* the executive branch, but not *of* it.

They carry out functions laid down in statute, but have a very complex set of formal and informal relationships with President and Congress of a quite different kind from the normal Executive Departments. The Commissions perform a wide range of regulatory functions over major areas of industrial and commercial life. They fix rates and fares, grant licences to common carriers, and television and radio stations, regulate business practices and labour relations. In the field of transport the Interstate Commerce Commission regulates the railways and bus and road transport, the Civil Aeronautics Board licenses and regulates airlines, and the Federal Maritime Commission sets rates and controls the practices of the shipping industry. The Federal Communications Commission deals with the enormously complex problem of the operations of radio and television stations and other communications media; the Federal Trade Commission has a general oversight of business practices including unfair and restrictive practices, control of advertising and labelling of goods, and a number of other aspects of business regulation. The National Labor Relations Board regulates the whole field of collective bargaining, supervising the activities of trade unions, preventing 'unfair labor practices', conducting secret ballots among employees to determine who shall represent them, and dealing with jurisdictional disputes between unions. Public utilities are regulated by the Federal Power Commission and the Atomic Energy Commission, and the whole field of banking and finance is dealt with by the Federal Reserve System and the Securities and Exchange Commission.

Congress has placed this enormous amount of regulatory power over the economic life of the country in the hands of a number of Commissions whose authority is derived from statute and whose responsibility to the President is far from clear. Any President is bound to be concerned with the way in which these bodies regulate economic life, but what power has he over them? Each of the Commissions is headed by a board, averaging five members, who are appointed by the President for fixed terms of office. Thus when a new President takes office he will be faced with a whole complex of agencies whose heads have been appointed by his predecessor. It may be two or three years before the process of retirement enables him to appoint a majority of members of each of the Commissions. Furthermore, he does not have the power to dismiss these men, as he does in the normal Executive Departments. This was settled by the Supreme Court in 1935, when it ruled in the case of *Humphrey's Executor v. U.S.* that President Roosevelt did not have the power to dismiss a member of the Federal Trade Commission appointed by President Hoover, except on the grounds of 'inefficiency, neglect of duty, or malfeasance'. This view was reiterated by the Court in 1958. However, it must be noted also that the turnover among members of the Commissions is very high, and a President will not have to wait till all the members have completed their terms of office before their posts fall vacant. One further limitation on the President written into the legislation regulating the composition of the Commissions is the requirement that the members should be drawn from both political parties.

Why did Congress set up agencies enjoying this degree of independence? Undoubtedly there were a number of motives. A desire to place limits to the increasing power of the President during the New Deal period, when some of the major Commissions were established, no doubt played a part, but there were other and more complex reasons. In one sense the Regulatory Commissions were the response to a new type of industrial society and to the unprecedented role which the government was called upon to play in regulating the economic affairs of private industry. It was felt necessary to break away from the traditional machinery of government, with its normal division into three parts, and to create a new instrument for this purpose which would be an industrial pattern of organization to meet the needs of an industrial society. Another reason for making these Commissions independent was the fact that they are by no means simply 'executive' agencies. Their regulatory role requires that they should make regulations, that is exercise a rule-making power, that they should decide in a judicial fashion whether these rules were being broken in particular cases, and also that they should administer and police the rules. Thus in lawyers' language, in addition to their administrative functions, they exercised quasi-legislative and quasi-judicial powers. These reasons reinforced the point of view of those who believed that it was time administration was taken out of politics and recognized as a distinct technique, which could be objectively and efficiently applied to the solution of largely technical problems.

However, the hope that agencies whose decisions could make fortunes for some and deny them to others, and which might affect the whole economic climate of the nation, could be insulated from politics, was inevitably still-born. Presidents have made strenuous attempts to exercise a much closer control over the Commissions than Congress ever intended. As we have seen, the turnover of membership is such that the President is able to make many more appointments during his term than was envisaged. The President's power to re-appoint members might influence their behaviour, and other influences can be brought to bear. President Eisenhower's Assistant, Sherman Adams, when asked whether he had found it necessary to ask commissioners to hand in their resignations, replied, 'If you insist on the question I should have to answer it in the affirmative'. Professor Bernard Schwartz has provided a great deal of evidence of the informal links between the White House and the Commissions, and it can also be shown that members of Congress have brought pressure to bear on the Commissions in much the same way, using the ultimate legislative power of Congress over the Commissions as the threat to gain compliance. Nevertheless, pressures from President and Congress, however they might conflict with the theory behind the Commission form of government, are perhaps more to be excused than the pressures which come from those being regulated: business and labour interests. A few cases of actual corruption have come to light, but the problem is more one of the personal relationships between the men who make decisions on the Commissions and those who can offer them much higher rewards in industry when they leave their government posts. There are examples, perfectly legal, of serving members of the Commissions openly offering their expertise to the highest bidder. Thus the Commissions are neither truly independent, nor subject to the control and direction of the President to the extent that is the case in the Executive Departments. They disappoint those who would like to see them making their decisions free from all pressures, and equally those who believe that a President should have effective control of his Administration's economic policy.

GOVERNMENT CORPORATIONS

It should already be clear that *laissez-faire*, if that be interpreted as complete non-interference by government in economic affairs, is certainly not characteristic of the United States. Extensive regulation of many aspects of economic life is undertaken by the American government, but there is yet another administrative dimension to add to the executive departments and the independent regulatory commissions – the government corporations. Whilst it is true that the United States has strictly avoided the nationalization of private industry that has taken place in Britain and elsewhere, the Federal Government has nevertheless become involved in conducting numerous activities which are commercial or industrial in nature, and for this purpose the corporation has been chosen as the appropriate form to enable these activities to be carried out according to the dictates of commercial or industrial needs. It was intended in this way to give to those directing public enterprises the same sort of freedom to act, the same flexibility, which directors of private enterprises enjoy. The best known of these corporations are the Tennessee Valley Authority, the Saint Lawrence Seaway Development Corporation, and the Panama Canal Company, but there are many others and their combined turnover runs into many billions of dollars anually.

However, as with public corporations in Britain, the attempt to give the necessary autonomy to government corporations to run their affairs along purely commercial lines has not been wholly successful. The corporations have been subjected to increasing legislative and administrative supervision, and the passage of the Government Corporation Control Act of 1945 integrated them more closely into the normal machinery of the Executive branch.

*

This then is the general picture of the administrative machinery of American government. As we have seen it is a complex organization which has grown in a haphazard and sporadic fashion. In recent years the 'Great Society' programmes of President Johnson's Administration added new accretions to the system, and its growth continues. The problem of coordination and control that this structure presents has increasingly been the subject of study by academic students of government and administration, and by government commissions. Before we turn, however, to their recommendations we must look at another aspect of the administrative machine, the characteristics of the civil service.

THE FEDERAL CIVIL SERVICE

We have seen some of the structural problems that the development of 'big government' has created in the United States. The same dilemmas are reflected in the field of the personnel of the Federal Government. How far should 'politics' enter into the choice and promotion of those who must run the government? Is 'efficient government' best served by utilizing the services only of neutral, career civil servants or by politically committed men who will whole-heartedly dedicate themselves to Presidential policies? In the early years of the Union, President Washington attempted to establish that ability should be the major criterion of appointment to office under the Federal Government, provided that loyalty to the new Constitution was ensured. Succeeding Presidents, who like Washington were 'aristocrats', broadly followed his example, although Thomas Jefferson, after taking office in 1801, ensured that the Republicans were well represented in the Federal service to an extent that his Federalist predecessors had not. In 1829, however, with the election of Andrew Jackson as a 'man of the people', a different principle of making appointments was explicitly recognized. Jackson claimed the right to reshape the civil service to conform more closely to the composition of American society, and to remove from office the 'unfaithful or incompetent'. The era of the 'spoils system' had begun. The justification of political appointment to government jobs was that the civil servants must be in sympathy with the policies of the Administration, but at the same time the triumph of the spoils system was the result of a grass roots political movement which aimed at using the government service as a means of maintaining political power through patronage at State and local level, and then in the Federal government. Although the spoils system is today much reduced in its overall impact on the structure of government, these two rather mixed motives continue to play a part in the way in which the system is operated. It is a means of satisfying the demands of the party faithful, and at the same time assuring that an important part of the civil service is strongly motivated towards supporting the President, either out of personal loyalty and gratitude, or because they believe passionately in his policies.

During the mid nineteenth century the spoils system became firmly established and increased in importance. When Lincoln took office in 1861 he made almost a clean sweep of the top-level positions and his successors generally followed suit. In the post-Civil War period there was a rising tide of corruption, which became associated with the patronage system, and as a result there developed a demand for reform of the civil service, and in particular for the introduction of a 'merit system' of appointment and promotion. After a number of abortive measures, including the appointment of a short-lived Civil Service Commission in 1871, the Civil Service Act of 1883 (the Pendleton Act) was passed into law. This legislation, which forms the basis of the present civil service system, was essentially an adaptation of the English system of recruitment and tenure established as a result of the Northcote-Trevelyan Report and the Macaulay Report of 1854. The Pendleton Act established a Civil Service Commission to conduct competitive examinations for entry to the service and gave a degree of security of tenure to civil servants. However, the Americans did not follow the British precedent altogether. The American examinations were to be 'practical in character', unlike the system which emerged from the English reports, with its emphasis on languages and mathematics. The American system provided also for freedom of entry to the service at all levels. Only certain classes of employees were included in the new merit system, representing initially only ten per cent of the total Federal civil servants, the rest remaining under the patronage system.

In that part of the civil service untouched by the reforms the spoils system continued with undiminished vigour, but the gradual classification of positions on a merit basis had extended to over forty per cent by the turn of the century. By 1932 the process of reform had progressed to the point where eighty per cent of the service was taken out of the realm of political appointment, and although the New Deal and the war brought about a resurgence of the number of unclassified posts, during the postwar years the merit system forged ahead to the point where it now includes eighty-five per cent of Federal posts. Of the remaining fifteen per cent, however, many posts could, in their nature, not be brought under the system; posts abroad and temporary or part-time posts, for example. There remain a substantial number of posts, including many of the most important jobs in the Executive branch, which are at the disposal of an incoming President. Estimates have varied from 7,000 to 15,000 jobs, and although this represents only a fraction of one per cent of the total size of the civil service, it represents quite a formidable task of selection for the new Administration. Furthermore, there is constant pressure upon Presidents to increase the amount of patronage available, particularly when there is a change of party in office. President Eisenhower gave way to such pressure in 1952 by declassifying some thousands of positions which had recently been given security of tenure by the previous Administration.

President Eisenhower also introduced a new category, a buffer-zone, as it were, between the great mass of career civil servants and the top-level political appointees. It was argued that the new Republican Administration found it difficult to exercise control over policy-making posts near the top of the service because they were filled with career officers who had been appointed under the Democratic Presidents of the preceding twenty years. A large number of key posts were transformed into 'semi-political appointments': posts occupied by advisers on policy, confidential assistants to the heads of agencies, or people whose job was publicly to defend controversial policies. Thus it is important to realize that the personnel of the Federal Govern-

ment is not divided simply into a thin layer of political appointees at Cabinet level directing the activities of the professional
civil servants. Political appointments reach well down into the
upper layers of the administrative hierarchy, but to different
levels in different areas. Indeed, within the same Department
some appointments may be made under Civil Service rules,
whilst others of a similar grade may be political or semi-political
in character.

The American Civil Service differs from the British, therefore, in that the higher levels are not wholly professionalized,
but it differs also in another important way from the service
which has evolved in Britain over the past century. The
British service was divided into a number of different classes,
and the most senior of these, the administrative class, was composed of officers who were generalists, able to move from one
department to another, advising Ministers on policy, and supervising its execution. Because the service was fully professionalized these men became a permanent, coherent body of top
administrators, forming almost a distinct caste in the hierarchy.
The United States Civil Service was not divided in this way.
It is a unified structure, with a number of salary grades within
which appointments are made. These are known as the General
Schedule Grades, from 1 to 18. Above these are five salary levels
for Federal executive posts. The latter range from members of
the Cabinet in Level I down to the heads of the smaller agencies.
Particular positions are classified as GS 1 to 18 according to the
evaluation that is made of the position. Thus there is nothing
comparable to the 'class structure' of the British Civil Service,
and the upper reaches of the two services are very different.
These differences provide the basis for a fascinating comparison
of developments in the two countries. American students of
administration have used the British service as a model for the
reform of their own system, proposing the creation of a Higher
Civil Service which would be politically neutral, and whose
members would not be specialists as they are today, but would
move from one department to another, each carrying his status
and tenure with him wherever he was moved. This proposal
was made by the Second Hoover Commission on the Organiza-

tion of the Executive Branch in 1955, but it has not found favour with Congress, and many students of administration, who would deplore excessive use of patronage, nevertheless are worried about a 'neutral' service, without a deep commitment to Presidential programmes. In Britain, on the other hand, the Fulton Committee, reporting in 1968, took the American Federal Service as a model for some of their proposed reforms. They proposed to abolish the class system and substitute for it a unified grading structure, and although they did not wish to see a large number of political appointees in the service they did express concern about the problem of strengthening the Minister's control of departmental policy-making.

CONGRESS AND THE FEDERAL SERVICE

We have already seen, at various points, how Congress affects the working of the Administration and the people who compose it. Congress sets up the administrative structure by legislation or by approval of Presidential reorganization plans; the President's nominations to senior positions must be confirmed by the Senate, and must, therefore, be cleared with influential Senators; the legislature provides the funds by which the Administration operates, and may scrutinize estimates very closely, probing the working of departments and agencies at committee hearings. Congress does not have the problem which the British Parliament faces, the anonymity of civil servants who do most of the actual business of government. Congressional committees continually call civil servants before them and subject them to very close questioning.

Although individual members of the civil service may form quite close connexions with members of Congress, there is a built-in distrust of 'bureaucrats' among Senators and Representatives. Most legislators, as we have seen, feel a very close affinity to the people in their constituencies, sometimes over two thousand miles away from Washington, D.C. They have much sympathy with the State and local governments with whom they will have been in close contact throughout their political careers. The 'Federal Government', therefore, remains in some sense the enemy still, even when they themselves become members of the national legislature. Most of them resent, and are fearful of, 'big government', and the power that it gives to a vast, impersonal and *permanent* bureaucracy. Few members of Congress, therefore, resist the temptation to attack civil servants when the opportunity arises, and the period since the Second World War has provided on occasion extreme examples of this tendency.

The internal and international strains of the post-war period, the Cold War and the fear of Communism, provided the backdrop for the phenomenal rise to prominence of Senator Joseph McCarthy. McCarthy, as chairman of the Permanent Subcommittee on Investigations of the Senate Government Operations Committee, pursued a vendetta against civil servants, accusing them of Communist sympathies and causing a number of them to resign or be dismissed. He particularly attacked civil servants in the Department of State, the Central Intelligence Agency and the Department of the Army. The extent and bitterness of McCarthy's attacks eventually led to a reaction against him, and after the extraordinary public battle between McCarthy and the Army in 1954 he was censured by the Senate. This was an extreme example of an attack on the service, but the House Committee on Un-American Activities (later re-named the Internal Security Committee) concerned itself actively over a period of thirty-seven years with the loyalty of Federal Government employees until its abolition in January 1975. It exemplified the way Congress, in certain circumstances, is able to exercise considerable influence on the administrative process.

PRESIDENTIAL CONTROL OF THE ADMINISTRATION

Thus to the problem of attempting to coordinate the legislative and executive policies of the Federal Government is added the problem which the President faces in attempting to control his own Administration. The fragmented character of the administrative structure that we have described presents a challenge of vast proportions to a President attempting to direct the government. This question of control has received a great deal of attention during this century, as the size of government has grown and the problem of coordination has escalated. The report of the Hoover Commission in 1949 put the problem as follows. 'Responsibility and accountability are impossible without authority – the power to direct. The exercise of authority is impossible without a clear line of command from the top to the bottom, and a return line of responsibility and accountability from the bottom to the top.'

This concern for stronger, more effective Presidential direction of the Administration has been a recurrent theme of official studies. In 1937 the Committee on Administrative Management (the Brownlow Committee) recommended that the administrative and legislative functions of the independent regulatory commissions should be transferred to the Executive Departments, leaving the commissions only the judicial part of their duties. However, when Congress passed the Reorganization Act of 1939, implementing some of the Committee's proposals and giving to the President the power to formulate Reorganization plans for submission to Congress, it withheld from the President the power to reorganize the independent commissions. In 1949 the Hoover Commission on the Organization of the Executive Branch, after an exhaustive survey of the machinery of government, laid great stress on the need for greater coordination and control in the administrative structure, and in the same year a new Reorganization Act gave new power to the President to propose reforms in the Administration. This time the independent regulatory commissions were not excluded by the Act. Successive Presidents submitted a large number of reorganization plans to Congress, perhaps the most important being the one creating the new Department of Health, Education and Welfare in 1953.

In 1955 the Second Hoover Commission went further than its predecessors and recommended that the problem of the regulatory functions of the commissions should be dealt with by the creation of an Administrative Court to take over their judicial role. Before taking office in 1960, President-elect John Kennedy asked James M. Landis to report on the problem of controlling the independent agencies, and he submitted a report which proposed that the Executive Office of the President should have a coordinating authority over the commissions, with three offices responsible for transport, communications and energy policy. In addition, an Office of Oversight over all the regulatory agencies would be created in the Executive Office, the authority of the chairmen of the commissions would be strengthened and they would be more directly responsible to the President. After taking office, President Kennedy included some of these recommendations in a series of Reorganization Plans which he submitted to Congress. There was a powerful reaction in Congress against the strengthening of Presidential power over the Commissions and the President failed to get his proposals for three of the commissions accepted. The ideas which Landis put forward for making the Executive Office into a general supervisor of the commissions were dropped.

Thus although there has been a good deal of reform, and much concern for the greater integration of the Administrative machine, the fundamental problems still remain. Indeed, the changes that have been made have not kept pace with the problem. Every new burst of government activity sees the proliferation of new agencies, and the problem of the Presidency becomes more and more formidable.

ADMINISTRATION AND THE FEDERAL SYSTEM

The inter-relationships between 'politics' and 'administration' are not, however, restricted to the internal operations of the Federal Government, for as we have seen in every other sphere of the American political system, the fact of federalism introduces another dimension, the effect of State and local politics on the national government. It is necessary to realize at this point that just as the *politics* of national and local affairs are inextricably interwoven, so also the administration of American government is a vast complex of national, State and local programmes, most of which involve more than one level of government. Only in a very few areas do Federal programmes have no implications for the States and localities, for in many fields of domestic policy Congress has deliberately chosen to administer Federal programmes through, and in cooperation with, State and local authorities. In many areas of social policy the Federal Government provides money in the form of grants-in-aid, sets standards for the States to comply with, and supervises the administration, but the States and localities carry out the programmes and also provide money from their own resources. Even when no cooperative programme is in operation there is usually a State programme running alongside the Federal one, so that the two levels of government may be in competition with each other, or may complement each other.

This network of administrative relationships necessitates that Federal, State, and local officials will constantly be coming into contact with each other, and the way in which government programmes are carried out will depend very much on the quality of the cooperation between them. However, it is important to emphasize the word 'cooperation'. Although the Federal Government may have provided most of the money for a programme, and have laid down quite precise conditions about the way in which it should be carried out, it cannot give 'orders' to State and local governments. Its major sanction is the withdrawal of funds, and this is sometimes done. But this type of action is politically hazardous for Federal administrators to adopt. The State officials can call upon political support from their superiors in the State government, Congressmen and Senators can be mobilized to put pressure on the Federal Department concerned, and as a last resort Congress can, and sometimes does, act to reverse the decisions of Federal officials taken under legislation which Congress itself had previously acquiesced in. Thus 'administrative' relationships between the levels of government are very political, and sometimes highly sensitive.

The problems that face the Federal Administration in dealing with State and local authorities are intensified by the very nature of State and local administration. In the first place, the structure of most State administrations is even more fragmented than that of the Federal Government itself. The Governor is usually much less in control of his administrative machine than the President is of his. The former has to contend with senior members of his administration who are separately elected by the people, and who may not share his views on policy. State legislatures have been even more assiduous than Congress in creating a multitude of independent agencies hardly subject at all to gubernatorial authority. Furthermore, many local authorities enjoy a high degree of autonomy, and are not easily controlled by the State government, so that where two or more levels of government are involved in administering a programme, overall Federal control may be very remote. It is true that in recent years the Federal government has tended to bypass State authorities in some programmes, and to work directly with local authorities, particularly with city governments in urban renewal programmes, but this has political drawbacks as well, for it tends to arouse resentment in the State administration, which does not relish direct Federal-local relationships.

Another complication in this situation is that the merit system has not been accepted to anything like the same extent for State and local employees as it has for the Federal civil service. Patronage, either openly or in disguised forms, is still characteristic of a great area of State and local government. The impact of State and local political situations upon politically appointed officials is, therefore, likely to be considerable, and at one remove the Federal administrators will be aware of these pressures. In such circumstances the administrative machinery becomes the vehicle through which political compromises are worked out. The Federal legislature may be following a policy which is only grudgingly accepted by the State legislature because of its desire to attract the Federal grants which go with the programme. In such circumstances Federal and State administrators have to work out a *modus vivendi* which will not offend their respective political masters, and in practice the Federal officials may be in a position to be much more flexible than their State colleagues. Indeed this is almost inevitable, for Federal programmes must be implemented across the whole continent in widely differing conditions, and without such flexibility it is unlikely that it would be possible to administer such a programme at all.

Politics and the Judiciary

9

It may seem strange to link the description of the structure and functions of the judicial system with the further elaboration of the working of American politics; but in fact no proper understanding of the political system can be attained without a clear realization of the role of the judges, and in particular of the Justices of the Supreme Court of the United States, in the way in which policies are made and implemented. Politics, in the broadest sense, has an impact at all levels of the American judicial system, and equally the courts play a vitally important part in the way in which the government of the country is carried on. This is not to suggest that judges are necessarily politically motivated, in a narrow partisan sense, in coming to decisions. A large section of the American judiciary, certainly most Federal judges, are of an extremely high calibre, but they cannot escape the responsibility of making decisions which in most countries are usually taken by the legislature or by executive officials. Some of the most significant decisions in American political history have been taken, not by President or Congress, but by the Supreme Court, acting in its judicial capacity to settle disputes arising under the laws and Constitution of the United States. The extent of this power, the way in which is it exercised, the motivations and opinions of the men who exercise it, and its results for the American polity, are all factors which the political scientist must attempt to assess.

THE SUPREME COURT AND JUDICIAL REVIEW

The Constitution of the United States briefly sets out certain broad, and rather vague, principles for the organization and operation of the government. It set up three branches of the government, a legislature, a chief executive, and a judiciary; it recognized a division of power between Federal and State governments and set out broad categories of Federal power; it guaranteed certain rights to the individual, and set certain limits to the exercise of power by the Federal and State governments. These rules still stand today, hardly altered at all in formal terms, yet applying to a country which has changed dramatically since 1787. However, these rules by their very nature are virtually meaningless without interpretation. What is the exact meaning of 'No person shall be ... deprived of life, liberty or property, without due process of law', a provision of the Fifth Amendment to the Constitution adopted as part of the Bill of Rights in 1791? What exactly is entailed by 'due process of law'? Or take the Commerce Clause of the Constitution which gives to Congress the power 'to regulate commerce with foreign nations, and among the several States, and with the Indian Tribes'. What exactly is 'commerce'? Does it include the manufacture of goods or simply trading in the finished products; does 'commerce' include ships, trains and aeroplanes, banks, insurance companies and atomic energy plants? The problems are endless. Who then should decide what the Constitution means, and then apply that interpretation to specific cases? The Constitution makes no direct reference to this problem other than the provision of Article III that 'the judicial power shall extend to all cases, in law and equity, arising under this Constitution, the laws of the United States, and treaties made, or which shall be made, under their authority . . .'. However, in the Federal Convention in Philadelphia in 1787 and in contemporary writing there is evidence that the members of the Convention were aware that the Supreme Court would have the power to interpret the Constitution and to declare null and void Congressional acts which conflicted with the Constitution. Alexander Hamilton, in number 78 of the *Federalist Papers*, published in 1788 before the ratification of the Constitution, gave a very clear explanation and defence of the right of the Supreme Court to act as the arbiter of the constitutionality of the acts both of the legislature and of the executive, concluding that the duty of the Court 'must be to declare all acts contrary to the manifest tenor of the Constitution void'.

The power of the Supreme Court to exercise this 'judicial discretion', in Hamilton's words, by no means went unchallenged. The Court was accused of aspiring to 'judicial supremacy', and bitter attacks were made upon it. Even its power to invalidate the acts of State legislatures was contested, in spite of the 'supremacy clause' of the Constitution, which provides that the Constitution and laws of the United States 'shall be the supreme law of the land ... the laws of any State to the contrary notwithstanding'. Gradually, however, the Court asserted itself. In *Chisholm v. Georgia* in 1793, and *Fletcher v. Peck* in 1810 it established its authority to set limits to the power of State governments; in 1803 in *Marbury v. Madison* the Court for the first time announced that the Federal Congress had acted unconstitutionally; in later cases the Supreme Court made clear that it would enforce the Constitution against the acts of Federal and State officials and uphold the rights of the individual, as it interpreted them, against the power of government. Thus the Court did establish a form of judicial supremacy over the parts of the government, but, as we shall see, this does not mean that the Court is completely unchecked by these other parts. There is, of course, the ultimate power to amend the Constitution, vested in Congress and the State legislatures, or in State Conventions. Even then, however, the interpretation of constitutional amendments and their application to judicial disputes is in the hands of the Court. Thus the Court came to exercise a formidable power through which non-elective justices can overrule the decisions of the elected representatives of the people.

There are, however, practical and political limits to the power of the Court. Its composition, and to a great extent its jurisdiction, are controlled by Congress. The Justices are nominated by the President, and appointed by him after confirmation by the Senate, holding their office 'during good behaviour'. Congress can remove the Justices through the cumbersome method of impeachment, or their authority can be restricted, or indeed the Court could be abolished by constitutional amendment. All these methods of controlling or influencing the Court have been attempted, and it inevitably operates, therefore, in a political context. As its decisions often have far-reaching political implications the justices can hardly be unaware, at one level of consciousness or another, of the role that they play in the political system. What then is that role?

THE SUPREME COURT AS POLICY-MAKER

The Supreme Court has made decisions affecting every aspect of American life, decisions which have shaped the course of development of every sphere of government activity. It has been the instrument of a great expansion of the power of the Federal Government, it has imposed restrictions upon the powers of the States, it has reached deeply into the economic affairs of the nation and regulated the social relationships between individual citizens. Yet the instruments which it has used for this work have been very few. Its major weapons have been the Commerce Clause, the General Welfare Clause, and in recent years the Fourteenth Amendment. Other provisions of the Constitution that the Court has used to change the balance of powers between Federal and State Governments, or between President and Congress, or to limit all of them, are the War Power, the Treaty Power, the First, Fourth and Fifth Amendments and the general enabling clause which gave to Congress the authority 'to make all laws which shall be necessary and proper for carrying into execution' the powers enumerated in the Constitution.

The Commerce Clause, quoted above, provides the most striking example of the way in which the Court has taken a brief, vague grant of power and transformed it into something of which the Founding Fathers could not have conceived, enabling the Federal Government to deal with the economic problems of the modern state. In the early years of the Union the Court was called upon to decide whether the power to regulate 'commerce' put the ferries which plied between New York and New Jersey under the control of the Federal Government. In 1824, in *Gibbons v. Ogden*, it decided that it did. Over a century later, the gradual extension of the commerce clause culminated in the application of Federal power to manufacturing industries, to banks, insurance companies and stock exchanges, to television and radio, to the production of atomic energy, indeed to almost every aspect of economic life that Congress wishes to regulate. The power of Congress 'to lay and collect taxes ... to pay the debts and provide for the common defense and general welfare of the United States' is the basis for the social welfare and security programmes of the Federal Government which are extensive, and expensive. The Fourteenth Amendment, ratified in 1868, states that 'no State shall make or enforce any law which shall abridge the privileges or immunities of citizens of the United States; nor shall any State deprive any person of life, liberty or property, without due process of law; nor deny to any person within its jurisdiction the equal protection of the laws.' On the basis of this Amendment the Court has moved into the whole sphere of civil rights, outlawing racial segregation in the schools and other public facilities, regulating State police and court proceedings, and attempting to assure political equality to the citizens of the United States. In these, and in many other areas, the Court has to give an authoritative interpretation of the Constitution, albeit one which may change from time to time. Let us look at the Court's functions in the American political system by reviewing three important cases through which the Court influenced the policy-making of the post-war period.

BROWN V. BOARD OF EDUCATION OF TOPEKA, 1954

The Fourteenth Amendment was incorporated into the Constitution after the Civil War in order to ensure that the newly freed slaves would be recognized as American citizens and accorded their proper rights by the governments of the States. As we have seen, the Amendment provided, among other things, that no State might 'deny to any person within its jurisdiction the equal protection of the laws'. However, this broad instruction could be interpreted in differing ways. The Southern States in particular wrote into their statute books laws which provided for segregation of the white and black races in the schools, on public transport, and in other areas of social life. Did such laws conflict with the Amendment? In 1896 the Supreme Court considered this problem in the case of *Plessy v. Ferguson*. The State legislature of Louisiana had required all railroads to provide 'equal but separate' accommodation for the two races and the Supreme Court upheld the constitutionality of the Louisiana statute, arguing that although the Fourteenth Amendment had ensured the *political* equality of the black and white races, it was impossible to ignore the *social* inequality of Negroes and whites and that therefore it could not say 'that a law which authorizes or even requires the separation of the two races in public conveyances is unreasonable'. Although the Court was dealing in this case with public transport it made reference in the decision to segregation in education, and over the following half century *Plessy v. Ferguson* was the constitutional basis for all sorts of State-enforced racial segregation. Provided that the State laws required *separate but equal* facilities the Constitution offered no barrier to such legislation.

In the period following the Second World War, however, the National Association for the Advancement of Colored People developed a growing campaign against segregation. The N.A.A.C.P. had been working towards a judicial confrontation on this issue for many years, and in a carefully planned scheme of attack the Association gradually set the scene for a reconsideration by the Supreme Court of the basic constitutional principle upon which segregation was established. In a series of cases the Court whittled away the supporting argument for segregation by refusing to accept the 'separate but equal' formula in the field of university and professional education. Then, in 1954, the Court squarely faced the question of segregation in the elementary schools. The Court considered a number of cases from various States in which the Negro plaintiffs argued that segregated public schools were not equal and could not be made equal, and that therefore the 'equal protection of the laws', which the Fourteenth Amendment was intended to guarantee, was far from being a reality.

In the *Brown* case the Court reviewed the history of the Amendment, relied heavily upon psychological and sociological evidence of the effect of segregation upon Negro children, and then proceeded explicitly to overrule *Plessy v. Ferguson*. The unanimous Court, speaking through Chief Justice Warren, found that segregated schools, even though physical facilities and other tangible factors were equal, deprived the children of the Negro minority of equal educational opportunities. 'Separate educational facilities are inherently unequal', and therefore a denial of the equal protection of the laws.

Thus without any legislation having been passed by Congress, and without any Presidential initiative, a new policy was instituted by the judiciary. The Court did not order an immediate desegregation of all schools, and the process of desegregation by judicial action has been going on slowly over the years since 1954, but the implications of this case for American politics can hardly be exaggerated. It was the forerunner of other decisions which outlawed segregation in other walks of life; it brought down upon the Court the wrath of the defenders of segregation, and it certainly opened an era of more and more insistent demands for the recognition of Negro rights which has often spilled over into violence, although this is not to say that the Court's decision was the cause of this violence – its action probably prevented a more severe outbreak.

BAKER V. CARR, 1962

Few cases decided by the Court in recent years have had such far-reaching political implications as that of *Baker v. Carr*. As we saw in Chapter 4, the State legislatures, which control their electoral law and also provide the framework of the Federal electoral system, had allowed themselves to become unrepresentative because of the wide disparities in the sizes of the electoral districts in many States. Usually far greater weight was given to rural areas than was justified on a population basis, and the gerrymandering of district boundaries in order to gain party advantage had reached the point where, in the words of Justice Clark, the apportionment of State legislatures had produced 'a crazy quilt without rational basis'. Because these unrepresentative State legislatures also determined the boundaries of Federal

Congressional Districts a similar, though less extreme, mis-
representation was to be found at the Federal level also. The
entrenchment of rural interests had been challenged in the courts
on a number of occasions before 1962, but the Supreme Court
had avoided ruling on the matter. In 1946 in *Colegrove v.
Green* a majority of the Court refused to interfere in the way in which
the State of Illinois had drawn the boundaries of the Congressional Districts within the State, although the largest District
contained over eight times as many people as the smallest. The
majority on the Court was not agreed on the reasons why it
refused to deal with this problem, but Mr Justice Frankfurter
argued that 'Courts ought not to enter this political thicket'.
Frankfurter pointed out that legislative apportionment is heavily
'embroiled in politics, in the sense of party contests and party
interests', and concluded that this was a problem best left to the
executive and legislative branches to deal with, subject to the
vigilance of the people in the exercise of their political rights.
The Court had always declined to interfere in a rather miscel-
laneous collection of 'political questions' involving for the
most part matters concerning foreign affairs, or international
boundaries or disputes. The labelling of a question 'political'
did not mean, of course, that the Court normally avoided a
problem just because it was politically controversial; this
would rule out most of the Court's constitutional business;
but Justice Frankfurter maintained that legislative apportionment was a question in which the Court should not intervene
because to do so 'would cut very deeply into the very being of
Congress'.

    In 1961 and 1962, however, the Court was faced with a chal-
lenge to the composition of the legislature of Tennessee which
had not been reapportioned since 1901. The State's electoral
districts had remained unchanged in spite of considerable shifts
in population within the State, so that there were great inequali-
ties in the representation of counties in the State legislature.
After long deliberation the Court decided that the 'equal protection of the laws' clause of the Fourteenth Amendment laid on
the Federal Courts the duty of ensuring that the States made
provision for a fair representation of the electorate. What con-

stituted 'fair representation' and how it would be enforced was not made clear in *Baker v. Carr*, but the decision immediately provoked an outburst of litigation, in which the constitutionality of State electoral laws was challenged. The courts were faced with the problem of determining whether State legislatures were fairly apportioned and of passing judgement upon schemes for the redistricting of State legislatures. This has led the courts into an incredibly complicated area of the legal and political structure. If a State's legislative apportionment is challenged and found to be unconstitutional the legislature must then produce a scheme for its own reapportionment which is satisfactory to the Federal Courts. If the new scheme is not satisfactory the Court can reject it and demand that a new one be prepared. The nature of the judicial process is such that although the courts can continually reject such schemes until a satisfactory one is forthcoming they do not themselves have the power, or the ability, to produce their own plans for legislative apportionment. An example of what then happens is illustrated by the case of Florida. In 1964 the Supreme Court found the districting provisions in that State to be unconstitutional. In the following year the Florida legislature reapportioned the State, but its plan was ruled unconstitutional. In 1966 the Florida legislature again adopted a reapportionment scheme and in January 1967 the Supreme Court again rejected it as unsatisfactory.

Since the original decision in *Baker v. Carr* the Supreme Court has gone on to tighten up very considerably its view of the requirements of the Fourteenth Amendment in this field. In later cases it laid down that the basic rule of 'one man one vote' must be implemented for primary elections as well as for general elections, for both the upper and lower houses of State legislatures, for elections for State executive offices, and for the House of Representatives at the Federal level. Although the Court, in the case in which this basic principle was first adopted, *Reynolds v. Sims* in 1964, said that it would not insist on mathematical exactness in applying this rule, but in two cases in 1969, *Wells v. Rockefeller* and *Kirkpatrick v. Preisler*, the Court insisted that the States must 'make a good faith effort to achieve precise mathematical equality' in apportionment. Thus the Supreme Court has to grapple with the complexities of State politics, for its decisions may be of vital importance to the groups contending for control of State legislatures. Justice Brennan when delivering the Court's opinion in the *Baker* case acknowledged that 'what is actually asked of the Court is to choose among competing theories of political philosophy'. Having chosen, the Court is then faced with the task of putting that philosophy into practice.

THE STEEL SEIZURE CASE:
YOUNGSTOWN SHEET AND TUBE CO. V. SAWYER, 1952

The rather humdrum title of this case conceals one of the most dramatic, cliff-hanging episodes in the history of the Supreme Court. In 1951 during the Korean War, the steelworkers' trade union began negotiations for an increase in wages as part of a contract with the steel companies due for renewal the following year. The managements of the steel mills were not prepared to increase wages unless there was a simultaneous increase in the price of steel. President Truman and his Administration had two major concerns in this dispute. They wished to keep the steel mills in production to maintain supplies for the armed services, but they wished also to keep the price of steel down in order to check inflation. In order to press their demands the union threatened strike action, but repeatedly called the strike off, until eventually they announced that they would strike on 9 April 1952. At 10.30 p.m. on 8 April President Truman appeared on television and announced that he intended to take possession of the steel mills and to keep them in operation. The President explained that he considered that the unions' wage demands were fair, and that the steel companies had refused to grant this increase without a price rise, which, the President said, was 'about the most outrageous thing I ever heard of'. The seizure of the steel mills was effected by Executive Order No. 10340 under the President's authority as Chief Executive and Commander-in-Chief. But did the President have such authority? The steel companies immediately filed a complaint in the Federal District Court, and the legal battle continued until the Supreme Court announced its decision on 2 June.

Whilst the lawyers argued, the steel mills were operated under the direction of Charles Sawyer, the Secretary of Commerce, in the midst of a political furore. Members of Congress introduced bills to withhold appropriations from the Department of Commerce to prevent it from implementing the Executive Order. The unions announced that they would strike immediately if the steel mills were returned to the companies. A turmoil of political and constitutional debate raged around the President. In this highly charged political atmosphere the Supreme Court handed down its decision, ruling by a majority of six to three that the President had exceeded his constitutional powers by attempting to take possession of the steel industry without statutory authority. The President does not have the power to make laws, the Court said, for this function was entrusted by the Constitution to the Congress. 'In the framework of our Constitution, the President's power to see that the laws are faithfully executed refutes the idea that he is to be a lawmaker.' Thus the Court, in a time of crisis, reasserted the nature of limited government in the United States, and its own authority to set limits to Presidential power. The President immediately returned the mills to the owners, the men went on strike and remained out for seven weeks.

THE NATURE OF JUDICIAL REVIEW

Undoubtedly, then, the Supreme Court 'makes policy' in a variety of fields, and it is therefore 'involved in politics', because in many instances it is the Court which decides the policies that are put into effect. But there have been differing views about the nature of the function that the Court performs when it decides that Congress, President, or State legislature has acted constitutionally or unconstitutionally. One view of the role of the judiciary is that stated as long ago as 1748 by Montesquieu when he said that the judges should be 'no more than the mouth that pronounces the words of the law, mere passive beings, incapable of moderating either its force or rigour'. In its modern form this view of the function of the judges can be described as the *mechanical* theory of jurisprudence. The judges are seen simply as highly skilled experts in the law, who learn a complex body of rules and then deduce almost automatically the application of the law to particular cases. From this point of view the judge is a neutral instrument; he does not interpose his personality between the general rules of the law and the solution of the practical problems which he must solve. The best statement of this view by a modern judge was made by Justice Roberts in 1936.

When an act of Congress is appropriately challenged in the courts as not conforming to the constitutional mandate the judicial branch of the Government has only one duty – to lay the article of the Constitution which is invoked beside the statute which is challenged and to decide whether the latter squares with the former. All the Court does, or can do, is to announce its considered judgement upon the question.

But is there a 'higher law' which can be discovered, studied, and applied by the judges independently of their personal ideas and attitudes? The view of the nature of law as simply an exercise in deductive logic was challenged by the school of legal realism. This school of jurisprudence argued that it is impossible to deduce unequivocally the application of legal rules in particular cases from very general and vague statements like those to be found in the Constitution. The exact decisions made, and therefore the general development of the law, depend on the way in which the judges exercise their discretion to choose one possible interpretation rather than another. This is not to say that the judges would simply decide cases in an arbitrary, erratic fashion. They would be influenced, and should be, by developments in society, by the needs of the time and the attitudes of society to the way in which they should be satisfied. This *sociological* view of the evolution of the law tends to foster a more flexible approach to the activity of judicial review, leading eventually to the acceptance by the Supreme Court of sociological and psychological evidence as relevant to the solution of judicial problems.

A view of the role of the judges in the political system which is at the other extreme from that of the mechanical view of jurisprudence, has been developed by the *behaviourists*. These students of judicial motivation approach the way in which decisions of the courts are arrived at neither by looking at the internal logic of the law, nor by simply observing the influence of the broad developments of social forces upon the law. They attempt to explain judicial behaviour, as other types of political behaviour, by the analysis of the personal characteristics of the judges, their social background and education, or their party orientation and ideological attitudes. The voting records of the judges and their personal characteristics are studied by statistical and mathematical techniques in the same way as the behaviour of members of the legislature. If it could be shown that judges with similar personal characteristics consistently vote in a particular way in cases involving disputes between employers and labour unions, in civil rights cases, or cases relating to individual freedom or communist control, then the explanation of the nature of law will be very different from either of the other types of explanation we have discussed. The role of 'politics' in the working of the judicial system is clearly quite distinct according to which explanation you choose.

The true description of the judicial processes is probably a construction of all three of these conceptions. The structure of legal rules and institutions does have an internal logic and a function in the political system which places considerable restraints upon the judges who have the responsibility for maintaining them; a judiciary which failed to be influenced by the essential changes which take place in society would soon be bypassed or replaced; at the same time individual judges, *within the limits which the system allows them*, must surely be influenced, marginally at the very least, by their personal experience and deeply held convictions. From the interplay of these three factors the American judicial system has been able, for a century and three quarters, with varying degrees of success at different times, to keep the structure of constitutional rules broadly in line with the enormous changes that have taken place in the society to which they are applied.

Nevertheless, the policy-making aspect of the work of the courts is bound to focus attention upon the motives of the judges, particularly by those opposed to their decisions. Critics of the way in which the Supreme Court overruled congressional legislation in the 1930s accused the Court of being 'a third chamber of the legislature', or pictured them as nine irresponsible judges exercising an arbitrary power to overrule the popular will. Members of the Court themselves have had different views of their function, some stressing the responsibility of the Court to act positively in defence of the principles of the Constitution, others stressing that it is the function of the executive or legislative branches of the government to make policy and to solve social and economic problems. These two attitudes, *judicial activism* and *judicial restraint* respectively, have, in the history of the Court, been reflected in the attitudes of different groups of justices, sometimes one gaining the ascendency, sometimes the other. Judicial activism can lead, as in the 1930s, to the Court striking down innovatory moves by the Congress, or it can lead, as in the period since 1954, to the Court itself initiating policies at a time when the legislature is relatively quiescent or even actively opposed to such policies. Such activism can call down upon the Court the anger of very different groups: on the one hand those who wish to see the legislature pursue strong and effective policies, and on the other those who wish the *status quo* to remain undisturbed. The fact that the Court has been under attack at different times, or even at the same time, by progressive and conservative forces alike is in fact a major source of its great strength.

We have established, therefore, the 'political' role of the Court and the sense in which it must be understood. We shall look more closely at this connexion between politics and law in the American judicial system, but it is necessary now, in order fully to understand the processes of decision-taking, to describe the judicial system as a whole and the nature of the judicial process.

We have concentrated so far upon the role of the Supreme Court of the United States, but that august body stands at the head of a complex judicial system in which is reflected the overall characteristics of American government, and in particular its federal structure. There are in fact fifty-one judicial systems in the United States: there are the Federal courts headed by the U.S. Supreme Court, and a separate judicial hierarchy in each of the States each with its own State Supreme Court. The relationship between these judicial structures, and between the laws that they administer, is complex indeed. As far as structure is concerned the Federal system is relatively simple. There are three levels of courts; at the bottom are the District Courts, eighty-nine of them across the continent including the District of Columbia, each consisting of from one to twenty-four District Judges. Above the District Courts are the Circuit Courts of Appeal, arranged in eleven circuits, each with from three to nine Justices. Above these the Supreme Court with its nine Justices forms the apex of the Federal system. In addition there are special Federal courts to deal with customs and patents, military cases, and claims against the United States. The Supreme Court has original jurisdiction only in a few important types of case. For the most part cases reach it on appeal either from the lower Federal courts or from the Supreme Courts of the States.

The State judicial systems tend to be much more complicated, and vary very considerably from State to State. The States are responsible for passing and enforcing the major part of the criminal and civil law in America. For every prisoner in Federal prisons there will usually be eight in State prisons. Basically the function of the Federal courts is to apply Federal laws, and of State courts to apply the laws of that State, but the relationships of the systems are much more complex than this. The systems are not separate and distinct. The Federal Constitution lays the duty upon all courts, Federal and State alike, of enforcing the Constitution of the United States and the laws made under it. The Constitution is the supreme law of the land, and when State laws conflict with it, or with Federal laws made under that Constitution, then the State laws must give way.

State courts must, therefore, take account of Federal statutes, and decisions of Federal courts, in so far as they affect the cases that come before them. If, however, no 'Federal question' is involved the matter will be dealt with entirely in the State system, and the final court of appeal will be the Supreme Court of the State. Issues involving Federal law will normally be initiated in the Federal District Court and appealed up to the United States Supreme Court. However, particular cases will not fall neatly into one or other of these categories. Federal laws and decisions of the Federal courts overlap very considerably in many areas with State law, and State law must always be applied in a way which is consistent with the Constitution as interpreted by the Supreme Court. Where a dispute exists between citizens of different States the Federal courts may have jurisdiction of the dispute even though no Federal law is involved.

Thus cases may be initiated in a State court, decided by the State Supreme Court, and then appealed to the Supreme Court of the United States on the grounds that the State has decided the matter in a way that conflicts with the Constitution or Federal laws; a case may be started in the Federal courts on the ground that a State or one of its officials has infringed the Constitution or valid Federal law; and in a few instances a case started in a State court may be transferred to a Federal court. The broad outlines of the American judicial system are illustrated by the chart opposite.

Such a complex system inevitably involves difficult questions of jurisdiction, and, as we shall see later, it raises also the problem of the way in which the decisions taken by the highest court in the land are put into effect in lower courts. It leads to rather similar consequences in the judicial sphere as in other aspects of the Federal system. The Federal and State courts work together, but they are also in competition with each other, and in extreme cases litigants can attempt to play off one system against the other, which leads sometimes, in the words of Dean Griswold, 'to a sort of legal battledore and shuttlecock, with cases bouncing back and forth almost endlessly between the State and the Federal jurisdictions'.

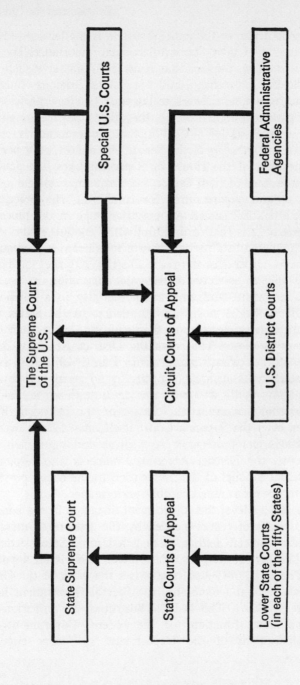

The Judicial System of the U.S.A.

An essential part of the judicial system is the legal profession, which has in the United States a particular importance. The complexity of the law, the fact that court decisions have such vital significance for government, and the general litigious tendencies of Americans give much work to lawyers. The legal profession is also the path to public office in the other branches of government. In the 1967 session of the Ninetieth Congress nearly seventy per cent of the members of the Senate and almost sixty per cent of the members of the House of Representatives had practised law at some stage of their career. Furthermore, the legal system provides unique opportunities for combining the practice of law with a political career. An essential stage in the process of law enforcement is that of deciding when enough evidence has been accumulated in a particular case to warrant a prosecution. This function is entrusted to the District Attorneys, who are therefore able to exercise considerable discretion in deciding whom to prosecute, and who are potentially in a position of considerable political power and influence. In the States these officers are usually elected and they can and do use their office for electoral purposes. The crusading District Attorney, or the District Attorney who is subservient to local political interests, may be stereotypes of fiction, but are by no means unknown in real life. Many political careers are begun at this level, and the State Governor's mansion, the Senate or the House of Representatives, even the Supreme Court itself, may be the eventual haven of a former prosecutor. As well as deciding which cases to prosecute, the District Attorney's office is also responsible for the actual conduct of the prosecution in the court, providing an opportunity for a dramatic public performance.

At the Federal level the enforcement of law is in the hands of the Department of Justice headed by the Attorney-General. In each Federal judicial district there is a United States Attorney who, unlike his counterpart at the State level, is an appointed official. The Solicitor-General supervises the work of the United States Attorneys and represents the Federal Government before the Supreme Court. The Federal Bureau of Investigation performs the police functions of the Federal Government, and other sub-divisions of the Department of Justice supervise various areas of law enforcement such as civil rights, anti-trust actions, and the laws regarding immigration.

THE JUDICIAL PROCESS

Considerable emphasis has been placed in the present chapter on the policy-making role of the American judiciary, and its importance is indeed considerable; however, it must be noted that there are considerable limitations upon the ability of courts to perform this function. The nature of the judicial process restricts the courts to a rather different role from that of the other branches of government. The courts cannot initiate action. They must wait for cases to be brought before them for decision. If the constitutionality of a particular piece of legislation is not challenged in court, then the courts cannot pronounce upon it. The courts do not have the resources for gathering and assessing information that are available to the legislature or the executive, but must depend upon the briefs which litigants submit to them. On the other hand, they are not subject to the same overt pressure as other branches of government. This is not to say that pressure-groups ignore the courts – far from it – but it means that the 'politics of access', as David Truman has termed it, have to be conducted in a very different way. The long involved process of the law can lead to the passage of years before a case is finally decided, although on occasion the courts can move with remarkable speed.

Perhaps the greatest advantage of the judicial process as a decision-making mechanism, in particular in a highly pluralistic political system like that of the United States, is that although the courts may become the centre of great political controversy, the way in which they go about their work gives their decisions a prestige and a disinterested quality very different from that of the other branches of government. On the other hand, the fact that the Supreme Court reaches its decisions by majority vote, that quite often very important decisions are reached by a five-to-four majority, and that the dissenting justices may write powerful and persuasive opinions, indicates to those who are interested that the judicial process is by no means a completely mechanical one, and that informed and learned judges can reach widely differing conclusions about the law.

One very important aspect of the judicial process is that the courts do not operate by pronouncing general abstract rules in advance of particular situations. They decide specific cases, and although in doing this they formulate general rules, interested parties can still argue that *their* particular case is rather different and should be decided differently. If they are prepared to risk the costs involved they may fight their case in the courts and possibly right up through the system to the Supreme Court. At the very least this can provide them with a powerful delaying tactic. Thus a general pronouncement against segregation like that contained in the *Brown v. Board of Education* decision does not result in the immediate desegregation of all segregated schools. It results instead in a large number of cases in the courts, fought out over a long period. It can be argued that this leads to an intolerably slow and patchy application of the law, much less efficient than the administrative process applying statutory rules. On the other hand, it can be pointed out that this method allows for a very flexible application of the law, enabling local conditions and special circumstances to be given full weight.

Another dimension of the way in which the courts apply the law is the way in which decisions of the Supreme Court are enforced by lower Federal courts and State courts. Although the rule of *stare decisis* applies to the lower courts, requiring them to observe Supreme Court rulings, in practice it is very difficult for the Supreme Court to ensure compliance with its decisions in the thousands of cases which come before courts all across the country. The only weapon it has is its power to overrule lower court decisions on appeal, but only a tiny percentage of cases can be reviewed by the Supreme Court. Even lower Federal courts may modify and moderate the application of Supreme Court decisions because of their closeness to the political situations involved in judicial decision making, but State courts, particularly where the judiciary is elective, are naturally more responsive to the local political atmosphere. State appeal courts may be more sympathetic to the lower State courts whose decisions they must review than to the Federal Supreme Court

whose rulings they should apply. Nevertheless it must be said
that, given the pressures of State politics upon the judiciaries,
particularly in the case of civil rights in the Southern States,
State courts have followed Federal precedents reasonably well,
and would certainly seem to have been more sympathetic to the
protection of the rights of Negro citizens than other branches of
the State governments.

Thus the overall picture of the judicial process is one of slow
development and flexibility in the way in which decisions are
applied. This is profoundly disturbing to those who look for
clear and unambiguous decisions, applied promptly and uni-
formly. But in the United States the complexity of the political
system, and the diversity of local political situations, make it
quite impracticable, and impolitic, to impose a rigid administrative policy in many areas of government activity. This consideration leads us back, then, to look a little more closely at the way
in which politics affects the work of the judiciary.

POLITICS AND THE JUDGES

The extreme view of the judges as simply politicians in robes is
an untenable one; nevertheless, the policy-making role of the
judiciary does involve it in overtly political manoeuvres. Nowhere is this more evident than in the selection of judges, both
Federal and State. Federal judges are nominated by the President
and confirmed by the Senate. These positions, with life tenure
and a prestige above that of any other office of the government
other than the Presidency itself, are the choicest patronage plums
that the President has at his disposal. During a four-year term a
President may, on average, expect to appoint three Supreme
Court Justices and make perhaps fifty to a hundred appointments
to District and Appeal Courts. No President can afford to ignore
either the partisan advantages of such appointments or the fact
that the men he appoints will be able, to say the least, to give a
particular emphasis to the way in which policy is carried out.
Party allegiance is certainly a very important factor in the
selection of candidates for judicial office. The overwhelming
majority of appointments to the Supreme Court are made from

supporters of the party of the appointing President, and in the case of the lower Federal judiciary the proportion is even greater. Over ninety-five per cent of the appointments that President Eisenhower made to District Court judgeships were of Republicans, and over ninety per cent of the appointments that President Kennedy made during his three years of office were of Democrats.

In making their nominations to the Supreme Court Presidents are almost inevitably influenced by their estimate of the attitude of the nominee to the kind of policies of which the President approves. The character of the Supreme Court was changed considerably by the appointments which President Roosevelt made from 1937 onwards. But the President's power to influence the course of judicial decisions should not be over-estimated. Once appointed, the Justices are by no means the mere creatures of the men who appointed them, and many Presidents have been incensed by the opinions of Justices that they had raised to the supreme bench.

The Senate's power to reject judicial nominees is not something that can be taken lightly, and the Administration must consult with Senatorial leaders, and in the case of lower court appointees the approval of the Senator from the nominee's home State must be obtained. The President delegates the selection of lower court judges to the Deputy Attorney-General, but the selection of Supreme Court Justices will be a matter for his personal attention. Although the Senate treats the President's nominations with respect it exercises its right to reject them. There was a bitter contest over the nomination of Justice Brandeis in 1916, and in 1930 John J. Parker was rejected by the Senate. The most spectacular exercise of the power of the Senate occurred in 1968 when it forced President Johnson to withdraw the nomination of Justice Abe Fortas for the position of Chief Justice. President Nixon was subjected to defeat on two successive nominations, those of Clement F. Haynsworth and G. Harold Carswell.

The selection process is complicated even further by the part which is played by the Committee on the Federal Judiciary of the American Bar Association. The Deputy Attorney-General cooperates with the Committee by informing it of prospective nominees, whose record is then investigated by them. The Committee grades the nominees as 'exceptionally well-qualified', 'well-qualified', 'qualified' or 'not qualified'. Sometimes the Committee's findings will lead the President to withhold a nomination, but political pressures may make him persist, and a number of 'not-qualified' candidates are confirmed. Nominations are considered by the Senate's Judiciary Committee, usually with public hearings during which the nominee's views on many issues may be probed. The Committee then reports to the Senate itself which will usually accept its recommendations.

Appointments to the Supreme Court is seen as the climax of a political career – one Chief Justice, Taft, had previously been President of the United States. The main routes to appointment on the Court are membership of the Senate or House of Representatives, a Cabinet post, lower Federal or State courts, and State legislative or gubernational office. The overwhelming majority of Justices have had what would be described as a political career, rather than a straightforward legal background before appointment. Indeed a few of the greatest Justices who have sat on the Court have had no previous judicial experience at any level.

The political nature of the State judiciaries is more explicit. In over two thirds of the States the judges are elected, either directly by the electorate, or by the State legislature. Studies of the decisions of elected judges have suggested that political considerations may affect the sentences which they impose, for in varying circumstances either a harsh or a lenient sentence may arouse considerable popular support. This last consideration leads us to look in more detail at the studies of judicial behaviour which have recently become fashionable: what are the factors which determine judicial decisions?

STUDIES OF JUDICIAL BEHAVIOUR

The subjection of the judiciary to the techniques of the quantitatively oriented political scientist has certainly made more precise the arguments that were in the past directed against the idea of the complete objectivity of the judges. Stuart S. Nagel has explored the relationship between the political party back-

ground of Federal and State Supreme Court Justices and their
decisions in fifteen different kinds of case. He suggests that the
data show that in all fifteen types of case, Democratic judges
tended to favour the 'liberal' position more than Republican
judges. Harold J. Spaeth has concluded that voting patterns in
the Supreme Court on cases concerning the regulation of business reveal a group of literally oriented Justices who were 'anti-
business, pro-competition, and pro-union', and another group
who were 'conservative'. Of course the existence of 'blocs' or
'coalitions' on the Court has long been known and understood,
although mathematical techniques can demonstrate the extent
and durability of such coalitions. As with legislative coalitions
they can be shown to form and reform according to the issues to
be decided, with differing judges exhibiting differing degrees of
consistency in their voting behaviour. On some issues certain
Justices can almost always be found on one particular side of
the question, whereas the behaviour of others may be less
predictable. Thus in the 1957 term of the Court, Justice Douglas
voted for litigants claiming protection for their civil rights on
forty occasions, whilst Justice Clark voted *against* on thirty-nine
occasions. Studies of judicial voting behaviour in cases involving
a number of issues which cut across each other, like States' rights
and the control of business by the Federal Government, show
very complex voting patterns on the part of the Justices.

However, it should not be assumed that the evidence of the
behaviourists leads to the simple conclusion that the judges
simply use their high office to pursue narrow political ends. One
of the foremost behaviourist students of judicial decision-
making, Glendon A. Schubert, has shown in two different ways
that the nature of the judicial function is far more complex.
Schubert has conducted an extremely detailed analysis of the
way in which blocks formed and reformed on the U.S. Supreme
Court and on the Supreme Court of the State of Michigan.
Schubert's conclusion was that 'the partisan political affiliations
of the justices appear to have been irrelevant to the group behaviour of the United States Supreme Court [to 1957]; while
bloc analysis suggests its primary importance in the case of the
Michigan Supreme Court'. The Michigan Justices are popularly

elected for eight-year terms of office, and nominated in State party conventions with other candidates for office, so that the comparison of the behaviour of the two courts leads Schubert to conclude, 'there may, after all, be validity in the assumption that life tenure makes for independence of judges'.

In another study Schubert looked at the cross-pressures to which Justices are subjected when their views of the merits of a particular issue come into conflict with their respect for a norm of judicial behaviour such as *stare decisis*. After looking at the way in which the Supreme Court had decided cases concerning Acts of Congress involving the jurisdiction of military courts over civil rights questions, Schubert observed that, in this important area, after the Court in 1955, 1957 and 1958 invalidated sections of Congressional Acts, a number of Justices were clearly influenced by their wish to respect earlier Court decisions even though they had not originally supported them. In particular Justice Clark accepted the rule of *stare decisis* in a case where his vote was decisive, even though he was not sympathetic to the aims of the majority of the Court. Schubert concludes from this study:

In measuring judicial attitudes, we must be concerned not only with the externally oriented values which represent the recurrent issues of law and policy raised before the Court for decision; we must also be concerned with the internally oriented values which represent the institutional identifications of the justices with the Court, its customs and traditions, and their attitudes toward each other as members of the same small decision-making group.

The institutional forces which make the Supreme Court so much more than a mere group of legal politicians give it also the power to assert itself against the executive and legislative branches, and at times to brave public uproar in defence of constitutional principles in which they believe. The years since 1954 have been a period in which the Court has used this institutional power to the full, and incurred the deep anger of Congress.

THE NEW JUDICIAL ACTIVISM

In the early years of the New Deal the court actively used its power to block Congressional action on a wide range of matters affecting the economic life of the nation. In two years, 1935–6, the Court invalidated seven major statutes which had been intended to deal with the economic problems of the depression, and the President's programme lay in ruins. The attack upon the Court, and the new appointments made by Roosevelt, led to the dominance of the philosophy of judicial restraint on the Court until the *Brown v. Board of Education* decision in 1954 ushered in a new era of judicial activism. In view of the political repercussions of the desegregation decision the Court might well have rested on its laurels and not ventured into other controversial areas, but instead it undertook to innovate in a number of other extremely politically sensitive fields of constitutional law. Having incensed Southern Senators and Congressmen, the Court proceeded to anger both conservatives concerned about the threat of Communism, and all those across the country who were fearful of further Federal intrusion into the affairs of the States.

In a series of decisions in 1956 the Court moved further into the field of civil rights. It held that defendants in criminal cases, against whom F.B.I. agents had testified, should be given access to the Bureau's files to enable them to check for discrepancies between the testimony and the reports upon which it was based (*Jencks v. U.S.*); it placed restrictions upon the investigatory powers of Congressional committees in a decision specifically directed at the Un-American Activities Committee of the House of Representatives (*Watkins v. U.S.*); the convictions were reversed of fourteen leaders of the Communist Party convicted under the Smith Act which was aimed at persons conspiring to teach the violent overthrow of the government (*Yates v. U.S.*); the Justices freed a university professor who had been convicted under a New Hampshire law for refusing to answer questions concerning his political beliefs (*Sweezy v. New Hampshire*); and the Court invalidated the laws of forty-two States directed against subversive activities, on the grounds that Congress had legislated in that field to the exclusion of State power (*Pennsylvania v. Nelson*).

In the following year the Court turned its attention to safeguarding other rights of the individual against the power of government. It invalidated legislation which revoked the citizenship status of naturalized citizens who had offended the government (*Trop v. Dulles*); and it overturned the decision of the State Department to withhold the passports of those it wished to prevent from travelling abroad (*Kent v. Dulles; Dayton v. Dulles*). In a string of cases the Court has invalidated sections of congressional statutes which it considered infringed the civil rights of the citizen, in particular sections of the Nationality Act of 1940 and the Smith Act. In 1965 the Court invalidated an Act of 1959 which disqualified members of the Communist Party from becoming officers or employees of a labour union (*U.S. v. Brown*).

The Court has been even more active in striking down State laws and controlling State court procedures. It has ruled that the States may not prescribe prayers in the public schools (*Engel v. Vitale*), or bible-readings at the beginning of the school day (*School District v. Schempp*). In the 1960s the Supreme Court used the Fourteenth Amendment to 'nationalize' the procedures and safeguards which have long been applied in the Federal courts, by ruling that they must be appplied also in State courts, and applying strict tests to police procedures. The citizen must be protected against unreasonable search and seizure (*Mapp v. Ohio*), against cruel and unusual punishments (*Robinson v. California*), and must be provided with counsel by the State if he is unable to afford it himself (*Gideon v. Wainwright*). These developments culminated in the case of *Miranda v. Arizona* in 1966, which applied the procedures that the F.B.I. has used in Federal cases, to the activities of State police. The Court asserted the right of an individual under interrogation to have a lawyer present, and laid upon the State the duty of supplying one at State expense if the person under interrogation could not afford it himself.

CONGRESS AND THE COURT

In the space of fourteen years, therefore, the Supreme Court initiated new policies in a wide variety of ways, all of which were likely to offend conservative elements in the community. As a

result the Court came under fierce attack both outside and inside the Congress. The Constitution had provided for an independent judiciary by providing that the judges should hold office
during good behaviour, that is they could be removed only by
impeachment. However, the Constitution gave Congress a potential power to discipline the Court either through legislation or
by proposing constitutional amendments. From time to time
throughout its history the Court has come into conflict with the
legislature. Congress has increased, or decreased, the number of
judges. On one occasion the legislature by statute withdrew jurisdiction from the Court whilst a case was actually under consideration by the Justices. However, most of the attacks upon
the Court have failed, though some only by a very narrow margin.
They have taken the form of the introduction of bills or proposed
constitutional amendments which would have required a two-
thirds majority, or some other high proportion of the Court's
membership, before a State or Federal statute could be declared
unconstitutional. Broad attacks have been mounted on the
Court's appellate jurisdiction that would have removed large
areas from the Court, or would even have removed altogether its
power to overrule the decisions of State Supreme Courts.
Attempts have been made to fix a retiring age for the Justices, to
make their positions elective, or to give them short fixed terms
of office. Other proposals would have made the Senate into an
appellate court to review Supreme Court decisions, or would
have given to Congress the power to set these decisions
aside.

These attacks have come at the Court from every direction. In
its early years the Jeffersonians attacked the Court for its centralizing influence; the abolitionists attacked the Court for its
support of the property rights of slave-owners; after the Civil
War the Radical Republicans wished to curb the power of the
Court because of its apparent sympathy for the Southern com-
plaints about arbitrary arrests and restrictions upon freedom of
speech; in the last quarter of the nineteenth century the Pro-
gressives attacked the Court because of its support for business
and commercial interests; in the 1930s liberals attempted to
transform the Court because of its attack upon the New Deal

legislation; since 1954 Southerners and Conservatives have bitterly attacked the Court because of its decisions on segregation, apportionment, Communist control and individual rights.

THE COURT AND PUBLIC OPINION

The Supreme Court wields considerable power in the American political system, and it plays a vital policy-making role in the government. What then is the place of the Court in a democracy? How is it that nine non-elected judges with life tenure can wield this power in the most election-conscious nation in the world? Undoubtedly the Court has been able to exercise a degree of leadership, because of its prestige and its relative aloofness from the hurly-burly of political life, which the other branches of government have often been incapable of mobilizing. Nevertheless the power of the Court depends in the last resort upon its success in refashioning the rules of the Constitution in such a way that the informed public, and in particular those who are responsible for the operation of the machinery of government, are prepared to accept. To some extent the Court, like other parts of the system of government, moderates its policies when they meet fierce opposition, or when its own position is seriously threatened. After each of the Court's periods of controversial activism it has, to a greater or lesser degree, retreated from its most exposed positions and made its judgements more palatable. However, the explanation of the Court's power is not to be found simply in terms of its ability to gauge public opinion accurately. Its role has to be seen in the general context of the pluralist political system of the United States. The Court is able to exercise its power because it rarely comes squarely into conflict with a truly united opposition, either inside or outside the formal institutional structure of government. Such a coalition of interests determined to attack the Court has not yet had the continuity or cohesion which would be required to put through the legislation or constitutional amendment which would be necessary to curb the Court. Every attack which has been made upon the Court so far has been based upon the current dissatisfactions of those who are at present outraged by its decisions, but they have

not overcome the reservations of the rest of the community who
fear the long-run results of reducing the Court's power. Many of
the problems which the Court is able to tackle appear to be quite
intractable as far as action by the more overtly 'political' branches
are concerned. Thus the Court remains, and is likely to remain,
at the centre of the policy-making process in the United States.

American Politics
after Watergate

10

The American political system is emerging from its most traumatic decade since the Civil War. In 1974 the Presidency seemed
at its lowest ebb: the effect of the Vietnam war on American
society, closely followed by the Watergate affair, shook the self-
confidence of the American people in their institutions, and led
them to look very closely at the relationships between President
and Congress which lie at the very heart of their system of government. The resignation of President Nixon, coming as it did
barely in time to forestall his impeachment, the conviction of
some of the most powerful members of his Administration, and
the apparently endless revelations of criminal or corrupt activities
by those in government service, underlined the claim by congressional leaders that the Presidency was out of control and
should be subjugated to a reinvigorated Congress. To the outside
observer, perhaps the most striking aspect of this episode in
American history is the fact that the Constitution and political
system have managed to survive these extraordinary events, and
to remove highly-placed wrongdoers so effectively. Few if any
other systems of government in the world would have made it
possible relentlessly to expose the misdeeds of those still actually
engaged in the exercise of power, and to remove them, without
violence, through proper legal procedures. Naturally enough,
however, the scandals produced a strong reaction against what
Arthur M. Schlesinger Jr has labelled 'the Imperial Presidency'.

However, the desire to reduce the power of the Presidency
represents an oversimple reaction to an extremely complex situation. The Watergate Affair, though not of course in any sense
inevitable, represents an extreme possibility inherent in the way
in which an eighteenth-century constitution has evolved under
the strains of twentieth-century conditions. The proximate cause

of Watergate was, no doubt, the character of President Nixon and
of the men with whom he surrounded himself, but to understand
the more fundamental causes it is essential to see recent events
within the context of long-term trends in the American political
system.

The American political system is extremely intricate. It has
evolved in response to the needs of a society which was expanding
rapidly in quite unique circumstances. In comparison with other
nations the United States was able to establish itself in an environ-
ment which was in some ways very favourable – an 'open' society
with the possibility of expansion, a wealthy society, and one
which was for most of the nineteenth century free of foreign
entanglements and able to devote its energies to the solution of
the problems of settling and developing the continent. As a result
the political system which emerged is able to do certain things
very well indeed, and copes with other problems much less efficiently. The structure of the electoral system, of the parties and
pressure-groups, the organization of Congress, all these are
superbly adapted to the task of registering and reflecting the
interests and opinions of innumerable groups throughout the
country, and of aggregating those interests in a way which will
facilitate the emergence of compromise policies, policies which
often represent the lowest common denominator of interested
opinion. As a mechanism for this purpose the system is unsur-
passed in the modern world. The other side of this coin, however, is that the compromises which work so well in many fields
are potentially disastrous in those areas which demand coordinated and continuous policies. The compromise politics of consensus give to interested groups the opportunity to delay, and to
modify substantially the policies which eventually emerge. In
this way minorities defend themselves from attack, but at the
same time they gain the ability to veto effective action on behalf
of other minority groups. When confronted by a head-on clash
of interests the political system instead of being able to resolve
such conflicts can only shelve them. The President, and the
Supreme Court, can exert considerable leverage, and by a cour-
ageous act of leadership may sometimes move the political situation. Their autonomy, somewhat apart from the pluralist battle,

and their prestige, endows them with this possibility, but in the process they must often subject themselves to vicious attack. Their ability to exercise this leadership is limited by their personal courage and skill, and by the institutional factors which hem them in.

The limitations on the power of the President, as we saw in Chapter seven, are considerable. As powerful as the President is in the field of foreign affairs, he is in a very different situation indeed in regard to domestic policy. He may find himself frustrated by Congress on those matters which he considers essential to the national interest, and unable to ensure the passage of legislation whether trivial or vital in importance. To pursue a vigorous policy in respect of domestic legislation requires a tremendous commitment on the part of the President, backed by all the charisma that he can muster. A John F. Kennedy can put all his enormous appeal into his relations with Congress and the public, and then fail miserably. A Johnson can use all his ability as a wheeler-dealer to get a large legislative programme through Congress only to see the results dissipated in the impossible complexity of the administrative arrangements necessary to win congressional approval. An Eisenhower without the urge to build great domestic programmes can withdraw to the golf-course; a Nixon can withdraw into an aloof, remote world apart. For all of them the temptation to spend more and more of their time and effort on foreign policy is almost overwhelming.

The roots of this situation are to be found in the institutional and political developments which have dominated the twentieth century. There has undoubtedly been a vast centralization of government authority and an increase in the power and functions of the Federal Government in this period. There has also been a consequent expansion in the statutory powers and functions of the President. It is to the Federal Government, and hence to the President, that Americans look increasingly for the solutions to the problems of their society. However, at the same time, as this centralization of constitutional and legal authority has been taking place there has been underway an increasing *decentralization* of *political* power, making it more and more difficult for the Federal Government to exercise effectively the authority which

it has accumulated. *The most significant fact of American Government in the twentieth century is that there has been a centralization of government authority without a corresponding
centralization of political power.* On the contrary, the power base
of the President, the only truly national political figure in the
country, has been weakened during the present century. The
Congress has become more and more a collection of individualistic,
undisciplined Senators and Congressmen who do not feel committed to support the President of their own party, or their own
leadership in Congress. Although there are signs that this situation may be changing as a result of the successes of liberal Democrats in recent elections, it is far too early to be sure that party
discipline will be revived in Congress. Even were this to be the
case it could raise more problems than it would solve, if a Republican President were to be faced by a disciplined Democratic
majority in Congress. This decentralization of political power
has resulted from the ending of the patronage system, from the
evolution of the American Welfare State and the disappearance of
machine politics, and from the introduction of primary elections.
The whole basis of the coherent political structure which was
relevant to the problems of politics in the nineteenth century has,
quite rightly, been removed, but it has not been replaced by any
other coherent organizing principle of politics. A President with
a strong character can battle against this system and try to impose
his will upon it by sheer force of character; a weak man will turn
to other means of maintaining his ego.

Finally the organizational changes which have been made since
1939 to help the President in his attempt to deal with Congress
and to coordinate his own Administration have resulted in his
being isolated more and more from the day-to-day political life of
the country. The machinery of the White House Office can be a
vital tool with which a President can direct a national campaign to implement his policy – at the other extreme it can be a
wall between him and those who wish, quite legitimately, to influence him. In the period 1971–4 all these factors, long-term and
short-term, institutional and personal, combined to create a situation in which the President, isolated and aloof from the political
life around him, allowed or encouraged his closest political aides

to undertake acts which led them to convictions and prison sentences, and led to his own resignation.

Thus the central problem of the American political system is not that the President is too powerful; it is that his power is both too small and too uncontrolled. Surely what is necessary is to try to achieve a more coordinated, and a more controlled exercise of power by President and Congress working together. This is not a plea for the introduction of the parliamentary system into the United States, for such a proposal would be both unrealistic and inappropriate to the American political culture. It is a suggestion that the President should conduct the business of government, together with his Cabinet, in direct face-to-face contact with the Congress, rather than at arms-length as at the present time.

The problem of the political system, however, goes much more deeply into the very fabric of the American political culture, and the problems which the political parties face in attempting to articulate opinion. The divisions within American society are apparently deep and serious. The great majority of the electorate remains firmly in the centre, retaining their belief in the traditional politics of America. They vote Democratic or Republican largely as a result of their historical allegiances, or as a result of the impact of a particular personality upon them. On the right, however, the dissatisfactions of a number of different groups who feel their position in life threatened, whether by the advance of the Negro, or more nebulously by Communism, lead them to opt out of the traditional party system. The surprising strength of Governor Wallace in 1968 was indicative of the importance of this feeling in the South, and in the nation at large. This sense of being under attack provides the potential basis of a relatively coherent third party which could at least hope to dominate the politics of enough Southern States to provide a constant threat to the stability of the political system by creating deadlock in the Electoral College. Although Wallace won many votes outside the South it is the latter area which would be the crucial basis for such a third party operation. It could provide the hard core of institutional support for such a party, which could, for a time at least, transform the traditional two-party system into something very different. The South has been edging towards such a situa-

tion since the end of the Second World War, sometimes flirting
with 'Presidential Republicanism', sometimes hoping to hold the
balance of power between the two parties by keeping itself independent of both of them. Wallace's success suggests that the third
party strategy might be the more profitable, but if this alternative
is chosen the South must pay a considerable price for it. If the
South really opts for a third party it would eventually have to
accept the logic of this situation at the congressional level, as
well as in Presidential politics. If the Democratic party in the
North could no longer hope to gain advantage in Presidential
elections by maintaining the coalition with the South, then its
party links with the South in Congress would be of little use,
indeed they would be a positive embarrassment. If the Wallace
forces can secure the election of members of Congress in sufficient
numbers, the end of the Southern Democracy would be in sight.
The *quid pro quo* which the South would have to pay for its
independence would be the loss of its important committee chairmanships in Congress, through which it is able to influence much
of the legislation which affects its interests, and the loss also of
the patronage which Democratic Presidents have provided.

The problem on the left of the two major parties is just as
serious although in some ways not so intractable. There is an
equal dissatisfaction with traditional politics, but of a kind which
makes it more difficult for the dissatisfied elements to coalesce into
a coherent minor party. In 1968 many of these elements found a
focal point in the candidacy of Senator Eugene McCarthy because
of his outspoken views on Vietnam, but with the end of the Vietnam War it is by no means clear what institutionalized expression of these dissatisfactions, if any, will emerge, for they seem to
lack any positive directional force which would be widely acceptable to all of them. If political leaders can devise pragmatic solutions to the central problems facing America, then the traditional
processes of American politics by which the two great parties
absorb protest and dissent by meeting the policy demands of
the protestors could well work again.

In electoral terms, therefore, the major problem of American
politics is on the right, but in social terms, the major problems
are on the left. This is a serious dichotomy for the American

political system, filled with danger. How far would a realignment of the parties into a more 'European' left-right division help the situation? The assumption behind this argument usually is that the Republican party could absorb the right-wing elements across the nation, that the Democratic Party would offer a more attractive haven for the dissident left, and that a more 'responsible' politics would emerge, oriented towards the solution of particular issues by advocating and carrying through clear policy mandates. The major objections to this line of argument are, first that it would require a considerable change of public opinion and of congressional attitudes to bring it about, and second that it might result not so much in healthy competition between the parties as in a desperate and potentially disastrous fight for existence. The moderating influence of the traditional parties would be lost, and the attempt to define two political camps more clearly could lead to intense political bitterness and frustration.

The reforms which have been proposed in order to try to bring about a more responsible policy-oriented political system have been intended to strengthen the position of the President in relation to Congress and to give to national party leaders a greater ability to discipline and control the lower echelons of the party. The centralization of party finances, the attempt to create stronger national party organizations, and to subject members of Congress to party discipline are major aims of such reforms. In order to increase the stature of the President reformers have proposed that Presidential candidates should be selected by a nationwide direct primary rather than by the present political infighting of the national conventions, whilst others would like to see closer links between President and Congress either by providing for the election of the President by Congress, or by a more radical movement towards a cabinet system of government. A more pressing and widespread demand for reform comes from those who see the Electoral College as a potential obstacle to the expression of the popular will in Presidential elections.

The danger of most of the proposals for reform of the party system is that they might tend to cause a disintegration of that system rather than a solidification of it, making the parties *less* responsible, and less responsive, than at present. There is always the danger that the latent multi-party system, which lies beneath the deceptively straight-forward two-party system, might emerge and take over American politics. Any proposed reform of the Electoral College ought to give careful consideration to this point. It is also doubtful if the model of British, or European, politics is a good one for the United States to try to emulate. The ideological differences which have so far sustained British parties seem increasingly stale and irrelevant. Should America move backwards into the past in this way? A more likely solution is perhaps to be sought in the American tradition, partly by the forceful assertion of the values of American constitutionalism, by the active pursuance of political equality, and of the social and economic equality of opportunity, which have been the overt goals of American society from the beginning. If these American values are applied to all Americans irrespective of colour or creed, then the party or parties which adopt them as a central credo will surely eventually overcome the extremists of left or right, who, whatever they say, are asserting values quite alien to the American tradition. If the Democratic Party were to accept this view wholeheartedly, it would mean the final break with the South that has been building up for over twenty years, and the end of the old Roosevelt coalition. But it would be the essential starting point for the building of a new coalition (the American way of realignment), the raw materials of which lie to hand – idealistic youth, the moderate negroes, the independents in the suburbs, the liberal working-class, the city-dwellers, Southern moderates, particularly Southern businessmen – an unlikely sounding group to work together it may seem, but no more unlikely than the previous coalitions that have dominated the American political scene. This is surely the only way forward for American politics. It requires a leader of exceptional power and ability to create such a coalition, and it is fervently to be hoped that the present turmoil of American society will throw up such a man in time.

The Constitution
of the United States
# of America

(The passages in italics have been replaced
by subsequent Amendments)

We the People of the United States, in Order to form a more
perfect Union, establish Justice, insure domestic Tranquility,
provide for the common defence, promote the general Welfare,
and secure the Blessings of Liberty to ourselves and our
Posterity, do ordain and establish this Constitution for the
United States of America.

ARTICLE I

Section 1. All legislative Powers herein granted shall be vested
in a Congress of the United States, which shall consist of a Senate
and House of Representatives.

Section 2. The House of Representatives shall be composed
of Members chosen every second Year by the People of the Several
States, and the Electors in each State shall have the Qualifications
requisite for Electors of the most numerous Branch of the State
Legislature.

No person shall be a Representative who shall not have attained
to the Age of twenty five Years, and been seven Years a Citizen
of the United States, and who shall not, when elected, be an
Inhabitant of that State in which he shall be chosen.

Representatives and direct Taxes shall be apportioned among
the several States which may be included within this Union,
according to their respective Numbers, *which shall be determined
by adding to the whole Number of free Persons, including those
bound to Service for a Term of Years, and excluding Indians not
taxed, three fifths of all other persons.*[1] The actual Enumeration
shall be made within three Years after the first Meeting of the
Congress of the United States, and within every subsequent Term

1. See 14th Amendment.

of ten Years, in such Manner as they shall by Law direct. The Number of Representatives shall not exceed one for every thirty Thousand, but each State shall have at Least one Representative; and until such enumeration shall be made, the State of New Hampshire shall be entitled to chuse three, Massachusetts eight, Rhode-Island and Providence Plantations one, Connecticut five, New-York six, New Jersey four, Pennsylvania eight, Delaware one, Maryland six, Virginia ten, North Carolina five, South Carolina five, and Georgia three.

When vacancies happen in the Representation from any State, the Executive Authority thereof shall issue Writs of Election to fill such Vacancies.

The House of Representatives shall chuse their Speaker and other Officers; and shall have the sole Power of Impeachment.

Section 3. The Senate of the United States shall be composed of two Senators from each State, *chosen by the Legislature thereof*,[2] for six Years; and each Senator shall have one Vote.

Immediately after they shall be assembled in Consequence of the first Election, they shall be divided as equally as may be into three Classes. The Seats of the Senators of the first Class shall be vacated at the Expiration of the second Year, of the second Class at the Expiration of the fourth Year, and of the third Class at the Expiration of the sixth Year, so that one third may be chosen every second Year; *and if Vacancies happen by Resignation or otherwise, during the Recess of the Legislature of any State, the Executive thereof may make temporary Appointments until the next Meeting of the Legislature, which shall then fill such Vacancies*.[3]

No Person shall be a Senator who shall not have attained to the Age of thirty Years, and been nine Years a Citizen of the United States, and who shall not, when elected, be an Inhabitant of the State for which he shall be chosen.

The Vice-President of the United States shall be President of the Senate, but shall have no Vote, unless they be equally divided.

The Senate shall chuse their other Officers, and also a President

2. See 17th Amendment.
3. See 17th Amendment.

pro tempore in the Absence of the Vice-President, or when he shall exercise the Office of President of the United States.

The Senate shall have the sole Power to try all Impeachments. When sitting for that Purpose, they shall be on Oath or Affirmation. When the President of the United States is tried, the Chief Justice shall preside : And no Person shall be convicted without the Concurrence of two thirds of the Members present.

Judgment in Cases of Impeachment shall not extend further than to remove from Office, and disqualification to hold and enjoy any Office of honor, Trust or Profit under the United States: but the Party convicted shall nevertheless be liable and subject to Indictment, Trial, Judgment and Punishment, according to Law.

Section 4. The Times, Places and Manner of holding Elections for Senators and Representatives, shall be prescribed in each State by the Legislature thereof; but the Congress may at any time by Law make or alter such Regulations, except as to the Places of chusing Senators.

The Congress shall assemble at least once in every Year, and such Meeting shall be on the first Monday in December, unless they shall by Law appoint a different Day.[4]

Section 5. Each House shall be the Judge of the Elections, Returns and Qualifications of its own Members, and a Majority of each shall constitute a Quorum to do Business; but a smaller Number may adjourn from day to day, and may be authorized to compel the Attendance of absent Members, in such Manner, and under such Penalties as each House may provide.

Each House may determine the Rules of its Proceedings, punish its Members for disorderly Behaviour, and, with the Concurrence of two thirds, expel a Member.

Each House shall keep a Journal of its Proceedings, and from time to time publish the same, excepting such Parts as may in their Judgment require Secrecy; and the Yeas and Nays of the Members of either House on any question shall, at the Desire of one fifth of those Present, be entered on the Journal.

Neither House, during the Session of Congress, shall, without the Consent of the other, adjourn for more than three days, nor

4. See 20th Amendment.

to any other Place than that in which the two Houses shall be sitting.

Section 6. The Senators and Representatives shall receive a Compensation for their Services, to be ascertained by Law, and paid out of the Treasury of the United States. They shall in all Cases, except Treason, Felony and Breach of the Peace, be privileged from Arrest during their Attendance at the Session of their respective Houses, and in going to and returning from the same; and for any Speech or Debate in either House, they shall not be questioned in any other Place.

No Senator or Representative shall, during the Time for which he was elected, be appointed to any civil Office under the Authority of the United States, which shall have been created, or the Emoluments whereof shall have been encreased during such time; and no Person holding any Office under the United States, shall be a Member of either House during his Continuance in Office.

Section 7. All Bills for raising Revenue shall originate in the House of Representatives; but the Senate may propose or concur with Amendments as on other Bills.

Every Bill which shall have passed the House of Representatives and the Senate, shall, before it become a Law, be presented to the President of the United States; If he approve he shall sign it, but if not he shall return it, with his Objections to that House in which it shall have originated, who shall enter the Objections at large on their Journal, and proceed to reconsider it. If after such Reconsideration two thirds of that House shall agree to pass the Bill, it shall be sent, together with the Objections, to the other House, by which it shall likewise be reconsidered, and if approved by two thirds of that House, it shall become a Law. But in all such Cases the Votes of both Houses shall be determined by Yeas and Nays, and the Names of the Persons voting for and against the Bill shall be entered on the Journal of each House respectively. If any Bill shall not be returned by the President within ten Days (Sundays excepted) after it shall have been presented to him, the Same shall be a Law, in like Manner as if he had signed it, unless the Congress by their Adjournment prevent its Return, in which Case it shall not be a Law.

Every Order, Resolution, or Vote to which the Concurrence of the Senate and House of Representatives may be necessary (except on a question of Adjournment) shall be presented to the President of the United States; and before the Same shall take Effect, shall be approved by him, or being disapproved by him, shall be repassed by two thirds of the Senate and House of Representatives, according to the Rules and Limitations prescribed in the Case of a Bill.

Section 8. The Congress shall have Power to lay and collect Taxes, Duties, Imposts and Excises, to pay the Debts and provide for the common Defence and general Welfare of the United States; but all Duties, Imposts and Excises shall be uniform throughout the United States.

To borrow Money on the credit of the United States;

To regulate Commerce with foreign Nations and among the several States, and with the Indian Tribes;

To establish an uniform Rule of Naturalization, and uniform Laws on the subject of Bankruptcies throughout the United States;

To coin Money, regulate the Value thereof, and of foreign Coin, and fix the Standard of Weights and Measures;

To provide for the Punishment of counterfeiting the Securities and current Coin of the United States;

To establish Post Offices and post Roads;

To promote the Progress of Science and useful Arts, by securing for limited Times to Authors and Inventors the exclusive Right to their respective Writings and Discoveries;

To constitute Tribunals inferior to the Supreme Court;

To define and punish Piracies and Felonies committed on the high Seas, and Offences against the Law of Nations;

To declare War, grant Letters of Marque and Reprisal, and make Rules concerning Captures on Land and Water;

To raise and support Armies, but no Appropriation of Money to that Use shall be for a longer Term than two Years;

To provide and maintain a Navy;

To make Rules for the Government and Regulation of the land and naval Forces.

To provide for calling forth the Militia to execute the

Laws of the Union, suppress Insurrections and repel Invasions;

To provide for organizing, arming, and disciplining, the Militia, and for governing such Part of them as may be employed in the Service of the United States, reserving to the States respectively, the Appointment of the Officers, and the Authority of training the Militia according to the discipline prescribed by Congress;

To Exercise exclusive Legislation in all Cases whatsoever, over such District (not exceeding ten Miles square) as may, by Cession of particular States, and the Acceptance of Congress, become the Seat of the Government of the United States, and to exercise like Authority over all Places purchased by the Consent of the Legislature of the State in which the Same shall be, for the Erection of Forts, Magazines, Arsenals, Dock-Yards, and other needful Buildings; – And

To make all Laws which shall be necessary and proper for carrying into Execution the foregoing Powers, and all the Powers vested by this Constitution in the Government of the United States, or in any Department or Officer thereof.

Section 9. The Migration or Importation of such Persons as any of the States now existing shall think proper to admit, shall not be prohibited by the Congress prior to the Year one thousand eight hundred and eight, but a Tax or duty may be imposed on such Importation, not exceeding ten dollars for each Person.

The Privilege of the Writ of Habeas Corpus shall not be suspended, unless when in Case of Rebellion or Invasion the public Safety may require it.

No Bill of Attainder or ex post facto Law shall be passed.

No Capitation, or other direct, Tax shall be laid, unless in Proportion to the Census or Enumeration herein before directed to be taken.

No Tax or Duty shall be laid on Articles exported from any State.

No Preference shall be given by any Regulation of Commerce or Revenue to the Ports of one State over those of another: nor shall Vessels bound to, or from, one State, be obliged to enter, clear, or pay Duties in another.

No Money shall be drawn from the Treasury, but in Consequence of Appropriations made by Law; and a regular Statement and Account of the Receipts and Expenditures of all public Money shall be published from time to time.

No title of Nobility shall be granted by the United States: And no Person holding any Office of Profit or Trust under them, shall, without the Consent of the Congress, accept of any present, Emolument, Office, or Title of any kind whatever, from any King, Prince, or foreign State.

Section 10. No State shall enter into any Treaty, Alliance or Confederation; grant Letters of Marque and Reprisal; coin Money; emit Bills of Credit; make any Thing but gold and silver Coin a Tender in Payment of Debts; pass any Bill of Attainder, ex post facto Law, or Law impairing the Obligation of Contracts, or Grant any Title of Nobility.

No State shall, without the Consent of the Congress, lay any Imposts or Duties on Imports or Exports, except what may be absolutely necessary for executing its inspection Laws: and the net Produce of all Duties and Imposts, laid by any State on Imports or Exports, shall be for the Use of the Treasury of the United States; and all such Laws shall be subject to the Revision and Controul of the Congress.

No State shall, without the Consent of Congress, lay any Duty of Tonnage, keep Troops, or Ships of War in time of Peace, enter into any Agreement or Compact with another State, or with a foreign Power, or engage in War, unless actually invaded, or in such imminent Danger as will not admit of delay.

ARTICLE II

Section 1. The executive Power shall be vested in a President of the United States of America. He shall hold his Office during the Term of four Years, and, together with the Vice-President, chosen for the same Term be elected as follows:

Each State shall appoint, in such Manner as the Legislature thereof may direct, a Number of Electors, equal to the whole Number of Senators and Representatives to which the State may be entitled in the Congress but no Senator or Representative, or

Person holding an Office of Trust or Profit under the United States, shall be appointed an Elector.

The Electors shall meet in their respective States; and vote by Ballot for two Persons, of whom one at least shall not be an Inhabitant of the same State with themselves. And they shall make a List of all the Persons voted for, and of the Number of Votes for each; which List they shall sign and certify, and transmit sealed to the Seat of the Government of the United States, directed to the President of the Senate. The President of the Senate shall, in the Prescence of the Senate and House of Representatives, open all the Certificates, and the Votes shall then be counted. The Person having the greatest Number of Votes shall be the President, if such Number be a Majority of the whole Number of Electors appointed; and if there be more than one who have such a Majority, and have an equal Number of Votes, then the House of Representatives shall immediately chuse by Ballot one of them for President; and if no Person have a Majority, then from the five highest on the List the said House shall in like Manner chuse the President. But in chusing the President, the Votes shall be taken by States, the Representation from each State having one Vote; A quorum for this purpose shall consist of a Member or Members from two thirds of the States, and a Majority of all the States shall be necessary to a Choice. In every Case, after the Choice of the President, the Person having the greatest Number of Votes of the Electors shall be the Vice President. But if there should remain two or more who have equal Votes, the Senate shall chuse from them by Ballot the Vice President.[5]

The Congress may determine the Time of chusing the Electors, and the Day on which they shall give their Votes; which Day shall be the same throughout the United States.

No Person except a natural born Citizen, or a Citizen of the United States, at the time of the Adoption of this Constitution, shall be eligible to the Office of President; neither shall any Person be eligible to that Office who shall not have attained to the Age of thirty five Years, and been fourteen Years a Resident within the United States.

5. Superseded by the 12th Amendment.

In Case of the Removal of the President from Office, or of his Death, Resignation, or Inability to discharge the Powers and Duties of the said Office, the Same shall devolve on the Vice President, and the Congress may by Law provide for the Case of Removal, Death, Resignation or Inability, both of the President and Vice President, declaring what Officer shall then act as President, and such Officer shall act accordingly, until the Disability be removed, or a President shall be elected.[6]

The President shall, at stated Times, receive for his Services, a Compensation which shall neither be encreased nor diminished during the Period for which he shall have been elected, and he shall not receive within that Period any other Emolument from the United States, or any of them.

Before he enter on the Execution of his Office, he shall take the following Oath or Affirmation: 'I do solemnly swear (or affirm) that I will faithfully execute the Office of President of the United States, and will to the best of my Ability, preserve, protect and defend the Constitution of the United States.'

Section 2. The President shall be Commander in Chief of the Army and Navy of the United States, and of the Militia of the several States, when called into the actual Service of the United States; he may require the Opinion, in writing, of the principal Officer in each of the executive Departments, upon any Subject relating to the Duties of their respective Offices, and he shall have Power to grant Reprieves and Pardons for Offences against the United States, except in Cases of Impeachment.

He shall have Power, by and with the Advice and Consent of the Senate, to make Treaties, provided two thirds of the Senators present concur; and he shall nominate, and by and with the Advice and Consent of the Senate shall appoint Ambassadors, and other public Ministers and Consuls, Judges of the supreme Court, and all other Officers of the United States, whose Appointments are not herein otherwise provided for, and which shall be established by Law: but the Congress may by Law vest the Appointment of such inferior Officers, as they think proper,

6. See 25th Amendment.

in the President alone, in the Courts of Law, or in the Heads of Departments.

The President shall have Power to fill up all Vacancies that may happen during the Recess of the Senate, by granting Commissions which shall expire at the End of their next Session.

Section 3. He shall from time to time give to the Congress Information of the State of the Union, and recommend to their Consideration such Measures as he shall judge necessary and expedient; he may, on extraordinary Occasions, convene both Houses, or either of them, and in Case of Disagreement between them, with Respect to the Time of Adjournment, he may adjourn them to such Time as he shall think proper; he shall receive Ambassadors and other public Ministers, he shall take Care that the Laws be faithfully executed, and shall Commission all the Officers of the United States.

Section 4. The President, Vice President and all civil Officers of the United States, shall be removed from Office on Impeachment for, and Conviction of Treason, Bribery or other high Crimes and Misdemeanors.

ARTICLE III

Section 1. The judicial Power of the United States shall be vested in one supreme Court, and in such inferior Courts as the Congress may from time to time ordain and establish. The Judges, both of the supreme and inferior Courts, shall hold their Offices during good Behaviour, and shall, at stated Times, receive for their Services, a Compensation, which shall not be diminished during their Continuance in Office.

Section 2. The judicial Power shall extend to all Cases, in Law and Equity, arising under this Constitution, the Laws of the United States, and Treaties made, or which shall be made, under their Authority; – to all Cases affecting Ambassadors, other public Ministers and Consuls; – to all Cases of admiralty and maritime Jurisdiction; – to Controversies to which the United States shall be a Party; – to Controversies between two or more States; – *between a State and Citizens of another State*[7]; –

7. See 11th Amendment.

between Citizens of different States; – between Citizens of the same State claiming Lands under Grants of different States, *and between a State or the Citizens thereof, and foreign States, Citizens or Subjects.*[8]

In all cases affecting Ambassadors, other public Ministers and Consuls, and those in which a State shall be Party, the supreme Court shall have original Jurisdiction. In all the other Cases before mentioned, the supreme Court shall have appellate Jurisdiction, both as to Law, and Fact, with such Exceptions, and under such Regulations as the Congress shall make.

The Trial of all Crimes, except in Cases of Impeachment, shall be by Jury; and such Trial shall be held in the State where the said Crimes shall have been committed; but when not committed within any State, the Trial shall be at such Place or Places as the Congress may by Law have directed.

Section 3. Treason against the United States, shall consist only in levying War against them, or in adhering to their Enemies, giving them Aid and Comfort. No Person shall be convicted of Treason unless on the Testimony of two Witnesses to the same overt Act, or on Confession in open Court.

The Congress shall have Power to declare the Punishment of Treason, but no Attainder of Treason shall work Corruption of Blood, or Forfeiture except during the Life of the Person attainted.

ARTICLE IV

Section 1. Full Faith and Credit shall be given in each State to the public Acts, Records, and judicial Proceedings of every other State. And the Congress may by general Laws prescribe the Manner in which such Acts, Records, and Proceedings shall be proved, and the Effect thereof.

Section 2. The Citizens of each State shall be entitled to all Privileges and Immunities of Citizens in the several States.

A Person charged in any State with Treason, Felony, or other Crime, who shall flee from Justice, and be found in another State, shall on Demand of the executive Authority of the State from

8. See 11th Amendment.

which he fled, be delivered up, to be removed to the State having Jurisdiction of the Crime.

No *Person held to Service or Labour in one State, under the Laws thereof, escaping into another, shall, in Consequence of any Law or Regulation therein, be discharged from such Service or Labour, but shall be delivered up on Claim of the Party to whom such Service or Labour may be due.*[9]

Section 3. New States may be admitted by the Congress into this Union; but no new State shall be formed or erected within the Jurisdiction of any other State; nor any State be formed by the Junction of two or more States, or Parts of States, without the Consent of the Legislatures of the States concerned as well as of the Congress.

The Congress shall have Power to dispose of and make all needful Rules and Regulations respecting the Territory or other Property belonging to the United States; and nothing in this Constitution shall be so construed as to Prejudice any Claims of the United States, or of any particular State.

Section 4. The United States shall guarantee to every State in this Union a Republican Form of Government, and shall protect each of them against Invasion; and on Application of the Legislature, or of the Executive (when the Legislature cannot be convened) against domestic Violence.

ARTICLE V

The Congress, whenever two thirds of both Houses shall deem it necessary, shall propose Amendments to this Constitution, or, on the Application of the Legislatures of two thirds of the several States, shall call a Convention for proposing Amendments, which, in either Case, shall be valid to all Intents and Purposes, as Part of this Constitution, when ratified by the Legislatures of three fourths of the several States, or by Conventions in three fourths thereof, as the one or the other Mode of Ratification may be proposed by the Congress; Provided that no Amendment which may be made prior to the Year One thousand eight hundred and eight shall in any Manner affect the first and fourth

9. See 13th Amendment.

Clauses in the Ninth Section of the first Article; and that no State, without its Consent, shall be deprived of its equal Suffrage in the Senate.

ARTICLE VI

All Debts contracted and Engagements entered into, before the Adoption of this Constitution, shall be as valid against the United States under this Constitution, as under the Confederation.

This Constitution, and the Laws of the United States which shall be made in Pursuance thereof; and all Treaties made, or which shall be made, under the Authority of the United States, shall be the supreme Law of the Land; and the Judges in every State shall be bound thereby, any Thing in the Constitution or Laws of any State to the Contrary notwithstanding.

The Senators and Representatives before mentioned, and the Members of the several State Legislatures, and all executive and judicial Officers, both of the United States and of the several States, shall be bound by Oath or Affirmation, to support this Constitution; but no religious Test shall ever be required as a Qualification to any Office or public Trust under the United States.

ARTICLE VII

The Ratification of the Conventions of nine States, shall be sufficient for the Establishment of this Constitution between the States so ratifying the Same.

Done in Convention by the Unanimous Consent of the States present the Seventeenth Day of September in the Year of our Lord one thousand seven hundred and eighty seven and of the Independence of the United States of America the twelfth. In witness whereof We have hereunto subscribed our Names.

*

Amendments

AMENDMENT I

[Ratification of the first ten amendments was completed 15 December 1791.]

Congress shall make no law respecting an establishment of religion, or prohibiting the free exercise thereof; or abridging the freedom of speech, or of the press; or the right of the people peaceably to assemble, and to petition the Government for a redress of grievances.

AMENDMENT II

A well regulated Militia, being necessary to the security of a free State, the right of the people to keep and bear Arms, shall not be infringed.

AMENDMENT III

No Soldier shall, in time of peace be quartered in any house, without the consent of the Owner, nor in time of war, but in a manner to be prescribed by law.

AMENDMENT IV

The right of the people to be secure in their persons, houses, papers, and effects, against unreasonable searches and seizures, shall not be violated, and no Warrants shall issue, but upon probable cause, supported by Oath or Affirmation, and particularly describing the place to be searched, and the persons or things to be seized.

AMENDMENT V

No person shall be held to answer for a capital, or other infamous crime, unless on a presentment or indictment of a Grand Jury, except in cases arising in the land or naval forces, or in the

Militia, when in actual service in time of War or public danger; nor shall any person be subject for the same offence to be twice put in jeopardy of life or limb; nor shall be compelled in any criminal case to be a witness against himself, nor be deprived of life, liberty, or property, without due process of law; nor shall private property be taken for public use, without just compensation.

AMENDMENT VI

In all criminal prosecutions, the accused shall enjoy the right to a speedy and public trial, by an impartial jury of the State and district wherein the crime shall have been committed, which district shall have been previously ascertained by law, and to be informed of the nature and cause of the accusation; to be confronted with the witnesses against him; to have compulsory process for obtaining witnesses in his favor, and to have the Assistance of Counsel for his defence.

AMENDMENT VII

In Suits at common law, where the value in controversy shall exceed twenty dollars, the right of trial by jury shall be preserved, and no fact tried by a jury, shall be otherwise re-examined in any Court of the United States, than according to the rules of the common law.

AMENDMENT VIII

Excessive bail shall not be required, nor excessive fines imposed, nor cruel and unusual punishments inflicted.

AMENDMENT IX

The enumeration in the Constitution, of certain rights, shall not be construed to deny or disparage others retained by the people.

AMENDMENT X

The powers not delegated to the United States by the Constitution, nor prohibited by it to the States, are reserved to the States respectively, or to the people.

AMENDMENT XI   [Ratified 8 January 1798]

The Judicial power of the United States shall not be construed to extend to any suit in law or equity, commenced or prosecuted against one of the United States by Citizens or Subjects of any Foreign State.

AMENDMENT XII   [Ratified 25 September 1804]

The Electors shall meet in their respective states and vote by ballot for President and Vice-President, one of whom, at least, shall not be an inhabitant of the same state with themselves; they shall name in their ballots the person voted for as President, and in distinct ballots the person voted for as Vice-President, and they shall make distinct lists of all persons voted for as President and of all persons voted for as Vice-President, and of the number of votes for each, which lists they shall sign and certify, and transmit sealed to the seat of the government of the United States, directed to the President of the Senate; – The President of the Senate shall, in the presence of Senate and House of Representatives, open all the certificates and the votes shall then be counted; – The person having the greatest number of votes for President, shall be the President, if such number be a majority of the whole number of Electors appointed; and if no person have such majority, then from the persons having the highest numbers not exceeding three on the list of those voted for as President, the House of Representatives shall choose immediately, by ballot, the President. But in choosing the President, the votes shall be taken by states, the representation from each state having one vote; a quorum for this purpose shall consist of a member or members from two thirds of the states, and a majority of all the states shall be necessary to a choice. And if the House of Representatives shall not choose a President whenever the right of choice shall devolve upon them, *before the fourth day of March next following,*[10] then the Vice-President shall act as President, as in the case of the death or other constitutional disability of the President. – The person having the greatest number of votes as Vice-President, shall be the Vice-President, if such number be a majority of the whole number of Electors appointed, and if no person have a majority, then from the two highest numbers on the list, the Senate shall choose the Vice-President; a quorum for the purpose shall consist of two-thirds of the whole number of Senators, and a majority of the whole number shall be necessary to a choice. But no person constitutionally ineligible to the office of President shall be eligible to that of Vice-President of the United States.

AMENDMENT XIII   [Ratified 18 December 1865]

Section 1. Neither slavery nor involuntary servitude, except as a punishment for crime whereof the party shall have been duly convicted, shall exist within the United States, or any place subject to their jurisdiction.

Section 2. Congress shall have power to enforce this article by appropriate legislation.

AMENDMENT XIV   [Ratified 28 July 1869]

Section 1. All persons born or naturalized in the United States, and subject to the jurisdiction thereof, are citizens of the United States and of the State wherein they reside. No State shall make or enforce any law which shall abridge the privileges or immunities of citizens of the United States; nor shall any State deprive any person of life, liberty, or property, without due process of law; nor deny to any person within its jurisdiction the equal protection of the laws.

Section 2. Representatives shall be apportioned among the

10. Altered by the 20th Amendment.

several States according to their respective numbers, counting the whole number of persons in each State, excluding Indians not taxed. But when the right to vote at any election for the choice of electors for President and Vice President of the United States, Representatives in Congress, the Executive and Judicial officers of a State, or the members of the Legislature thereof, is denied to any of the male inhabitants of such State, being twenty-one years of age, and citizens of the United States, or in any way abridged, except for participation in rebellion, or other crime, the basis of representation therein shall be reduced in the proportion which the number of such male citizens shall bear to the whole number of male citizens twenty-one years of age in such State.

Section 3. No person shall be a Senator or Representative in Congress, or elector of President and Vice President, or hold any office, civil or military, under the United States, or under any State, who, having previously taken an oath, as a member of Congress, or as an officer of the United States, or as a member of any State legislature, or as an executive or judicial officer of any State, to support the Constitution of the United States, shall have engaged in insurrection or rebellion against the same, or given aid or comfort to the enemies thereof. But Congress may by a vote of two thirds of each House, remove such disability.

Section 4. The validity of the public debt of the United States, authorized by law, including debts incurred for payment of pensions and bounties for services in suppressing insurrection or rebellion, shall not be questioned. But neither the United States nor any State shall assume or pay any debt or obligation incurred in aid of insurrection or rebellion against the United States, or any claim for the loss or emancipation of any slave; but all such debts, obligations, and claims shall be held illegal and void.

Section 5. The Congress shall have power to enforce, by appropriate legislation, the provisions of this article.

AMENDMENT XV   [Ratified 30 March 1870]

Section 1. The right of citizens of the United States to vote shall not be denied or abridged by the United States or by any

State on account of race, color, or previous condition of servitude.

Section 2. The Congress shall have power to enforce this article by appropriate legislation.

AMENDMENT XVI   [Ratified 25 February 1913]

The Congress shall have power to lay and collect taxes on incomes, from whatever source derived, without apportionment among the several States, and without regard to any census or enumeration.

AMENDMENT XVII   [Ratified 31 May 1913]

The Senate of the United States shall be composed of two Senators from each State, elected by the people thereof, for six years; and each Senator shall have one vote. The electors in each State shall have the qualifications requisite for electors of the most numerous branch of the State legislatures.

When vacancies happen in the representation of any State in the Senate, the executive authority of such State shall issue writs of election to fill such vacancies: *Provided,* That the legislature of any State may empower the executive thereof to make temporary appointments until the people fill the vacancies by election as the legislature may direct.

This amendment shall not be so construed as to affect the election or term of any Senator chosen before it becomes valid as part of the Constitution.

AMENDMENT XVIII   [Ratified 29 January 1919]

Section 1. After one year from the ratification of this article the manufacture, sale, or transportation of intoxicating liquors within, the importation thereof into, or the exportation thereof from the United States and all territory subject to the jurisdiction thereof for beverage purposes is hereby prohibited.

Section 2. The Congress and the several States shall have concurrent power to enforce this article by appropriate legislation.

Section 3. This article shall be inoperative unless it shall have been ratified as an amendment to the Constitution by the legislatures of the several States, as provided in the Constitution, within seven years from the date of the submission hereof to the States by the Congress.[11]

AMENDMENT XIX   [Ratified 26 August 1920]

The right of citizens of the United States to vote shall not be denied or abridged by the United States or by any State on account of sex.

Congress shall have power to enforce this article by appropriate legislation.

AMENDMENT XX   [Ratified 6 February 1933]

Section 1. The terms of the President and Vice President shall end at noon on the 20th day of January, and the terms of Senators and Representatives at noon on the 3rd day of January, of the years in which such terms would have ended if this article had not been ratified; and the terms of their successors shall then begin.

Section 2. The Congress shall assemble at least once in every year, and such meeting shall begin at noon on the 3rd day of January, unless they shall by law appoint a different day.

Section 3. If, at the time fixed for the beginning of the term of the President, the President elect shall have died, the Vice President elect shall become President. If a President shall not have been chosen before the time fixed for the beginning of his term, or if the President elect shall have failed to qualify, then the Vice President elect shall act as President until a President shall have qualified; and the Congress may by law provide for the case wherein neither a President elect nor a Vice President elect shall have qualified, declaring who shall then act as President, or the manner in which one who is to act shall be selected and such person shall act accordingly until a President or Vice President shall have qualified.

11. Repealed by the 21st Amendment.

Section 4. The Congress may by law provide for the case of the death of any of the persons from whom the House of Representatives may choose a President whenever the right of choice shall have devolved upon them, and for the case of the death of any of the persons from whom the Senate may choose a Vice President whenever the right of choice shall have devolved upon them.

Section 5. Sections 1 and 2 shall take effect on the 15th day of October following the ratification of this article.

Section 6. This article shall be inoperative unless it shall have been ratified as an amendment to the Constitution by the legislatures of three-fourths of the several States within seven years from the date of its submission.

AMENDMENT XXI   [Ratified 5 December 1933]

Section 1. The eighteenth article of amendment to the Constitution of the United States is hereby repealed.

Section 2. The transportation or importation into any State, Territory, or possession of the United States for delivery or use therein of intoxicating liquors, in violation of the laws thereof, is hereby prohibited.

Section 3. This article shall be inoperative unless it shall have been ratified as an amendment to the Constitution by conventions in the several States, as provided in the Constitution, within seven years from the date of the submission hereof to the States by the Congress.

AMENDMENT XXII   [Ratified 1 March 1951]

Section 1. No person shall be elected to the office of the President more than twice, and no person who has held the office of President, or acted as President, for more than two years of a term to which some other person was elected President more than once. But this Article shall not apply to any person holding the office of President when this Article was proposed by the Congress, and shall not prevent any person who may be holding the office of President, or acting as President, during the term within which this Article becomes operative from holding the office of President or acting as President during the remainder of such term.

Section 2. This article shall be inoperative unless it shall have been ratified as an amendment to the Constitution by the legislatures of three-fourths of the several States within seven years from the date of its submission to the States by the Congress.

AMENDMENT XXIII   [Ratified 29 March 1961]

Section 1. The District constituting the seat of Government of the United States shall appoint in such manner as the Congress may direct:

A number of electors of President and Vice President equal to the whole number of Senators and Representatives in Congress to which the District would be entitled if it were a State, but in no event more than the least populous State; they shall be in addition to those appointed by the States, but they shall be considered, for the purposes of the election of President and Vice President, to be electors appointed by a State; and they shall meet in the District and perform such duties as provided by the twelfth article of amendment.

Section 2. The Congress shall have power to enforce this article by appropriate legislation.

AMENDMENT XXIV   [Ratified 23 January 1964]

Section 1. The right of citizens of the United States to vote in any primary or other election for President or Vice President, for electors for President or Vice President, or for Senator or Representative in Congress, shall not be denied or abridged by the United States or any state by reason of failure to pay any poll tax or other tax.

Section 2. The Congress shall have power to enforce this article by appropriate legislation.

AMENDMENT XXV   [Ratified 10 February 1967]

Section 1. In case of the removal of the President from office or of his death or resignation, the Vice President shall become President.

Section 2. Whenever there is a vacancy in the office of the Vice President the President shall nominate a Vice President who shall take office upon confirmation by a majority vote of both Houses of Congress.

Section 3. Whenever the President transmits to the President pro tempore of the Senate and the Speaker of the House of Representatives his written declaration that he is unable to discharge the powers and duties of his office, and until he transmits to them a written declaration to the contrary, such powers and duties shall be discharged by the Vice President as Acting President.

Section 4. Whenever the Vice President and the majority of either the principal officers of the executive departments or of such other body as Congress may by law provide, transmit to the President pro tempore of the Senate and the Speaker of the House of Representatives their written declaration that the President is unable to discharge the powers and duties of his office, the Vice President shall immediately assume the powers and duties of the office as Acting President.

Thereafter, when the President transmits to the President pro tempore of the Senate and the Speaker of the House of Representatives his written declaration that no inability exists, he shall resume the powers and duties of his office unless the Vice President and a majority of either the principal officers of the executive departments or of such other body as Congress may by law provide, transmit within four days to the President pro tempore of the Senate and the Speaker of the House of Representatives their written declaration that the President is unable to discharge the powers and duties of his office. Thereupon Congress shall decide the issue, assembling within forty-eight hours for that purpose if not in session. If the Congress, within twenty-one days after receipt of the latter written declaration, or, if Congress is not in session, within twenty-one days after Congress is required

to assemble, determines by two thirds vote of both Houses that
the President is unable to discharge the powers and duties of his
office, the Vice President shall continue to discharge the same as
Acting President; otherwise, the President shall resume the
powers and duties of his office.

AMENDMENT XXVI   [Ratified 30 June 1971]

The right of citizens of the United States, who are 18 years of
age or older, to vote shall not be abridged by the United States or
by any state on account of age.

Factual Tables

1. PRESIDENTS AND VICE-PRESIDENTS OF THE UNITED STATES

	Presidents	Vice-Presidents
1789–97	George Washington	John Adams
1797–1801	John Adams	Thomas Jefferson
1801–9	Thomas Jefferson	Aaron Burr
		George Clinton (from 1805)
1809–17	James Madison	George Clinton
		Elbridge Gerry (from 1813)
1817–25	James Monroe	D. D. Tompkins
1825–9	John Q. Adams	John C. Calhoun
1829–37	Andrew Jackson	John C. Calhoun
		Martin Van Buren (from 1833)
1837–41	Martin Van Buren	R. M. Johnson
1841	William H. Harrison[1]	John Tyler
1841–5	John Tyler	—
1845–9	James K. Polk	George M. Dallas
1849–50	Zachary Taylor[1]	Millard Fillmore
1850–3	Millard Fillmore	—
1853–7	Franklin Pierce	William R. King
1857–61	James Buchanan	J. C. Breckinridge
1861–5	Abraham Lincoln[2]	H. Hamlin
		Andrew Johnson (1865)
1865–9	Andrew Johnson	—
1869–77	U. S. Grant	S. Colfax
		H. Wilson (from 1873)
1877–81	Rutherford B. Hayes	W. A. Wheeler
1881	James A. Garfield[2]	Chester A. Arthur
1881–5	Chester A. Arthur	—
1885–9	Grover Cleveland	A. Hendricks
1889–93	Benjamin Harrison	Levi P. Morton
1893–7	Grover Cleveland	Adlai E. Stevenson

[1] Died in office.   [2] Assassinated.

	Presidents	Vice-Presidents
1897–1901	William McKinley[2]	G. A. Hobart
		Theodore Roosevelt (1901)
1901–9	Theodore Roosevelt	—
		C. W. Fairbanks (from 1905)
1909–13	William H. Taft	J. S. Sherman
1913–21	Woodrow Wilson	T. R. Marshall
1921–3	Warren G. Harding[1]	Calvin Coolidge
1923–9	Calvin Coolidge	—
		Charles G. Dawes (from 1925)
1929–33	Herbert C. Hoover	Charles Curtis
1933–45	Franklin D. Roosevelt[1]	John N. Garner
		Henry A. Wallace (from 1941)
		Harry S. Truman (1945)
1945–53	Harry S. Truman	—
		Alben W. Barkley (from 1949)
1953–61	Dwight D. Eisenhower	Richard M. Nixon
1961–3	John F. Kennedy[2]	Lyndon B. Johnson
1963–9	Lyndon B. Johnson	—
		Hubert H. Humphrey (from 1965)
1969–74	Richard M. Nixon[3]	Spiro Agnew[3]
		Gerald R. Ford (from 1973)
1974	Gerald R. Ford	Nelson A. Rockefeller

[1] Died in office.   [2] Assassinated.   [3] Resigned.

Note: Until the passage of the 20th Amendment in 1933 the inauguration of the President took place in the March following his election. Inauguration of the President now takes place on 20th January.

2. CHIEF JUSTICES OF THE UNITED STATES SUPREME COURT

1789–95	John Jay	1910–21	Edward D. White
1795	John Rutledge	1921–30	William H. Taft
1796–9	Oliver Ellsworth	1930–41	Charles E. Hughes
1801–35	John Marshall	1941–6	Harlan F. Stone
1836–64	Roger B. Taney	1946–53	Fred M. Vinson
1864–73	Salmon P. Chase	1953–69	Earl Warren
1874–88	Morrison R. Waite	1969–	Warren E. Burger
1888–1910	Melville W. Fuller		

3. PRESIDENTIAL ELECTIONS: THE POPULAR VOTE AND ELECTORAL COLLEGE VOTES, 1932–72

	DEMOCRAT			REPUBLICAN			OTHERS	
		Popular Vote 000's	Electoral College Vote		Popular Vote 000's	Electoral College Vote	Popular Vote 000's	Electoral College Vote
1932	F. D. Roosevelt	22,810	472	H. Hoover	15,759	59	1,163	
1936	F. D. Roosevelt	27,753	523	A. M. Landon	16,675	8	1,215	
1940	F. D. Roosevelt	27,308	449	W. Willkie	22,321	82	262	
1944	F. D. Roosevelt	24,607	432	T. E. Dewey	22,015	99	347	
1948	H. S. Truman	24,106	303	T. E. Dewey	21,970	189	2,615	39
1952	A. Stevenson	27,307	89	D. D. Eisenhower	33,848	442	149	
1956	A. Stevenson	26,017	73	D. D. Eisenhower	35,599	457	402	1
1960	J. F. Kennedy	34,227	303	R. M. Nixon	34,109	219	502	15
1964	L. B. Johnson	43,129	486	B. Goldwater	27,178	52	337	
1968	H. H. Humphrey	31,271	191	R. M. Nixon	31,770	301	10,145	46
1972	G. McGovern	29,170	17	R. M. Nixon	47,170	521	1,345	

Sources: *Statistical Abstract of the U.S.*; *Congressional Quarterly Almanac*; *Keesings Contemporary Archives*.

4. COMPOSITION OF CONGRESS, 1933-75

	PRESIDENT		CONGRESS	HOUSE			SENATE		
				Maj. Party	Min. Party	Others	Maj. Party	Min. Party	Others
1933-4	Roosevelt	D	73rd	D-313	R-117	5	D-59	R-36	1
1935-6	,,	D	74th	D-322	R-103	10	D-69	R-25	2
1937-8	,,	D	75th	D-333	R-89	13	D-75	R-17	4
1939-40	,,	D	76th	D-262	R-169	4	D-69	R-23	4
1941-2	,,	D	77th	D-267	R-162	6	D-66	R-28	2
1943-4	,,	D	78th	D-222	R-209	4	D-57	R-38	1
1945-6	{ Truman	D	79th	D-243	R-190	2	D-57	R-38	1
1947-8	,,	D	80th	R-246	D-188	1	R-51	D-45	—
1949-50	,,	D	81st	D-263	R-171	1	D-54	R-42	—
1951-2	,,	D	82nd	D-234	R-199	2	D-48	R-47	1
1953-4	Eisenhower	R	83rd	R-221	D-213	1	R-48	D-47	1
1955-6	,,	R	84th	D-232	R-203	—	D-48	R-47	1
1957-8	,,	R	85th	D-234	R-201	—	D-49	R-47	—
1959-60	,,	R	86th	D-283	R-154	—	D-66	R-34	—
1961-2	Kennedy	D	87th	D-263	R-174	—	D-64	R-36	—
1963-4	{ ,, Johnson	D	88th	D-258	R-176	—	D-68	R-32	—
1965-6	,,	D	89th	D-295	R-140	—	D-67	R-33	—
1967-8	,,	D	90th	D-248	R-187	—	D-64	R-36	—
1969-70	Nixon	R	91st	D-243	R-192	—	D-58	R-42	—
1971-2	Nixon	R	92nd	D-255	R-180	—	D-54	R-44	2
1973-4	{ Nixon Ford	R R	93rd	D-243	R-192	—	D-56	R-42	2
1975-6	Ford	R	94th	D-291	R-144	—	D-61	R-37	2

D=Democratic   R=Republican   Sources: *Congressional Quarterly Almanac; Keesings Contemporary Archives.*

5. THE PRESIDENTIAL ELECTION OF 1972:
THE POPULAR VOTE AND ELECTORAL COLLEGE
VOTE BY STATES

	Percentage of Popular Vote		Electoral Votes	
Richard M. Nixon	60·7		521	
George McGovern	37·5		17	
Others	1·8		—	

	Popular Vote		Electoral Vote	
State	Nixon	McGovern	Nixon	McGovern
Alabama	661,525	205,343	9	
Alaska	41,809	24,362	3	
Arizona	369,068	181,651	6	
Arkansas	427,014	190,598	6	
California	4,544,134	3,431,824	45	
Colorado	568,426	305,522	7	
Connecticut	763,880	507,331	8	
Delaware	139,796	91,907	3	
District of Columbia	29,697	109,974		3
Florida	1,751,210	690,565	17	
Georgia	766,899	330,607	12	
Hawaii	167,414	100,617	4	
Idaho	197,589	80,558	4	
Illinois	2,613,162	1,794,765	26	
Indiana	1,397,748	703,202	13	
Iowa	702,398	492,642	8	
Kansas	605,632	265,158	7	
Kentucky	670,937	369,082	9	
Louisiana	679,944	305,836	10	
Maine	251,327	160,845	4	
Maryland	795,358	486,195	10	
Massachusetts	1,104,310	1,323,843		14
Michigan	1,860,186	1,467,562	21	
Minnesota	881,326	789,473	10	
Mississippi	498,680	125,756	7	
Missouri	1,132,111	682,030	12	
Montana	177,926	116,490	4	
Nebraska	384,157	162,600	5	
Nevada	114,593	65,258	3	
New Hampshire	212,232	115,474	4	
New Jersey	1,769,458	1,058,451	17	

State	Popular Vote Nixon	Popular Vote McGovern	Electoral Vote Nixon	Electoral Vote McGovern
New Mexico	233,036	138,756	4	
New York	4,149,761	2,884,949	41	
North Carolina	1,051,583	437,299	13	
North Dakota	166,131	94,927	3	
Ohio	2,361,238	1,524,118	25	
Oklahoma	745,910	243,338	8	
Oregon	483,229	390,867	6	
Pennsylvania	2,703,975	1,788,034	27	
Rhode Island	209,166	185,239	4	
South Carolina	468,036	184,958	8	
South Dakota	163,746	137,432	4	
Tennessee	812,484	355,817	10	
Texas	2,147,970	1,091,800	26	
Utah	318,407	124,430	4	
Vermont	115,453	67,508	3	
Virginia	982,792	439,546	12	
Washington	679,156	475,553	9	
West Virginia	471,858	271,856	6	
Wisconsin	986,751	805,726	11	
Wyoming	100,561	44,341	3	

Source: *Congressional Quarterly Almanac*, 1973.

Select Bibliography

A. GENERAL

Beard, C., *An Economic Interpretation of the Constitution of the United States*, 1913

Benson, L., *Turner and Beard: American Historical Writing Reconsidered*, 1960

Farrand, M., *The Framing of the Constitution of the United States*, 1913

Grodzins, M., *The American System*, 1966

Hamilton, A., Jay, J., and Madison, J., *The Federalist Papers*

Hartz, L., *The Liberal Tradition in America*, 1955

Leach, R., *American Federalism*, 1970

Lees, J. D., *The Political System of the United States*, 2nd ed., 1975

Lerner, M., *America as a Civilization*, 1957

Lipset, S. M., *The First New Nation*, 1963

Rossiter, C., *1787: The Grand Convention*, 1966

Turner, F. J., *The Frontier in American History*, 1920

Vile, M. J. C., *The Structure of American Federalism*, 1961

Warren, C., *The Making of the Constitution*, 1957

B. POLITICAL BEHAVIOUR

Alford, R., *Party and Society: The Anglo-American Democracies*, 1963

Berelson, B., Lazarsfeld, P. F., and McPhee, W., *Voting*, 1954

Bone, H. A., and Ranney, A., *Politics and Voters*, 1963

Campbell, A., Converse, P., Miller, W., and Stokes, D., *The American Voter*, 1960

Campbell, A., Gurin, G., and Miller, W., *The Voter Decides*, 1954

Devine, D., *The Political Culture of the United States*, 1972

Fenton, J. H., *The Catholic Vote*, 1960

Glazer, N., and Moynihan, D. P., *Beyond the Melting Pot*, 1963

Hofstadter, R., *The Paranoid Style in American Politics*, 1966

Key, V. O., Jr, *The Responsible Electorate*, 1966

Lane, R. E., and Sears, D. O., *Public Opinion*, 1964

Lipset, S. M., *Political Man*, 1960
Lubell, S., *The Future of American Politics*, 1952
  Revolt of the Moderates, 1956
Mitchell, W. C., *The American Polity*, 1962
Wood, R. C., *Suburbia, Its People and Politics*, 1958

C. POLITICAL PARTIES

Bell, D. (ed.), *The Radical Right*, 1963
Burns, J. McG., *The Deadlock of Democracy*, 1964
Chambers, W. N., and Burnham, W. D. (eds.), *The American Party Systems*, 1967
Herring, P., *The Politics of Democracy*, 1940
Jacobs, P., and Landau, S., *The New Radicals*, 1966
Key, V. O., Jr, *Politics, Parties and Pressure Groups*, 5th edition, 1964
Leiserson, A., *Parties and Politics: An Institutional and Behavioural Approach*, 1958
Mills, W., *The Power Elite*, 1956
Ranney, A., *The Doctrine of Responsible Party Government*, 1962
Rossiter, C., *Parties and Politics in America*, 1960
  Conservatism in America, 1955
Schnattschneider, E. E., *Party Government*, 1942
Sorauf, F. J., *Party Politics in America*, 2nd ed., 1972

D. STATE AND LOCAL POLITICS

Banfield, E. C., *Big City Politics*, 1965
Dahl, R. A., *Who Governs?*, 1961
Fenton, J. H., *Mid-West Politics*, 1966
  Politics in the Border States, 1957
Grazia, A. de, *The Western Republic 1952 and After*, 1954
Heard, A., *A Two-Party South?*, 1952
Hunter, F., *Community Power Structure*, 1953
Key, V. O., Jr, *Southern Politics in State and Nation*, 1949
Lockard, D., *New England State Politics*, 1959
  The Politics of State and Local Government, 1963
Martin, R. C., Munger F. J., and others, *Decisions in Syracuse*, 1961
Polsby, N. W., *Community Power and Political Theory*, 1963
Sayre, W. S., and Kaufman, H., *Governing New York City*, 1965
Vidich, A. J., and Bensman, J., *Small Town in Mass Society*, 1958

E. ELECTIONS

David, P., Goldman, R. M., and Bain, R. C., *The Politics of National Party Conventions*, 1960

Davis, J. W., *Presidential Primaries: The Road to the White House,* 1967

Cummings, M. C. (ed), *The National Election of 1964,* 1966

Heard, A., *The Costs of Democracy,* 1960

Moos, M., *Politics, Presidents and Coat-tails,* 1952

Polsby, N. W., and Wildavsky, A. B., *Presidential Elections: Strategies of American Electoral Politics,* 1964

Scammon, R. M., and Wattenberg, B. J., *The Real Majority: An Extraordinary Examination of the American Electorate,* 1971

White, T. H., *The Making of the President, 1960,* 1961
     The Making of the President, 1964, 1965
     The Making of the President, 1968, 1969
     The Making of the President, 1972, 1973

Wilmerding, L., *The Electoral College,* 1958

F. PRESSURE GROUPS

Brock, C., *Americans for Democratic Action,* 1962

Broyles, J. A., *The John Birch Society,* 1964

Engler, R., *The Politics of Oil,* 1961

Garceau, O., *The Political Life of the A.M.A.,* 1941

Milbraith, L. W., *The Washington Lobbyists,* 1963

Salisbury, R. H. (ed.), *Interest Group Politics in America,* 1970

Truman, D. B., *The Governmental Process,* 1951

Vose, C. E., *Caucasians Only: The Supreme Court, the N.A.A.C.P., and the Restrictive Covenant Cases,* 1959

Ziegler, H., *Interest Groups in American Society,* 1964

G. CONGRESS

Bailey, S. K., and Samuel, H. D., *Congress at Work,* 1952

Berman, D. A., *A Bill Becomes a Law: The Civil Rights Acts of 1960,* 1962

Carr, R. K., *The House Un-American Activities Committee,* 1952

Farnsworth, D. N., *The Senate Foreign Relations Committee,* 1961

Fenno, R., *The Power of the Purse: Appropriations Politics in Congress,* 1966

Froman, L. A., *Congressmen and their Constituencies*, 1963
  The Congressional Process, 1967
Green, H. P., and Rosenthal, A., *Government of the Atom*, 1963
Harris, J. P., *The Advice and Consent of the Senate*, 1953
Matthews, D. R., *U.S. Senators and their World*, 1962
Mayhew, D. R., *Party Loyalty among Congressmen*, 1966
Polsby, N. W., *Congress and the Presidency*, 2nd ed., 1971
Reiselbach, L. N., *Congressional Politics*, 1973
Truman, D. B., *The Congressional Party: A Case Study*, 1959
Wahlke, J. C., and Eulau, H., *Legislative Behavior: A Reader in Theory and Research*, 1959
White, W. S., *The Citadel: The Story of the United States Senate*, 1957

H. THE PRESIDENCY

Adams, S., *First-Hand Report*, 1962
Fenno, R., *The President's Cabinet*, 1959
Finer, H., *The Presidency: Crisis and Regeneration*, 1960
Hughes, E. J., *The Ordeal of Power*, 1963
Koenig, L. W., *The Invisible Presidency*, 1960
Neustadt, R. E., *Presidential Power*, 1960.
Polsby, N. W. (ed.), *The Modern Presidency*, 1973
Rossiter, C., *The American Presidency*, 1956
Schlesinger, A. H. Jr, *A Thousand Days: John F. Kennedy in the White House*, 1965
  The Imperial Presidency, 1973
Tugwell, R. G., *The Enlargement of the Presidency*, 1960

I. THE ADMINISTRATION

Bernstein, M. H., *Regulating Business by Independent Commissions*, 1955
Jacob, C. E., *Policy and Bureaucracy*, 1966
Sayre, W. S. (ed.), *The Federal Government Service*, 2nd edition, 1965
Van Riper, P., *History of the United States Civil Service*, 1958

J. THE JUDICIARY

Berman, D. M., *It Is So Ordered*, 1966
Black, C., *The Making of Constitutional Law*, 1963
Cardozo, B., *The Nature of the Judicial Process*, 1921

Eulau, H., and Sprague, J. D., *Lawyers and Politics*, 1964
Jackson, R., *The Supreme Court in the American System of Government*, 1955
Lewis, A., *Gideon's Trumpet*, 1964
Mason, A. T., *The Supreme Court from Taft to Warren*, 1958
Murphy, W., *Congress and the Court: A Case Study in the American Political Process*, 1962
Peltason, J. W., *Federal Courts in the Political Process*, 1955
Pritchett, C. H., and Murphy, W. F., *Courts, Judges and Politics*, 1961
Rosenblum, V. G., *Law as a Political Instrument*, 1955
Schubert, G., *Judicial Policy-Making*, 1965
    Quantitative Analysis of Judicial Behavior, 1964
Wechsler, H., *Principles, Politics and Fundamental Law*, 1961
Westin, A., *The Anatomy of a Constitutional Law Case*, 1958

Index